The Accountant's Story

The Accountant's Story

Inside the Violent World of the Medellín Cartel

Roberto Escobar

with David Fisher

GⅼC

GRAND CENTRAL
PUBLISHING

New York   Boston

Grand Central Publishing
Hachette Book Group
237 Park Avenue
New York, NY 10017

Visit our Web site at www.HachetteBookGroup.com.

Printed in the United States of America

First Edition: February 2009
10 9 8 7 6 5 4 3 2 1

Grand Central Publishing is a division of Hachette Book Group, Inc.
The Grand Central Publishing name and logo is a trademark of Hachette Book Group, Inc.

Library of Congress Cataloging-in-Publication Data
Escobar Gavíria, Roberto.
   The accountant's story : inside the violent world of the Medellín cartel / Roberto Escobar with David Fisher. —1st ed.
      p. cm.
   Includes index.
   ISBN-13: 978-0-446-17892-1
   1. Escobar, Pablo. 2. Escobar Gavíria, Roberto. 3. Drug dealers—Colombia—Biography.
I. Fisher, David, 1946– II. Title.
   HV5805.E82E828 2008
   363.45092'2861—dc22
   [B]
                                    2008040087

Book design and text composition by L&G McRee

I dedicate this book to God Almighty, as gratitude and to the memory of three extraordinary people: my mother, Hermilda, dedicated to a life of social service as a teacher and a role model citizen in the community; my father, Abel, a good man who showed me the rewards earned by hard work and the values of fighting for what you believe; and finally my brother, Pablo, a good soul with a vision for the future that turned the impossible to possible, who planted in his heart a place for the poor and unprotected—and whose memory today is part of history.

ROBERTO ESCOBAR
October 2008

Author's Note

In our world of instant communications it has become relatively simple to become a legend. To be anointed a person has to perform a feat mammoth enough to earn the covers of all the celebrity magazines the same week and dominate twenty-four-hour coverage on cable news for at least several news cycles. One of these nouveau legends can emerge instantly from any field: politics, entertainment, sports, crime, and the bizarre. But in our eat-'em-up media yesterday's legends rapidly become tomorrow's *Dancing with the Stars* contestants.

But Pablo Escobar became a legend the old-fashioned way: He shot his way to the top of the charts. True legends, like that of Pablo Escobar, grow slowly through time and must be nurtured. The stories told about them have to continue to grow in scope and size until reality is simply too small to contain them. They have to burst beyond the borders of time and place and become famous enough to outlive the contemporary journalism of their life. The world has to come to know them on a first-name basis.

Pablo Escobar has joined the list of celebrity criminals, finding his place on the dark side of history with Blackbeard, Jesse James, and Al Capone. Movies about his life will be made, more in an ef-

fort to exploit him than explain him. Pablo Escobar gained infamy
as the most successful, most ruthless, and certainly the best known
drug trafficker in history, a man who was beloved by the poorest
people of Colombia while being despised by the leaders of nations.
He has become known as the richest outlaw in history, a man who
built neighborhoods while destroying lives, a multibillionaire who
was able to evade the armies searching years for him. When I began
working on this project I knew very little about Pablo Escobar other
than the broad facts that emerged above the clatter: He had become
synonymous with Colombian cocaine, which had flooded the United States, and as a result he was listed as one of *Forbes* magazine's ten
richest men in the world.

Before beginning my long series of interviews with Pablo's surviving brother, Roberto, I did considerable background research, most
of which confirmed what I knew and filled in substantial details. The
facts of Pablo Escobar's life are the bricks of legend: Born in 1949
during a period of tremendous violence that resulted in the deaths of
tens of thousands of Colombians, he grew up in a lower-middle-class
working family. By the early 1970s he had become involved in his
first serious crimes, and by the late 1970s he had entered the world
of drug trafficking. His genius for organizing enabled him to bring
together other traffickers to form what became the Medellín cartel.
This came at the perfect time, when affluent Americans fell in love
with cocaine. It was Pablo Escobar's cartel that supplied America's
habit, and even the countless thousands of tons of coke that were
successfully smuggled into America weren't enough to satisfy the demand. Pablo revolutionized the drug trade by creating new methods
to smuggle massive amounts of drugs into America and then Europe.
The business made Pablo and his partners billionaires. Pablo used
many millions of his dollars to aid the poorest people of Colombia,
building homes, buying food and medicine, paying school tuition,
and in so many different ways becoming their hero.

Meanwhile, his greatest fear, the greatest fear of all the traffickers, was that Colombia would enforce its extradition treaty with the United States and they would end up in an American prison.

In 1982 Pablo entered politics and was elected as an alternate to Congress; perhaps to serve the lower classes of his country as he claimed or perhaps to insulate himself from extradition as an elected official. Although Pablo claimed his money had been earned in real estate, in 1983 Minister of Justice Rodrigo Lara Bonilla accused him of being a drug dealer; for the first time the rumors had become public. When Lara Bonilla was killed in April 1984, Pablo was blamed and his political career ended.

For the first time the extraordinary violence for which the Medellín cartel would become known became part of Colombia's daily life; in 1985 almost 1,700 people were murdered in Medellín, a figure that would continue to grow. Pablo and the leaders of the cartel were forced into hiding for the next few years, at times spending months in the jungles, often escaping just minutes ahead of government forces. In November of 1985 rebels launched a massive attack on the Palace of Justice; hundreds of people died, among them justices of the Supreme Court. Pablo was accused of financing the attack in an effort to destroy all the evidence the government had collected against him, which was stored there. This attack on the government truly shocked Colombia, and people all over the world began learning the name Pablo Escobar.

In 1988 the rival Cali cartel also declared war on Medellín by bombing Pablo's houses. The killings throughout Colombia increased; at night the streets of the large cities were deserted. And still the flood of drugs into America continued growing. Pablo and his close associates, including his brother, Roberto, successfully managed to evade the enemies searching the country for them while he led his private army in battle. But one by one other leaders of the cartel were captured or killed.

By 1989 government officials were being killed and bombs were exploding in the big cities of the nation almost on a daily basis. But the civilized world was stunned once again when a commercial airliner, Avianca flight HK 1803, was bombed and all 107 passengers died. Pablo was blamed for this, adding to his growing reputation as one of history's most brutal criminals. A week later the headquarters of DAS, Colombia's FBI, was destroyed by a massive bomb; 89 people died. The Colombian government's war against Pablo Escobar was joined by American Special Ops teams.

Pablo retaliated by targeting police officers, and within a few months more than 250 policemen were killed. In 1991 the government finally outlawed the extradition treaty, and Pablo, Roberto, and a dozen other men surrendered and were housed in a prison that Pablo built and controlled, a prison known as the Cathedral.

In July 1992, the government attempted to invade the prison and capture the prisoners. While officially it was explained that Pablo was to be moved to a more strict prison, he believed this was an attempt to extradite him to America. Before he could be taken, he escaped into the jungles and the inner cities of Colombia, and the killing began once again.

The legend of Pablo Escobar continued to grow. As the world watched, Pablo Escobar successfully evaded thousands of soldiers from Colombia and America, as well as enemies from Cali and other groups organized to capture or kill him, for more than a year. One man against the organized armies of government. To draw him out some of these forces attacked his family, his friends, anyone who had ever been associated with him. In December 1993, as he tried to force the government to allow his family to leave the country, his hiding place was finally discovered. On December 2, one day after his forty-fourth birthday, he died on a rooftop trying to flee those soldiers who had found him.

Basically, that's the story of Pablo Escobar as it has been written.

But as I began speaking at great length with his brother, Roberto Escobar, who served as the accountant for Pablo's business, and later spoke with many others who knew him at various times of his life, I discovered a slightly different version of that story, the story told in these pages.

Roberto spoke with me as both a loving brother and a man desperately trying to correct history. The point he emphasized so many times was that the growing legend of Pablo Escobar was used by other groups to service their own needs, from the traffickers of Cali who were ignored while the focus remained on Pablo Escobar, to the various factions within the government who used the shadows that covered the search for him to settle old feuds and destroy growing opposition, and even by those men who once had worked for him and after being arrested provided information that would reduce their own sentences. It was easy for everyone to blame all the violence, all the killings, on Pablo Escobar. Americans certainly came to believe that Pablo Escobar was perhaps the primary source of the flood of cocaine from Colombia, and that killing or capturing him would end the problem. Few Americans knew the names of anyone outside the Medellín cartel. Obviously that has proved not to be true, as the cocaine tide never receded.

At times it was very difficult for Roberto to accept that the little brother he had protected as a child and loved dearly had become the criminal Pablo Escobar. For legal and security reasons there were people that Roberto could not identify by name and details that he could not reveal, so an occasional name has been changed and some details have been blurred to make them less identifiable, but no less accurate.

From others who knew Pablo well and worked for him or with him I heard stories that often differed from the accepted history and revealed a much more complex Pablo Escobar than I'd learned about through my research.

As with every legend, there are numerous competing stories. While it's sometimes impossible to determine which of these stories is true, there can be absolutely no doubt that Pablo Escobar was the mastermind behind the most successful criminal operation in history, as well as the brutal force behind the years of chaos and violence that plagued Colombia. He was the larger than reality figure vilified and loved by the people of his country.

But this is very much a brother's story.

DAVID FISHER

The
Accountant's
Story

This is the story of my family as I know it to be: More than one and a half centuries ago a woman named Ofelia Gavíria came from Vasco, Spain, to Colombia. She traveled legions of soldiers through the Gulf of Urabá, men intent on taking control of our beautiful lands and precious metals. Ofelia Gavíria was a wealthy woman, a landowner with many Indian slaves, who were well treated. She lived in the town of Murri but often visited nearby towns. But to do so she had to cross several rivers.

Is was a time of danger, and a group of Indians from the forests plotted her death. When she reached a certain bridge she was to be captured and pushed into the river, allowing those Indians to regain control of their native lands. But one of her loyal slaves warned her of this attack. This was a brave woman, and instead of avoiding these attackers, she went to them with sacks of gold. Eventually they came to work for her and adopted the surname Gavíria.

Several years later it was these Indians who found an infant in the forest who had been abandoned by his mother. They brought this child to Ofelia, who adopted him and raised him as her own blood. His name was Braulio Gavíria, who grew to be a handsome man and one day would marry a blue-eyed beauty named Ana Rosa Cobaleda Barreneche, herself from Spain. They had five children, and the last of them was Roberto Gavíria, who was to grow and become the grandfather of myself and my brother, Pablo Escobar, who was to become the most famous criminal in the world.

ROBERTO ESCOBAR, 2008

One

IN THE MONTH OF OCTOBER 2006 MY BELOVED MOTHER, Hermilda Gavíria, died. As she wished, she was to be buried next to my brother, the infamous Pablo Escobar Gavíria. The government of our country, Colombia, decided to use this opportunity to take a DNA sample from the body of my brother. The purpose was to prove to the world that the body in this grave was truly that of Pablo Escobar, the man who had risen from the streets to become the most powerful, the most beloved, and the man most despised by the ruling classes of Colombia. There were many people who believed my brother had not truly been killed on a Medellín rooftop by combined forces from America and Colombia in December 1993, but that another body had been substituted and Pablo lived free. Many others had claimed to be his children or a relative and so were entitled to some of the billions of dollars he had earned and hidden. This DNA sample would settle all of these claims.

Here Lies the King once had been inscribed on his tombstone, but the government had ordered it brushed away. Since his death the cemetery Monte Sacro has become a popular place for tourists. Countless thousands have come from around the world to have their picture taken at the grave of the legendary outlaw Pablo Escobar. Others have come to pray, light candles for his soul, leave written notes for him, or knock on the gravestone for good luck. And some have come to cry. But on the day of my mother's funeral only my family and witnesses from the government and military were there. And when Pablo's grave was opened they were shocked. A large tree had wrapped its roots around the coffin; it was as if long arms from the ground were clutching it tightly. As if it was being claimed.

I think about my brother every day. Pablo Escobar was an extraordinarily simple man: He was brilliant and kindhearted, passionate and violent. He was a man of both poetry and guns. To many people he was a saint, to others he was a monster. I think about him as a young child, lying next to me as we hid beneath our bed while the guerrillas came during the night to kill us all. I think about the drug organization he built and ruled, a business that stretched throughout much of the world and made him one of the richest men on earth. I think about the good things he did with that money for so many people, the neighborhoods he built, the many thousands of people he fed and educated. And, less often, I think about the terrible things for which he was responsible, the killings and the bombings, the deaths of the innocents as well as his enemies and the days of terror that shocked nations. I think about the sweet days and nights we spent with our families and our friends in the spectacular home he built called Napoles, Napoles with its animals and rare birds collected from around the world where even today a herd of rhinoceros runs free, and I think about the hard times we spent together living in the prison he built on a mountaintop and the many escapes into the jungle we made together as the army and the police searched desperately for us. At times our lives were like a dream, and then we lived in a nightmare.

I've never been a man of great emotions. I accept life in all its colors, I accept it all. Once I was a champion bicycle racer, and then a coach of our national team. I was a successful businessman who employed a hundred workers making bicycles and I owned five stores. It was then my brother asked me to handle the money he was earning from his business. For me, that's how it began. I have a lot of scars from those years, both on my body and my soul. And now I'm almost totally blind, the result of an attempt to kill me while I was in prison by sending me a letter bomb, and I live quietly on a ranch.

My brother will live forever in the history books, and in legend and lore. The greatest criminal in history, they call him. *Forbes* magazine listed him as the seventh richest man in the world, but even they had no concept of his true wealth. Each year we lost 10 percent of our earnings due to water damage, eaten by rodents, or simply misplaced. Robin Hood, the peasants of Colombia called him for the gifts he gave them.

Pablo controlled governments of other countries and set up a social security system for the poor of Colombia, he built submarines to transport cocaine, and he raised an army that waged war against the state and the other cartels. But some of the claims made against him are false. I don't excuse my brother for the terrible violence, but the truth is that he was not responsible for many of the crimes for which he has been blamed.

I was by his side much of the time, but not always. Many of the stories of his life I know to be true because I was with him, while others were told to me. The complete truth died on the rooftop with Pablo. But as I know it, this is the story of Pablo Escobar and the Medellín drug cartel.

There are many people who believe that it was Pablo who brought the terrible violence and death to Colombia but that isn't true. My brother and I were born into a civil war between the Conservatives and the Liberals, a period known in Colombia as La Violencia. In the decade ending in the mid-1950s peasant guerrilla armies murdered as many as 300,000 innocent people, countless thousands of them hacked to death with machetes. No one in Colombia was safe from these killers. Those murders were particularly hideous. Bodies were sliced apart and decapitated, throats were slit and tongues were ripped out and laid on the victim's chest, and in what became known as the *Corte Florero*, the Flower Vase Cut, limbs were cut off and then stuck back into the body like a macabre arrangement of flowers.

I will never forget the night the guerrillas came to our house in the town of Titiribu. Our father was a cattle rancher and Pablo and I were born on a cattle ranch that he had inherited from his father near the town of Río Negro, the Black River. We owned as many as eight hundred head of cattle. Our father was about work, hard work, and that was what was expected of us. It was our job to help with the cows. One of those cows, I remember, gave milk from its tail, or so we believed. Actually, an employee would wet down the tail with milk when we weren't looking, then when we came close he would shake it vigorously and spray us with milk. So for a time we believed this magic cow truly gave milk through its tail. Our father loved working on his farm, and our family would have stayed there if the herd had not been diseased. The cows caught a fever and more than five hundred of them died. Eventually my father had to declare bankruptcy and we lost the farm, we lost everything we owned.

My mother was a teacher, a role she loved equal to my father's love of farming, and we moved to Titiribu, where she was hired to teach. She would work in the school all week, and on weekends she would teach the children of poverty to read and write for free. While my father was a man of simple tastes, my mother was beautiful and elegant. She was blue-eyed and blond and had a very white complexion, and even with almost nothing to spend on herself she would always carry herself with great pride. The small wooden house in which we lived had one bedroom, which my brother, a sister, and I shared with our parents. We had two mattresses and one of them would be laid on the floor and the children would sleep on it. We barely had enough for food and Pablo and I would have to walk almost four hours each day to get to school. We left our house at four o'clock in the morning to be there at the beginning of class. Like so many others of Colombia, we were poor people. Our mother had to sew our school uniforms and often we wore old and torn clothes. Once, to her shame, Pablo was sent home from school because he had no shoes. Her teacher's pay had been spent, so she went to the plaza and took a pair of shoes for him, although when she had her salary she returned and paid for them. In Colombia, poor people have always tried to help each other. But our poverty made an impression on our lives that neither my brother nor I ever forgot.

When I was ten years old—Pablo was seven—I was given my first bicycle. It was a used bicycle that my mother paid for in many payments—and I would ride Pablo and myself to school. Our four-hour trip could be done in an hour. Each day I would challenge myself to get there a little faster; I began to race my friend Roberto Sánchez to school and it was then my love of racing bicycles was born.

It was that same year when the *Chusmeros*, the Mobs, came during the evening to kill us. The area in which we lived was the home of mostly liberals, and the guerrillas believed we shared those beliefs. That wasn't true, my parents had no politics. They wanted only to be left alone to raise their children. They had been warned to leave town or we would be cut into pieces, but there was nowhere safe for us to go. The most we could do was lock our doors at night. We were defenseless, our only weapon was our prayers.

They came to our town in the middle of the night, dragging people out of their houses and killing them. When they reached our house they started banging on the doors with their machetes and screaming that they were going to kill us. My mother was crying and praying to the Baby Jesus of Atocha. She took one of the mattresses and put it under the bed, then told us to lie there silently and covered us with blankets. I heard my father saying, "They're going to kill us, but we can save the kids." I held on to Pablo and our sister, Gloria, telling them not to cry, that we would be all right. I remember giving Pablo a baby bottle to calm him down. The door was very strong and the attackers failed to break through it, so they sprayed it with gasoline and set it on fire.

Our lives were saved by the army. When the soldiers knocked on our door and told us we were safe my mother didn't believe them, even though she eventually opened the door for them. They took all the survivors of the town to the schoolhouse. Our road was illuminated by our burning house. In that strange light I saw bodies lying in the gutters and hanging from the lampposts. The *Chusmeros* had poured gasoline on the bodies and set them on fire, and I will remember forever the smell of burning flesh. I carried Pablo. Pablo held on to me so tightly, as if he would never let go. We had left his baby bottle in the house and he was crying for it. I wanted to go back but my parents would not allow it.

So the killing in Colombia had started long before my brother. Colombia has always been a country of violence. It was part of our heritage.

A year after the attack my parents sent Pablo and me to live with our grandmother in the safety of the city of Medellín. Medellín was the most beautiful place I had ever seen. It is known as "the City of Everlasting Spring." And its climate was perfect, between 70 and 80 degrees throughout the year. Our grandmother had a large house, and part of it was used as a factory for her business of bottling sauces and spices, which she sold to the supermarkets.

At first the city frightened us. Medellín also is the second most populous city in Colombia. We were children of the country and knew nothing of city life. It was a big shock. We had never seen so many cars before, so many people always in a hurry. Our grandmother was a loving woman, but very stern. Each morning she would make us get up very early and go to church. I remember one morning after the first week she got sick and told me to take Pablo by myself to church: "You have to pray to God and come back." Coming out of the church I got confused and we were lost in the city. I didn't know my grandmother's address or her phone number. We walked many blocks looking for anything familiar, and then returned to the church to start again. I kept Pablo calm but inside I was scared. My prayers were not being answered. It was six in the evening before we finally found my grandmother's house.

That was the way our lives began in Medellín. Back in those early days it was impossible to believe that one day Pablo would rule the city and make it known throughout the world as the home of the Medellín drug cartel. Our mother and father eventually moved to Medellín to be with us, but my father would never be comfortable there. He returned to the country and found work on other people's farms. We would visit him, but we no longer belonged to the country. Medellín had become our city and eventually we would know every street, every alley. And eventually Pablo would die there.

It was on the streets of Medellín that we were formed. We were typical kids from the lower economic level. We built wooden carts from scrap wood and raced down hills. We stuck gum in the doorbells of our neighbors so they would ring continuously, then ran away. We would battle with eggs. We would make our own soccer balls by wrapping old clothes into a ball and putting them inside plastic bags. Pablo was always one of the youngest among us, but even then he was a natural leader. Sometimes, for example, when we were playing soccer in the street the police would come and take away our ball, and make us get out of the street. We weren't doing anything bad, we were kids playing. But Pablo had the idea that the next time the police came we should throw stones at their patrol car. And that's what happened.

Unfortunately, we cracked a window of the police car. We ran, but several of us—including myself and Pablo—were caught and taken to the police station. To scare us, the captain told us he was going to lock us in jail the whole day. Among us only Pablo spoke back to him. "We didn't do anything bad," he said. "We're tired of these guys taking our ball. Please, we'll pay you back." He was just a little kid, the smallest of us all, but he had no fear of talking directly to the commander.

Many of the friends we made as children would end up in the business with us, among them Jorge Ochoa, who with his brothers built his own organization, and Luis Carlos Maya, Mayín, we called him, who was very small and very thin. El Mugre, which means "dirt," which was the right name for him. Vaca, the cow, my closest friend, was tall and blond and had intense blue eyes and was the one of us the girls liked the most. When I was bicycle racing Vaca was my strongest supporter; before a race he would steal chickens from the local market and bring the chicken and some oranges to my house because he wanted me to be healthy for the competition. Our very close cousin Gustavo de Jesús Gavíria was the one who eventually started Pablo in the business and became his closest associate. Gustavo's father was a musician who was well known for his serenades, so Gustavo learned to play the guitar and sing so well that when he was eleven years old he won a talent competition on a popular radio station.

For some time I lived with Gustavo and his family. We would ride our bicycles together and one day as we reached a hill we grabbed on to the back of a bus to be pulled up. The driver had a different idea and after gaining speed he put on his brakes—Gustavo and I lost control and we went sailing through an open door into a house. We broke two vases and the lady called the police. But my grandmother paid for the damage and we went laughing into the streets.

We were good kids. We spent much of our time after school together, playing soccer until late at night, going to bullfights, flirting with beautiful young girls from our neighborhood. We all had our dreams; for me, I never wanted to get off my bicycle. The bicycle represented my freedom and I raced like the wind through the city. I wanted to be a professional bike rider; I wanted to represent Colombia in famous races in South America and Europe. But from our mother we learned the importance of an education. Even when we had nothing she knew we would go to college. For my profession I intended to be an electronics engineer. Mathematics has always been easy for me; I understood the language of numbers and enjoyed doing calculations, often in my head. I have always had the ability to remember numbers without having to write them down, which proved to be extremely important in the business. Pablo too knew what he wanted. Knowing poverty, he wanted to be rich. Even as a very young boy he would tell our mother, "Wait until I grow up, Mommy. I'm going to give you everything. Just wait until I grow up." And as he got older he decided, "When I'm twenty-two years old I want to have a million dollars. If I don't, I'm going to kill myself; I'm going to put a bullet in my head." Pablo had never seen a dollar bill in his life; he didn't know what a dollar bill looked like or how it felt in his hand. But he was determined to have a million dollars. And his other great ambition was equally improbable: He intended to become the president of Colombia.

As I've said, from our father we had learned the importance of hard work. One of the first true jobs that Pablo and I had was making deliveries on our bicycles from a factory where they made dentures to dentists all over Medellín. We'd race from dentist to dentist. I don't remember how much we were paid, but even after giving half of our salary to our mother, for the first time in our lives we had some money in our pockets to spend as we wished. The question was, what did we want the most?

We were teenagers, I was sixteen and Pablo thirteen. So that answer is obvious: girls. Pablo and I knew very little about sex. Our grandmother had a young and beautiful maid that we both admired.

As young men sometimes will do, when she was taking a shower we would put a chair by the window and take turns silently watching her. Once, I remember, when it was Pablo's turn he was standing on the chair when I heard our grandmother approaching. Naturally, I ran. Our grandmother caught Pablo and moved the chair, causing him to fall and break his finger.

But with our salary we decided we wanted to be with a woman. There was a club nearby called the Fifth Avenue Nightclub and we knew that prostitutes worked there. One night Pablo and I put on our best clothes and went to that club. This was it! We chose two beautiful women and paid them. They took us to a room then told us, "Wait." They went into the bathroom and returned carrying soap and hot water and towels. We didn't know what they were going to do, but it didn't seem good. So we got up and left. We practically ran away.

The next day we told the story to our friends, who laughed at us. "Don't be stupid," they told us. "These prostitutes wash you first because they want to make sure you're clean. Then they give you a massage and then have sex with you."

Oh. So Pablo and I saved for another two months before we had enough money to return. And this time neither of us ran away.

As my mother and I had dreamed, eventually I attended the Science and Electronics Academy in Medellín, where I became an electronics engineer. It was there I learned how to build and repair almost any electronic device. Later I was able to use those skills to design sophisticated security systems and even created the electronics for our submarines that carried cocaine to the Bahamas. For my thesis, I remember, I had to build a television set, a radio, and a stereo system from the pieces. While still at this academy I got a job working for the Mora Brothers, a large company that sold and repaired electronic equipment. Although I was one of the youngest workers, I became the head of their technical department.

This job came easily to me, and I took great pride in being the top student in my class. There was nothing beyond my skills, I believed—until the day a customer brought a Russian-made television into the store to be repaired. This I saw as a great challenge. I had never seen a TV like this one but I was sure I could fix it. I worked on it for more than a week but I couldn't solve the problem. Finally I brought it home with me to work on it at night. I pulled it apart and asked the housekeeper to clean the parts, which were covered with dust. As she was doing so she asked suddenly, "Mr. Roberto, what is this needle doing here?"

And that was how our housekeeper fixed the Russian television. Someone had stuck a small needle into a tube, and with all my tremendous expertise I had been unable to see what was right in front of me.

At the same time I was at the academy I enrolled in a second college to study accounting, University Remington. I didn't know exactly what I'd be doing in the future, but I was certain a knowledge of numbers would be helpful to me. The course came easily as the emphasis on numbers made it complementary to engineering. I learned all the systems necessary to run the business I intended to own someday.

While I enjoyed solving the complexities of electronics and the symmetry of numbers, the bicycle was my passion. When I started racing professionally Mora Brothers became my first sponsor. I was a champion racer; in 1966 I was named the second top cyclist in Colombia. I was a member of our national team and represented my country in competitions throughout Latin America, winning races in Ecuador and Panama as well as in Colombia. I was known as El Osito, the Bear, a nickname I earned in our national championships. That race had been held in the rain and as we came into the long, last stretch the streets were caked with mud. I took a bad spill, sliding through the wet clay, covering completely with that mud my face and my racing number. Near the end of the race I made a strong move and caught up with the leaders, but with my number being obscured the radio commentators couldn't identify me. So they said, we don't know who it is, but he is covered in brown like a bear, El Osito. Eventually I won the race and from that day forward in whatever I did that was my nickname. In fact, in the drug organization no one ever called me Roberto. Pablo was "the boss," "*el patrón*," sometimes "the doctor," but I was always El Osito.

Almost always when I raced Pablo was with me. He was my assistant. He'd wash my bicycle and prepare my uniform for the next race. And before the race he would kill a pigeon for me. Some people believed that the blood of pigeons provides energy, so Pablo would go to a park and capture a pigeon to give to me. Pablo would also make sure that big groups from our neighborhood would come to the races to cheer for me. In those days, I was his hero.

With the first salary I earned as a member of the national team in 1965 I purchased my first car—a blue German Warburt, and I saved my mother's house. Even with her teacher's salary and the money my father earned working on a farm, she had fallen months behind on the rent and was about to be evicted. It was the proudest day of my life when I was able to pay the overdue balance to the bank as well as several months in advance.

It's very difficult for me to describe the feelings that I experienced during a race, but in a life that has been full of extraordinary events I've never known anything comparable to it. Bicycle racing requires great physical stamina—but also an extreme mental toughness. And when everything is working perfectly in unison, the bicycle, your body, and your mind, the result is a sensation far beyond any kind of conscious thought.

It can be a dangerous sport too, and I was injured badly twice. Once while training I was racing behind a large truck on its way to a construction site. We used to like to do this because the body of the truck protected the rider behind it from the wind. What I didn't realize was that this truck was carrying pieces of wood. A small piece fell from the back and I couldn't avoid it. When my bike ran over it I lost control and went flying through the air. I landed on my right side and slid a long distance, basically ripping off a layer of skin from my legs, arms, and face. My helmet was cracked, the shoe on my right foot was destroyed, and I was bleeding very badly. They rushed me to the doctor. I hadn't broken any bones but it felt like my whole body was on fire. The doctor told me the therapy was going to be very painful. "Your skin is going to start growing back so you have to keep moving or your body will be very tight." To prevent the whole right side of my body from becoming one great scab I had to work out on a stationary bike for hours every day for more than a month. It was the most painful experience I'd ever gone through—until later.

When I retired as a racer I became the trainer of the team representing Antioquia, the second largest of the thirty-two departments or states that comprise Colombia, and later the trainer and assistant coach of the Colombian national team. While I was working with the national team we competed in Europe and Latin America and won several medals. By that time I was already married—the first of my three marriages—and was the father of two beautiful children, a son, Nicholas, and a daughter, Laura. My wife and I had dated two years and we were married on Halloween night because she was pregnant with Nicholas. We couldn't even afford a car at that time; we took the bus home from the small church in which we were married. Our dream was that someday we would be able to afford a home of our own.

I was a hard worker, and always honest in business. But also clever. To take advantage of the reputation I'd earned as a racer, in 1974 I took the money I'd saved and opened a shop in the beautiful mountaintop city of Manizales to build, sell, and repair bicycles. The El Ositto Corporation I named it—using two ts in the spelling because a popular Italian manufacturer used two ts in its name. The first thing I did was rent the outside of a large truck, I couldn't afford to rent the truck itself, and put a large advertisement on it. To begin building my business, one day I borrowed the truck and drove it to Bogotá, the capital of Colombia, and parked it directly in front of the biggest bicycle factory in the country. I asked to speak to the manager. After introducing myself I pointed to the truck and told him, "That's one of my trucks. I own the whole company." We were expanding, I explained, and we needed a reliable spare parts supplier to build more bicycles. I wanted to talk to them about forming a relationship. Well, naturally he was interested in obtaining my business. Eventually he agreed that I could take a large load of parts with me on credit. "I wish I could," I told him. "I can't because the truck is already full." Of course that wasn't true. I hadn't rented the inside of the truck so I was not permitted to use it. A few days later the manager delivered a truckload of parts to my store in Manizales, and I hired two additional workers and began building more bicycles. These were well-made bikes and because I was assembling them in Colombia I could sell them for substantially less than the bikes shipped from Europe.

But selling them still was difficult. Colombians loved the well-made Italian and Swiss bikes, and didn't want to buy bikes made in our country. I had a hard time getting Ositto bikes into the popular stores. I literally begged the owner of a major store to place a few of my bikes, telling him, "I'm going to sell them to you for much less than the bikes you bring in from Europe."

He refused, saying, "Nobody knows of Ositto bikes in Colombia." But finally he agreed to take five bikes, warning me that if they didn't sell within two weeks I should come and pick them up.

During the next week I sent five friends to the store to buy these bikes. The store owner placed a larger order and soon my bikes began selling to real customers. Eventually I was manufacturing seventeen different types of bicycles, including racing bikes, cross-country bikes, touring bikes, and even children's bikes. In addition to the factory I opened five stores; I had more than a hundred people working for me. In 1975 I even worked with our government sports minister to convert a soccer field that was not being used into a modern bicycle racing complex, where kids could race for free. I was being very successful on my own, working sixteen hours a day at my business and coaching the team. I owned two apartments and was able to help my mother with her expenses. My future was very promising. And this happened long before Pablo and I got involved in the drug business.

In 1974 Pablo was studying political science at the Universidad de Antiochia. There are many who believe Pablo was an uneducated man who succeeded only through drugs. That simply is not true. Pablo was very smart about many different subjects. He had a true understanding of subjects as different as history and poetry. He could talk easily about world politics and loved to recite the most beautiful poems. At times, Pablo would even surprise me; he spoke several languages and when we were imprisoned in La Catedral, the Cathedral, the fortress he built after we agreed to surrender to the government, he even studied Chinese. At the university he had decided that he would become a criminal lawyer, which would be his path into politics. He still intended to become the president of Colombia. He would often go to the public library to read law books and, when he could afford it, bought used books. It was there that he actually began his political career. Like many students, he would stand up at lunch or on the soccer field and make speeches to anyone who would listen. Pablo was never shy about speaking in public and always had great confidence in his ideas. I only heard him speak a few times, but I remember him saying in a loud and passionate voice, "I want to be president of Colombia, and when I am I'll take 10 percent of the earnings of the richest people to help the poor. With those funds we'll build schools and roads." He also said he wanted to encourage Japanese and Chinese manufacturers to build factories in Colombia, which would provide jobs for people who desperately needed them.

Pablo had very large dreams, but he had no money to make them come true. He was forced to drop out of the university because he could not pay the necessary fees. When you've grown up poor, as we did, the need to make money is always uppermost in your mind. Maybe it was ordained that eventually Pablo would work outside the law. It was an important part of our family history.

Colombia is a beautiful country and rich in the gifts of nature, but it is a place where corruption has always been an accepted part of our lives. Our country has always been ruled by a class of wealthy families that did very little to help the poor. There were very few social programs that assisted people in making their lives better. We have a system of laws in Colombia, but we lived by a different set of rules. From the time we were growing up the government was run by corrupt people who made themselves richer while claiming they were starting programs to help the less fortunate live a better life. From the highest offices of the political rulers to the leaders of the military, from the civil servants who controlled the government offices to the policeman on the street, people with even a little power have used it whenever possible for personal gain. The police, for example, were poorly trained, very badly paid, and were not at all respected, so just to survive, many of them accepted bribes to look away from illegal activities. If you wanted to get something done in Colombia and you had the money it was not difficult to get it done. Pablo and I grew up knowing that all the rules were for sale. It was not considered good nor bad, it's just the way it has always been.

In fact, the Colombian journalist Virginia Vallejo, a woman who became a loving part of my brother's life, once said she fell in love with him because "he was the only rich man in Colombia who was generous with the people, in this country where the rich have never given a sandwich to the poor."

I was named after my maternal grandfather, Roberto Gavíria, but it was Pablo more than me who inherited his history. Every family has its story, and the story of the Escobar-Gavíria family began the morning Roberto Gavíria decided to plant bananas in his backyard in the town of Frontino. So the story goes, he discovered a *guaca*, a treasure buried in the ground consisting of several clay pots filled with jewelry and precious stones. No one ever learned the source of these riches. At least, that's the way the story has been passed down to the family.

Rather than revealing his fortune, which would have been dangerous, Roberto slowly and quietly sold the jewelry. Some of the proceeds he used to make loans to other farmers—but he lost that money when they couldn't repay him. Then he bought wild animal furs from the Indians in Chocó and resold them in town. And finally he discovered his true calling: smuggling tobacco and liquor.

Like Al Capone in the United States, Roberto Gavíria was a bootlegger. He bought *tapetusa*, a favorite alcoholic drink of Colombians, directly from the Indians who distilled it and bottled it before it was sold to legal distributors. To bring it directly to his customers without paying the government fees that made it expensive, he would hide the bottles in a sealed coffin, and then hired men to carry it through a town and young women to walk alongside crying. The people of the town would quickly—and very happily, learn what was actually in those wooden boxes. In his hometown of Frontino he sold the *tapetusa* from the living room of his mother's home, hiding it from authorities by draining egg shells with a needle, then refilling them with his liquor. It was a very successful business—until a neighbor informed on him and he was arrested. And that was when the most important lesson was learned: A few days later my grandfather was released without punishment. Although truthfully we don't know all the facts of that situation, I think it is proper to assume that he shared his profits with those in power. In Colombia, that's the way business has always been done.

It was while Pablo was in college that he started earning money. As with all aspects of his life, many stories have been written that are based in truth but are not completely accurate. It has been accepted, for example, that Pablo began his career in crime by stealing tombstones, blasting off the inscription, and reselling them. In fact, our uncle had a small shop close to the largest cemetery in Medellín from which he engraved and sold marble tombstones. Rather than going in the dark of night and stealing tombstones, Pablo would buy the very old stones from cemetery owners who would remove bodies from the ground many years after the last person came to pay respects. And perhaps sometimes he did take stones from old graves, but most of them he bought legally and took to our uncle's shop to be cleaned and used again. With the money he earned from this business Pablo bought a motorcycle, the first vehicle he ever owned.

It has also been written in many books that Pablo would steal cars. Supposedly, he was so successful in that business that citizens and insurance companies agreed to pay him a fee not to steal the cars they insured, providing him with a list of protected cars. Now, as close as I was to my brother I don't know every detail of his life. At this time of our lives we were living in different cities and some things might have happened that I did not know about. But if he had been stealing cars I would have known about it. And additionally, a few years later when he began transporting kilos of cocaine he bought my used Renault 4 from me—which would not have been necessary if he stole cars. This story became popular in the early 1980s when Pablo decided to run for political office and his opponents began telling stories about his background. In addition to claiming that he was a drug dealer, they said he also was a car thief, a kidnapper for ransom, a brutal killer—and that he had stolen tombstones. Legends are built in many ways, but part of such legends consists of accusations made by enemies, and often for their own benefit. In America, for example, the stories that are told about the legendary heroes of the West, the famous outlaws like Billy the Kid and Jesse James, are based in truth but much of them are exaggeration. This is true for Pablo as well. In his death, so many people who never even knew him have made claims that just are not true.

But what Pablo did do illegally to make money, just like our grandfather Roberto, was become involved in contraband. The business of contraband means simply bringing goods into the country without paying the required government fees, the duties and taxes, which allows you to sell the goods to people for much less money than they would have to pay in the stores. It's very profitable. While contraband certainly is illegal, because it benefits people and hurts only the government, it has long been an accepted part of the Colombian economy. In fact, when the police caught someone doing contraband without paying their bribes they used to take the merchandise but didn't put any people in jail.

One of the most successful groups of smugglers in Medellín was run by a multimillionaire named Alvaro Prieto. He earned his fortune bringing cigarettes, electronic equipment, jewelry, watches, and clothing from America, England, and Japan. Shipping containers from these countries arrived in the Panamanian city of Colón, near the end of the canal, and were taken from there to the Colombian city of Turbo on the Gulf of Urabá. There the containers were unloaded and large trailer-trucks carried the merchandise to Medellín for distribution.

As with many parts of Pablo's life, there are different stories about the way he met Alvaro. One of the stories is that Pablo and some friends of his were captured by the police protecting Prieto's trucks. In the capture supposedly Pablo got shot twice. Instead of letting him die, Prieto bailed him out and saved his life. But the real story is that Pablo went to a soccer game to meet up with some associates. At this game Pablo was formally introduced to Alvaro, who immediately took a liking to Pablo and offered him a job as a bodyguard. The story continues that Prieto recognized Pablo's potential and decided to teach him the ways of smuggling. "The way to make money is to protect the merchandise for the guy who has the money, and that's who I am."

At first Pablo concentrated only on cigarettes, using connections he had to sell them at the small stores and many flea markets around the city. By doing this successfully Pablo established his credibility with the contraband organization. Eventually Alvaro asked him to help solve an expensive problem. The hardworking peasants who unloaded the containers and packed the merchandise in trucks were paid badly. There were about fifty of them and they didn't live much better than slaves. As a result they had absolutely no loyalty to the organization and sometimes stole more than half of the goods from the containers. Alvaro offered Pablo 10 percent of the value of the load if he could reduce the theft. Pablo surprised him by turning him down, instead volunteering to supervise a load for nothing to prove his value. That was the agreement they made.

His first day in Turbo, Pablo served a lunch of seafood and wine to the workers and told them, "I'm here to represent the boss. I'm not going to make trouble for you, but I need you to work with me. If the merchandise continues to disappear your work is going to end and my work is going to end." Then he made them an offer. "I'm going to give you half of my salary forever if you work with me. But this time if we show the boss that you don't take anything, I promise when I come back in two weeks to take care of you guys."

There are some stories that Pablo threatened these men if they stole from the load. Many people believe that Pablo was successful in his operations only because people were afraid of him. That's not true. Pablo knew that profits generated more loyalty than fear. People who did business with Pablo and were honest made a lot of money; only those people who cheated him, stole from him, threatened him, or betrayed him suffered at his hands. Anyone who knows how tough the workers of Turbo are, and understands the way they live and their pride, would know that they did not cooperate out of fear. This was long before Pablo had established his reputation for terror and he couldn't fight them on his own. In fact, it was because of his offer to pay these people a fair salary that most of them who had already taken merchandise from the containers even returned what they had stolen.

Pablo led the convoy of five or six trailers in a jeep. As was expected of him, he made the required payments to policemen in the small towns and on the roads along the way. After the contraband was delivered to warehouses in Medellín, Pablo told Alvaro, "The problem was the guys running this for you didn't care about your workers. They didn't even pay them on time. By being fair with these guys I delivered the whole load to you." Prieto was delighted—probably until Pablo told him his own offer to continue the business. "You said I could do it for 10 percent," he said. "I want 50 percent."

I wasn't there, but I could imagine how Alvaro responded. I know he wasn't used to having his workers make such large demands from him. Pablo told me he asked, "Are you crazy?"

"I think it's fair," Pablo said back. "Sometimes you've been losing more than half the products. This way you'll be getting it all, and even by giving me 50 percent you'll be making more money because nobody will be stealing anything."

Prieto said 50 percent was too much—they settled for 40 percent. It proved to be a beneficial deal for him as well as Pablo. Eventually Pablo expanded the business, adding products like washers and dryers, which then were not common in Colombia—to his deliveries. Pablo became a true partner in the contraband business, supervising loads from their delivery in Panama to the warehouses in Medellín. He became an expert at moving goods through the country. To secure the money he was paid, he built *caletas*, hiding places or safes, in the walls of his house in which he kept tens of thousands of dollars. They were protected with electronic doors that only he knew how to open.

Pablo developed a strong relationship with the workers in Turbo. He kept his word and gave half of his cut to the workers, who became the first people to bestow on him the title by which he became very well known, el patrón, the boss. He also gained the trust of the citizens of the towns his convoys had to pass through, winning their allegiance by paying them in cash and merchandise.

My brother was making a huge amount of money. Usually they ran two loads a month and Pablo could earn as much as $120,000 from each of them. And so he was able to achieve his teenage vow that he would become a millionaire by the time he was twenty-two. It's very difficult to explain to anyone who has not experienced it, the incredible feelings you have of being rich after you've grown up with having very little. Most people have some dreams come true, but suddenly Pablo was in a situation where he could pay for more than all his dreams. The first things he did was make a down payment on a house for our mother, he bought a car for himself, he bought a taxicab for our cousin, and for me he bought a very expensive titanium bicycle from Italy, a bicycle that weighed so little I could pick it up with two fingers. One day I went with him and some of our friends to an outdoor food market; we filled up a truck with lettuce and meat and fish and took it to the poorest neighborhood in Medellín. There was a large garbage dump where the rejects from the city were thrown and these people survived by picking through this mountain of trash for food or clothing that could be repaired and worn or goods that might be cleaned and sold. We went there and Pablo handed out this food. The people loved him for it. That was the type of thing he would often do with his money. Pablo would eventually do many terrible things, but he never forgot the poor people, and they loved him for it. And even until today they remember him and celebrate his life.

One other thing we did was take our entire family to Disney World in Orlando, Florida. We were about twenty people, including our mother, sisters, and my children. I don't remember all the rides we rode on, or other places we visited, although we did go to a dog show, but I remember the joy we shared. For my family this was one of the first of our many dreams that came true. Before the nightmares, of course. When we were growing up, like most Colombians, we had greatly admired the United States. But once we finally got here it seemed even more amazing than we had imagined. Everything we saw seemed so big and so beautiful, all of the people seemed to be so successful. And Disney World, I remember that it was so clean and so well organized. And most of all I remember how much fun we had and how free of worries we were.

Pablo worked in the contraband business for almost three years. During that time he earned more money than any of us had thought possible—except Pablo, of course—and to save it he had to open a lot of different bank accounts, many of them in assumed names. At that time our government paid little attention to the amount of money Colombians had in banks. No one tracked it. No one had a legal right to ask any questions about where money came from. Eventually Pablo asked me to manage this money. It was my job to make payments to all his employees, deposit the money in banks and other secure places, and to begin making smart investments. This was the time I first became the accountant.

Generally Pablo and I would meet once or twice a week. With my encouragement we eventually began investing the money in real estate, buying land and buildings and financing construction. This was something Pablo would do for the rest of his life. At one time, for example, he owned as many as four hundred farms throughout the country. I used the real estate deals to protect Pablo's money. If his contraband business should be discovered the government had the right to take the money he had earned from it, so I created a new set of books to prove he had earned his money from real estate. For example, if we sold an apartment for $50,000, in those books the sale was recorded as $90,000. In this way we were able to create very complicated paths that were impossible to follow to the source. I don't remember precisely how much money Pablo earned in the three years he worked in the contraband business, but in addition to becoming a wealthy man himself, he improved the lives of many people who worked with him.

It was during this time that we got guns for the first time. Pablo was given his gun by the contraband boss known as El Padrino. And Pablo gave me the first gun I owned as a birthday present, a Colt, in a gift bag along with a nice suit, tie, and shoes. "You need it," he said. "You're carrying around a lot of money. You gotta be careful, you gotta protect yourself." Growing up on the farm we had fired a gun at birds, but we didn't really know how to use it. Certainly, I didn't. A friend of Pablo's, a captain in the police, helped me get a permit to carry it. I was not comfortable with it, I hid it from my wife, but Pablo was right. I carried around a lot of cash. I had to be able to protect myself. Fortunately, at that time I never needed it.

Had his involvement in contraband continued anything might have happened. It's possible he would have used his profits to go directly into politics. He might have done special things. But the business ended suddenly. What happened was that a corrupt police official with whom he had been doing business betrayed him. This high-ranking member of the police force had been on Pablo's payroll for several years, being well paid to facilitate passage of goods through his region. But when he was transferred to another city he knew he would lose these payments, so to gain favor with his bosses he told them everything he knew about Pablo's business. Their plan was to intercept the next convoy. That would be worth a fortune to them.

By this time Pablo's convoys included as many as forty trucks. One thing about my brother, he always had luck. Usually he drove in his jeep in front of the trucks. But on this trip he decided he was going to stop for lunch in a nice restaurant. He told the drivers to keep going and eventually he would catch up and make the payoffs to the local police in towns along the route. At that time the police trusted Pablo so there should have been no problem with this. But while Pablo was eating, under orders from superiors, the police stopped the convoy and seized thirty-seven of the trucks. One of the three drivers who got away called Pablo and told him what had happened. "Tell the drivers not to say anything to anyone," Pablo said.

Alvaro accepted the loss. "Forget about the trucks," he said. "Just come back to Medellín."

There was nothing Pablo could do to save the merchandise. Instead of driving the jeep back to the city he took a public bus, which allowed him to get past the police who were waiting for him. Alongside the road he saw the thirty-seven captured trucks. Eventually Pablo hired lawyers and paid officials to get the drivers released. Their defense was that there was no proof they knew they were transporting contraband. They were just simple truck drivers. Eventually all the drivers were released. But for Pablo, this was the end of the contraband business. And the beginning of the life that made him infamous.

Today the cocaine business is a well-established part of the world culture. Everybody knows about it. Storms of cocaine use have rolled over countries like the United States. Because of Pablo and the Medellín and Cali cartels Colombia has become known mostly for the export of cocaine. But when Pablo started working in the cocaine business it was not that way at all. In the United States cocaine was not considered a big problem; in fact, most people didn't know very much about it at all. While in Colombia we knew much about cocaine, primarily because the paste from which it is made came from our region, the distribution business had not spread much beyond our borders. The cocaine we made was mostly sold and used in our country. No one was sending cocaine from Colombia to the United States. No one was earning a billion dollars' profit from it.

Once cocaine had been widely and freely used in America. A small amount was part of the original Coca-Cola and some cigarettes; it could be bought in drugstores. The first laws were passed against it in America in 1914, when people were told it made black people in the South crazy and caused them to attack white women. But mostly the police left people who used cocaine alone. Only in 1970 did the American government make it a so-called controlled substance, which caused the police to start making arrests for selling it and using it. Doing this made it more dangerous for dealers and more difficult for users to find it, which made it more expensive to buy. And much more profitable to sell.

Cocaine comes from the leaf of the coca plant, which grows best in the jungles of Peru, but also in Bolivia, Colombia, and Ecuador. It was everywhere in the mountains and jungles of Peru long before people started growing it to sell. The Indians have used it for medicine and chewed it for energy for all of known history. It was 150 years ago, in 1859, that a German scientist discovered a way to bring out from those leaves the exact white substance that made people feel so good. The base. He named it cocaine. Other people began adding it to many different products. It was only much later that people understood its dangers, that it was like a magnet, that once you were attracted to it you couldn't easily get free of it.

Neither Pablo nor I ever used cocaine when we were growing up. As we got older occasionally Pablo liked to smoke marijuana. He had a saying: "I love marijuana because it relaxes me—and it can't be bad because it comes from the earth."

Pablo did not tell me he had decided to become involved in the cocaine business. He just told me that contraband was getting too dangerous, that it required too much traveling and there were too many people involved, so he was going to do something different. In fact, I don't think transporting cocaine was something he had carefully been planning for a long time or even gave much consideration. Certainly he didn't think that this was going to become his life and he would become the biggest cocaine dealer in the world. I think the opportunity was there and Pablo recognized it. This was simply an easier way to make money than contraband. It was possible to make more money with a single load that one person could transport in a car than with all the merchandise in forty trucks. At that time Pablo was one of the few who brought the cocaine from Peru to Colombia, and then to the United States. But the other people doing it almost never transported more than a few kilos—a kilo is 2.2 pounds—at a time. There was a good profit to be made and it wasn't too difficult or too dangerous. There was no such thing then as a drug cartel, instead there were just some people who were bigger in the business. One of the most successful and most ruthless was a woman from Medellín that everybody knew about named Griselda Blanco, who was called the Black Widow because three of her husbands had died. Eventually she had moved to the United States and ran her business in Miami. So it took almost nothing to get started in the business except some money and some guts, and the chances of rewards were high.

The idea to do the business came originally from a man known as Cucaracho, the Roach, who asked Pablo and our cousin Gustavo Gavíria to go with him to Peru to arrange a deal. Gustavo's father was our uncle who owned the shop that produced tombstones. Pablo and Gustavo were especially close and would stay that way until Gustavo was kicked to death by the police in front of his residence in 1990. In the drug organization Pablo built, Gustavo was the closest to him at the top. Gustavo was a partner; the two of them started the business together on this trip. He was a great guy—funny, smart, and very clever. His official job before the business was as an English teacher in a lower school. The two of them spent a great amount of time together, and both of them were passionate about soccer and racing cars. Later, when they could easily afford it, they would often race against each other in anything that moved fast, from cars to Jet Skis.

In Peru, Cucaracho introduced Pablo and Gustavo to people who would sell them the cocaine paste, the base, which would be refined into something pure. Returning with this paste to Medellín required driving through three countries, Peru, Ecuador, and Colombia. To complete this trip in each country Pablo purchased yellow Renault 4s—one of them from me—and put the correct national license plate on each one. I still remember the license plate of my car, LK7272. He drove the first car to the Ecuador border and transferred his package. He drove the second car across Ecuador to the border with Colombia and again changed the package. And then he drove it to its final destination, the neighborhood Belén situated in Medellín where he had prepared a "kitchen," it was called, to make the drugs.

The Renaults were specially prepared to secret the package. The design of this car had very large wheel wells, meaning there was a lot of empty space right inside the fenders above the front wheels. A stash was made above the wheel on the passenger side to hold the package. On this first trip, and the many that followed, Pablo and Gustavo had to pass through police checkpoints. The police always approached the car on the driver's side, away from the drugs. Sometimes they would search the whole inside of the car, but never under the chassis. On his very first trip Pablo bought one kilo of the paste, which cost about $60.

To build his market, after the paste had been converted to cocaine, Pablo gave some of it to about ten people to try. Almost all of them liked it better than marijuana. They found out that when they were drinking they could take cocaine and it would calm them down. It also gave them energy. Most of them wanted to use it again and asked Pablo for more, and eventually they shared it with other people and this is how Pablo found his customers. I know Pablo never used it because he didn't like it.

And this was how Pablo Escobar began in the cocaine business.

Two

I SAW THE STRANGE PRIEST IN MY MIND for the first time the night in 1976 I was driving from Manizales to Medellín to try to get Pablo out of jail. He had been arrested for smuggling cocaine. But from that night until today the priest will still visit me with warnings.

All of this happened because people wanted cocaine. Pablo found he could easily sell as much as he could bring into our country. The business grew very rapidly, but at the beginning it was just Pablo and Gustavo. In fact, I remember that my brother asked our mother to make him a jacket with a double cover, a secret lining, so he could hide the merchandise and the cash he had to carry. One member of Pablo's organization, the Lion, remembers carrying as much as $3 million in cash in the lining as he made more than twenty flights between Medellín and New York, bringing the drugs to America and the cash back to Colombia. Hermilda, who made the first such jacket, certainly did not know what this jacket was for, she was very innocent about all of this. One night the family was at the dinner table when Pablo handed her some money. "Pablo," she said, "I heard you are washing the money. Is this money laundered?"

"Yes, of course," he said.

She shook her head. "Then why is it not wet?" I can still hear our laughter.

Soon the Renault 4s were too small so Pablo bought trucks that could carry as many as twenty kilos each journey. The drugs came through Ecuador to the agricultural city of Pasto in southwest Colombia. One of the biggest products of Pasto is potatoes and Colombians are used to seeing large trucks carrying loads of potatoes from the border. Pablo had the idea of secreting many kilos of cocaine in a large spare tire carried by the trucks. It worked very well for several months. Still at this time I didn't know what Pablo and Gustavo were doing.

Pablo and Gustavo hired several drivers and helpers, each pair of them being responsible for a different section of the trip, because they didn't want anyone else knowing their route. One of the drivers was known as Gavilán, meaning Vulture. Gavilán was stupid; with the money Pablo paid him he bought a car and a motorcycle and expensive clothes. Gavilán had an uncle who worked for the DAS, the Departamento Administrativo de Seguridad, Colombia's FBI, and he wondered what his nephew was doing to earn so much money. "It's nothing," Gavilán told him. "I'm working with this guy and all I do is drive a truck with potatoes from Pasto to Medellín." The DAS agent started an investigation. All the details were never known, but somehow they found out the truth. One day the DAS and the police stopped the truck outside Medellín. They told the driver that everything was set; he just had to call the boss and tell him that he had to pay a bribe for the truck to continue. As Pablo told me later, he was not surprised when he got the phone call, as this was often the way business was done in Colombia. But when he and Gustavo showed up at the designated meeting place they were arrested.

I didn't learn about this until the next day. I was in the city of Manizales meeting with the coaching staff of the national bicycling team, preparing for a speech I was to give that evening, when I saw the police picture of Pablo on the front page of the newspaper. I was stunned; I knew he was doing contraband, but not drugs. My first fear was what this would do to my own position with the team. I was worried I would be fired. But then I realized that no one at this meeting knew Pablo was my brother. I decided to be cool. I'd give my speech and then I would try to help.

I called my mother, who had been crying for hours. Remember, we had no cell phones then and she had not been able to find me. I told her I knew nothing about it, but that certainly I would do whatever I could to help my brother.

I tried to give my speech that night, but it was impossible. I apologized and said I was feeling sick and had to leave. The drive from Manizales to Medellín took about eight hours. I was with a good friend who eventually would work for Pablo in the cartel. We were driving a Dodge truck. I drove for several hours, then allowed my friend to take over. Today Colombia has nice highways, but at that time it was mostly narrow old roads. I sat back in the passenger seat and began thinking about what I would have to do right away. As soon as I got back to Medellín I had to make sure our financial records were the way we wanted them to be. The government was not going to check the source of Pablo's funds, but they might want to see how much he had earned from drug deals. I had to make sure that all the money he had in the banks was based on recent real estate transactions.

It was 3:30 in the morning and we were the only car on the road. I saw that we were running short of fuel and began looking around for a gas station. As I did I saw a man dressed in black, with a round black hat on his head, standing by the side of the road. To me, he looked like a priest. I thought that was very strange: What was a priest doing standing alone on the road in the middle of the night? As we came close to him my friend didn't even slow down. "Hey," I practically yelled at him, "stop the car! Stop the car!"

We raced right past the man. I saw his face looking at me. I said to my friend, "Man, I'm telling you to stop the freaking car!" Then I turned around and looked back—and the man was gone. He had disappeared.

A little while later we drove past an open gas station—and again he refused to stop. He didn't stop until we finally ran out of gas. I was furious with him. "What's the matter with you? Why didn't you stop to pick up that guy? I told you to stop at the gas station."

He looked at me like I was crazy. "What are you talking about? You never told me to stop. There was no guy on the road."

I got goose bumps. Even now when I think about it my body goes cold. I know what I saw that night. And more important, that was only the first time I would see the priest. And I would learn to understand what it meant when I saw him.

We had to walk back to the gas station but eventually we got home. I saw Pablo a day later at the Itagüi prison, one of the toughest jails in Medellín. He didn't want to talk about his situation, just telling me that he would take care of it. He spent eight days there, then paid someone to arrange his transfer to a more relaxed prison. This was more of a farm than a jail; the prisoners were allowed to walk free, play soccer, even eat their meals outside. He spent more than two months there waiting for his trial. During that time, I believe, some arrangements were made with the local judge. In addition, my mother became friends with the director of the prison, bringing him meals, because she was there so often. Unfortunately, because the crime began in Pasto, it was decided the trial would take place there. But that was much more dangerous for Pablo, as he was going to be tried by a military judge, and those judges were difficult to corrupt. If Pablo and Gustavo were convicted in a military court it was possible he would receive a long sentence.

Pablo's attorney informed him of this the day before the transfer was to take place. Pablo became concerned; he didn't know anybody in Pasto who could help him. It was possible he wasn't going to be able to make a deal for their freedom. So late that night he told one of the guards that he couldn't sleep and needed to take a walk around the soccer field. "I need to relax," he said. "I need to stretch my legs."

He stretched them a long distance. He escaped that night. I can imagine that people were paid to help him. He walked out of the jail. Several hours after his escape the director called my mother to plead for assistance. "I don't know what to do. I'm expecting an airplane from the air force to bring the boys to Pasto," he told her. "If he isn't here they might put me in jail myself. He has to return. I promise, nothing is going to happen to him.

"I was so good with them," he said. "I let them walk wherever they wanted to go. And now I'm going to be punished for it."

When Pablo finally called our mother to tell her he escaped she was angry. "I wonder who you think you are? You've got to do things right. You have to go back," she explained. "Things will be okay." Pablo agreed and she went to meet him. Many years later our mother would risk her life meeting without security with our enemies from Cali and from a group organized to kill Pablo, Los Pepes. Hermilda Gavíria was a brave woman who would do anything to protect her children.

She took a taxi to meet Pablo. She was worried how the director would explain his absence to the military, but Pablo came up with a plan. Instead of returning immediately to the prison they went to visit a doctor. Pablo paid the doctor a lot of money to make up some documents that Pablo had been very, very sick, some problem with his digestive system. The doctor put Pablo's name on X-rays of a patient who really had a problem. And by 11 A.M. Pablo and our mother showed up at the prison. Pablo apologized to the director and confessed he had been feeling very bad. "I thought I was going to die," he said.

Thankfully the air force plane had not been able to fly because of bad weather. Eventually Pablo and Gustavo and their drivers were taken by truck to Pasto. He was lucky because the government changed the system and he had the opportunity to use his money there. He bought the judge, although I don't know how much money it cost him. As part of the arrangement the driver, Frank, who had been caught with the merchandise in the truck, agreed to plead guilty to trafficking drugs and say that Pablo and Gustavo were not involved in the deal. Frank the driver was sentenced to less than five years.

Pablo told him, "During the time you're in jail you're going to have everything and your family is going to be taken care of. It's like you're working hard and there is money in the bank." Pablo arranged for him to be held in a nice jail. And for his family he gave them a house and car and a good bank account. It was my job to make certain that Frank and his family regularly received the payments.

The first Sunday Pablo was out of jail we had dinner together at our mother's house. It was then I tried to talk him away from cocaine. "This is bad. Don't do this," I told him. "There's no need. You're making so much money in contraband. Why do you want to get messed up with this stuff?" That's when he told me how everything had started.

But he promised me, "Don't worry, brother, I'm not going to do this for long. It's just to make some money. Then I'm going to stick to contraband, because if they catch me they just take the merchandise, they don't put you in prison."

I told him that he was hurting me too. I was a successful businessman, my stores were selling my bicycles and I was receiving my salary from the government for coaching. I wondered if the government would allow the brother of a drug dealer to coach the national team. He promised me that he was done with the cocaine deals. I don't remember if I believed him.

Pablo went right back to the business. By this time he was known to the police. More than a month later the same two DAS agents who had arrested Pablo and Gustavo earlier stopped them once again. This time their plans were different. They took them to El Basurero, the desolate area where a mountain of garbage was being created, tied their hands together, and made them get down on their knees. They were very hard with them. Pablo believed he was about to be murdered, but he stayed cool. He never begged for his life, rather he negotiated. Eventually the DAS kidnappers agreed to accept one million pesos to let them live. They set Gustavo free to go get the money. While waiting for Gustavo to return they spoke, and Pablo offered more money to learn who had set him up. The purchased answer was surprising: El Cucaracho. The man who had put Pablo in this business was worried that Pablo was taking control. To protect his business he had bought their death. Unfortunately, that also was the way this business was done.

Eventually they were paid their ransom and allowed Pablo and Gustavo to go free. The legend makes it clear that this was an insult Pablo could never forgive. Kidnapping for ransom was an accepted part of our lives, but by making him go down on his knees they paid him no respect. The story is that Pablo promised, "I'm going to kill those motherfuckers myself." Only a few days later these corrupt agents were planning to kidnap another worker of Pablo's. At that time the name Pablo Escobar wasn't known, so no one had reason to be afraid of him. For the agents he was just another drug dealer. But instead of being successful in this attempt, they were caught themselves. Pablo never told me this whole story. I have heard from others that Pablo had them brought to a house, made them get down on their knees, then put a gun to their head and killed them. Maybe. But I do know that the newspapers reported finding the bodies of these two DAS agents who had been shot many times.

From this time forward Pablo was in the business of distributing cocaine, at first only in Colombia but eventually to at least fifteen countries and through those countries much of the world. Toward the end of his life the cartel was even beginning to move into Eastern Europe, into the communist nations. At the height of its business the Medellín cartel was producing and delivering tons of cocaine weekly, tons, but for Pablo it began by producing a few kilos by hand in a small house.

I don't remember the day Pablo told me the whole truth about his business. It was soon. As I was the man taking care of the money, of course I had to know. Transforming the alkaloid from the coca leaf requires a process of several steps. It is a chemical process but it does not require experts to do it, just people who can follow simple steps. It is no more difficult than baking a cake. The process is done in a laboratory, which is called the kitchen. It is a laboratory in word only, as the process can take place anywhere from a nice house to the jungle. Eventually Pablo built many very large labs, employing hundreds of people, deep in the Colombian jungle, far away from any normally traveled roads. But his first lab was inside a two-story house Pablo purchased in the town of Belén. This was a normal house set in a residential neighborhood. The workers, known as the cooks, lived on the second floor and the kitchen was most of the first floor. Pablo had turned several old refrigerators into simple ovens that were used to cook the powder. What made this house different was that all the windows were covered all the time, making it impossible for anyone to see inside. In the beginning there was no need to pay anything to the police, who had no knowledge of what was going on.

The only problem was the very strong smell of the chemicals. Pablo was afraid the neighbors would complain to the police, so that's when he decided to build his laboratory in the jungle. This was when the business really began to grow. At that time there was no way of imagining what it would become, what incredible riches he would earn. There was nothing to which it could be compared.

The president of Colombia, Virgilio Barco, would later call it "a great and powerful organization the likes of which has never existed in the world."

Within only a few months Pablo and Gustavo had earned considerable money. I was putting Pablo's money in different banks, spreading it around as best I could. But there was no way for me to prepare to handle this amount of money. For anyone. Pablo had started purchasing nice things for himself; he bought a Nissan Patrol, which is a large jeep-type vehicle, and a beautiful house for himself in the wealthy neighborhood El Poblado, living among the wealthiest citizens of Medellín. I still tried to convince him not to continue in this business. Pablo and I were both very strong soccer fans, although we supported different teams from Medellín. Our whole lives we would go to the stadium whenever possible. Once, I remember, early in Pablo's story, we went together and were sitting side by side in the sun. There was just the two of us, two brothers, no bodyguards, no wives or children. This was one of the last times we were ever able to do this. I made one last plea: "You have enough money now," I said. "You can buy what you need. Why don't you just focus on the real estate business?"

He smiled to himself. As we were to learn, there are different ways to be addicted to drugs. Once Pablo was in the middle of the business, once he had tasted the power and the money and the renown, there was no way he could ever get out of it.

It was as he established his name that Pablo's life changed in another, very different way. In 1974 he had fallen in love with the most beautiful young girl of the neighborhood, María Victoria Henao. The difficulty was that Pablo was already twenty-five and she was only fourteen, and because of that age difference María Victoria's mother was very much against this relationship. She refused to speak with Pablo and tried to make it difficult for María to be with him. But Pablo was very much in love and pursued her very strongly. I remember one night he and a guitar player got very drunk and like a scene in a cheap movie serenaded her. In 1976 María Victoria became pregnant. One day, just like that, they decided they would be married. At that time I was outside Colombia, traveling with the national cycling team, so I missed the ceremony. It was a simple event. There was no planning, nothing special was organized. Three months later their son, Juan Pablo, was born. It took a couple of years before his mother-in-law would finally agree to join their new family, but eventually she accepted that Pablo truly loved her daughter.

It would be wrong to say that Pablo was always the most faithful husband to María Victoria, the world knows that, but there was not one day that he stopped loving his wife, his children, and his family. In fact, years later it was this love for his family and his fear for their safety that caused him to change his usual behavior and allow himself to be found and killed.

For the entire family, our lives changed forever the day my brother decided to send his drugs to America. By that time there had been a long-established marijuana business between Colombia and the United States, but there was not much of a market for cocaine. That began to change when Americans began growing much of their own marijuana, so the profit from the large loads was greatly reduced. Pablo had gone into his business at just the right time to take advantage of that. Some of the routes and the customers were already in place. Cocaine was the perfect product to replace marijuana: It was much easier to smuggle because it required so much less space, yet it was more profitable. One small load that could be carried by a "mule," a person carrying the drugs with him, or on a small airplane, was worth a lot more money than many bales of marijuana secretly packed onto a freight ship.

Also at that time most people didn't see much difference between cocaine and marijuana. They were both experience-enhancing drugs. This was before there was any violence attached to the cocaine trade and before cocaine had addicted America, long before the even stronger crack cocaine had been introduced to the American streets. Nobody thought it was much of a big deal. For smugglers it was just a more profitable substitute for marijuana. And in Colombia, there was the belief that sometime soon cocaine would be made legal both in our country and in America, just like it had been in the past. So when Pablo first came up with the idea to ship cocaine to America no one there seemed very worried about it.

The first way Pablo smuggled cocaine into the United States was by packing between twenty and forty kilos into used airplane tires and sending them to Miami on a small plane. He would find or buy used airplane tires in Colombia and store the drugs in them. When they arrived in Miami the pilots would throw them out as useless and buy new tires. In Miami the used tires had no value to anyone, so they would be thrown on a truck, driven to a garbage dump, and thrown away. An employee of Pablo's would follow the truck, and retrieve those packages from the garbage. It was a simple plan that worked well.

What was nice for Pablo was that he never touched the drugs. He had decided that he no longer was going to be doing the dirty work, he didn't want to risk going to jail again, and now he could afford to hire people to take those risks. It made the business much safer for him. So he employed regular people to bring the paste from Peru to Medellín and he had his cooks there to make the paste into the valuable powder. But some of the people who took the drugs from there to Florida later occupied important positions in the organization.

There were a few different people who drove the merchandise from the laboratory to the airport. The man in charge was Alosito and one of his main drivers was called Chepe. Chepe drove the big flatbed trucks and worked for Pablo from the beginning almost to the end. During the war with the enemies of the cartel Chepe was caught. We never knew exactly which of the many organizations fighting us had captured him, but we knew that they had tied his arms and ran over him with his own truck. They killed him like an animal in the street.

At the airport the men in charge of wrapping the cocaine into packages and packing those packages into the used tires were Prosequito and Juan Carlos. Juan Carlos was called Mr. Munster. Pablo named him that because he was tall and ugly, like Herman Munster from *The Munsters*. These two would write the brand name on the packages of cocaine; Pablo used names like Emerald and Diamond, so that if American drug agents overheard Pablo discussing a shipment they would believe he was referring to precious stones rather than drugs. Years later Prosequito was killed in just the same way as Chepe. For these jobs each of these people was paid $150 to $200 per kilo.

Pablo depended on several different pilots, and they were flying small private airplanes. The pilots mostly were paid by the kilo, at first about $2,500 per kilo but later as much as $6,000. For some flights a pilot could earn more than $1 million. Eventually Pablo and his partners in the cartel would have their many large airplanes and helicopters, but on these small planes it was only possible to carry three or at most four old tires.

The person who opened up Florida for Pablo was Luis Carlos, who had been a friend of his for a long time. It was Luis Carlos's job to get the drugs out of the tires and begin the distribution. Luis didn't speak English, but with all the Latinos in Miami that was not necessary. Particularly as long as he had a lot of money to give to the people who were needed. I remember that once he returned home to Medellín and brought some canned food from the market for Pablo to try. "You gotta eat this," he said. "It's delicious. It's what I've been eating for the past two months."

Pablo knew enough English to know that Luis Carlos had been eating cat food.

After Luis Carlos set up the operation in Miami he did the same thing in New York City.

At the beginning Pablo was sending only one airplane a week, but since the profit for each kilo was about $100,000, he was still earning almost $2 million a week. The business grew up so fast, much faster than anyone knew, and within a few months he was sending shipments two or three times a week, and even that was not enough to satisfy the fast growing market. Americans wanted cocaine. At first it was mostly high-class people, people of the entertainment business, people doing advertising, the Wall Street people, the record business, the people who went to the clubs like Studio 54. All people who could afford it easily. But soon everybody was doing it. The demand only went up. And because Pablo was almost the only person bringing coke into the country the supply was very small, so people were willing to pay big money for it. The further away it traveled from the route, from Miami, the more expensive it became. In the late 1970s in Colorado, for example, the cost was $72,000 a kilo. In California it was $60,000, in Texas $50,000. Anytime another person put his hands on the merchandise the price went up $1,000.

Pablo was smart enough to understand that he could not depend on one method of delivery for too long. The more people who knew even some of the details of his operation the more chance there was it would be betrayed. He used to figure that the United States Drug Enforcement Agency was between two and three years behind him, so before that amount of time passed he would find other ways of bringing cocaine into America. When the DEA started asking people at the airport questions he knew they were getting information from somewhere and that was the end of the used tires scheme. Instead he would send ordinary people with drugs in their suitcases or in their clothes on regular commercial airplanes. It was even more simple than it sounds. The travelers had to be people Pablo knew or who were recommended by people he trusted. The people who recommended them were responsible for their actions. The only requirement was that they already had to have a visa. They were both Colombian citizens and American citizens. People who were traveling from Colombia to the United States carried drugs in their suitcases, people coming to Colombia from America brought back the money in their suitcases. Anybody who wanted to come to the U.S., boom, drugs, anybody who wanted to go to Colombia, boom, money. Back then it wasn't that risky, the DEA or Customs was not looking for these people. They were much too busy searching freighters for big bales of marijuana. It was also much less expensive for Pablo to make his shipments this way than it had been with the tires. He didn't have to pay for the airplanes and the large fees. These people were paid around $1,000 plus their tickets.

In addition to the passengers, also the crew of the regular commercial airplanes carried suitcases for Pablo. That was even easier because they could just walk on and off the plane without having to go through a search. On some planes two or three stewardesses and a pilot or co-pilot might be carrying merchandise for us, but they never shared that information with each other. Each of them believed they were the only one on that flight. For these people it was an easy way of making additional money, particularly because they would fly both parts of the route and maybe make the trip twice a week.

The suitcases they were given were specially made. They had double walls and it was possible to secret as many as five kilos in one suitcase. All they had to do was make sure they handed the suitcase to the correct person at their destination.

Some people also were given special shoes made with hollow bottoms in which the drugs were carried. The grandfather of someone in our organization had a shoe manufacturing corporation; when he got sick his son took over and began working with us. In this factory they would make these shoes with the merchandise sewn inside. There was almost no way they could ever be discovered. We even put people in wheelchairs to carry the drugs, which was safe because no one ever suspected that they were sitting on close to a million dollars in cocaine. Sometimes our mules were dressed in costume, like a nun, for example, or even a blind person—who would be using a hollow walking stick filled with merchandise. Rarely were there any problems or discoveries with these people.

When Pablo started doing it this way he would send a few passengers every other day. Then it was an everyday thing and then twice a day. Only once did the DEA discover the cocaine in two suitcases, but nobody picked up those suitcases so they didn't catch anybody.

Another method, which eventually became well known, was having the mules eat the cocaine. The cocaine would be put in condoms and the mules would swallow them. The drugs were undetectable inside their bodies. When they arrived at their destination they would go to the bathroom and then, boom. While there were always enough mules willing to make this trip, this was the most dangerous method for them. If any of the condoms would start leaking, or if one opened up, the mule could die. People did die this way. It was written about in the newspapers in America and got a lot of attention.

But eventually Pablo decided it was not even necessary to send people with the suitcases; we could just send the suitcases. This was many years before the attack on 9/11 so security was easy, we paid the right people to put our suitcases on the flight. At the destination our people would just pick them up. One thing that Pablo found right away was that it was simple to convince people working in the right jobs to cooperate with us. Almost from the very first day Pablo knew he had to pay big bribes, just like in the contraband business. Pablo was generous with these payments, he wanted to make it so rewarding for people that they would never betray him. So many people earned their fortunes working for us that no one ever learned about. For example, when Pablo was flying our own airplanes the manager of a small airport we used in Colombia was paid up to $500,000 for each flight he arranged to land without any difficulty.

This was a man who earned a small salary from his job, but when he was finally arrested the authorities found he had $27 million in all his bank accounts. So obviously it was never a problem recruiting the people we needed. People in positions to assist would come to us and make offers. These people would include airplane maintenance people who would put our merchandise aboard the plane for us, military and police officers and guards who would look in a different direction when they were told to, even an American who sold Pablo the flight schedules for the surveillance planes that flew above Florida searching the skies for our planes.

Tito Domínguez, who ran a smuggling operation for the cartel in Florida, remembers how simple it was to recruit the people we needed and deliver the cocaine. When he was making preparations to land planes in the Bahamas to refuel he wanted to guarantee the safety of this part of the operation. He found out from a Customs agent that he had been working with in the marijuana business that the government official who ran the airport would go to a certain bar every Friday afternoon. Tito often traveled with his pet mountain lion, by the name of T.C., which could be an intimidation, but this time he went there by himself and sat two seats away from this official at the bar. He didn't need the threat, he had a better weapon: cash. He didn't speak to him for a time, then finally said, "Excuse me, but I'd like to talk to you for a second."

The official said, "About what, man?"

"We have a mutual friend who said I could speak to you about something sensitive."

"What's his name?" the man asked carefully.

"Frankie," Tito told him.

The man shook his head. "Nah, I don't know any Frankie."

Tito stood up. He was holding about $20,000 in hundred-dollar bills in his hand. One by one he started laying them out on the bar. "You might recognize his picture," he said.

"Stop, man. What do you want to talk about?"

It was that easy. "I want to talk about making you rich."

The man moved over one seat and spoke in a low voice. "What do I have to do for this, man?"

"Nothing. You do nothing when I land my airplane full of cocaine at your airport. You go get a cup of coffee and you do nothing at all."

He considered that. "What does this mean?"

Tito told him flat out: "$500,000 up front."

The official nodded. "How many times a month can you do this?"

That was the way Pablo built up the organization. The money he earned brought even more money. At this time, in the late 1970s, there was no Medellín cartel, just Pablo running his own business. And drug smuggling was not nearly as difficult or dangerous as it was to become because the United States was very slow to recognize the size of the business. They still believed it was mostly small shipments, and operated that way.

There were some other people selling small amounts of Colombian coke to the United States but it was only Pablo who controlled the entire operation from buying the paste in Peru to delivering the product to Miami. And once Pablo had set up his system he invited others to take advantage of it. For example, he would allow other Colombians to invest their money in the business. If someone that could be trusted wanted to invest $50,000, Pablo would tell them he would return $75,000 in two weeks. He would use that $50,000 to finance a drug run. Because his operation was so safe, he also was able to guarantee to people that if the American DEA or Customs intercepted the shipment he would refund 50 percent of their money. It was very profitable for everyone who invested with Pablo. Mostly for Pablo, though, who would own the biggest share of the profits. There were so many people who were almost begging him to take their money, regular people with all types of normal jobs. These people didn't know about drugs, they knew about Pablo. People were handing over to Pablo their life savings, they were selling their car and their house to raise money to invest with him. And nobody lost money. Nobody. Pablo helped many people have their dreams come true.

Pablo was starting to build a much bigger operation. Two of the other dealers in Medellín were a good friend of Pablo's named Dejermo and another person Pablo did not know named Rodrigo. Dejermo was good at bringing drugs from Panama into Medellín by car; he had made valuable connections with the police in the city. Rodrigo was a great pilot. These two men started fighting a war between them, for what reason I don't know. They wanted to kill each other but didn't succeed, so instead they started killing each other's families and the innocent people who worked for their enemy, cutting off the heads of the bodies. Dejermo went to Pablo, who by then was getting a reputation in the city for being very strong in doing whatever needed to be done, and having the men with the ability to get it done. He asked him to be the middle guy and negotiate an end to this war.

Pablo spoke with Rodrigo. "You guys have to stop this war," he said. "Dejermo wants me to be on his side to use my guys to fight you." Rodrigo knew that Pablo was strong enough to crush him so he agreed to meet with Pablo and Dejermo in Panama. "Let's start working together," Pablo told them both. Pablo put them in charge of a route from Panama to Haiti and Haiti to Miami. While the two men never became friends, they did become partners—working for Pablo Escobar.

The great desire from America for coke created the market, and others in addition to Pablo went into the business. There is a great misunderstanding about what is known as the Medellín cartel. Generally it's believed that the cartel was a typical business, with management at the top giving out the instructions and employees carrying them out. The profit is returned to the company. The Medellín cartel was actually many independent drug dealers who got close together for their mutual profit and protection, but each of them continued to run his own operation. But it was never discussed how much money each of the main people earned or their total wealth. Often they would use each other's manufacturing, supply, and distribution capabilities. For example, Pablo would charge other traffickers 35 percent of the value of the shipment if they contracted with him to bring it into the United States, but he gave them the insurance that if the load was intercepted by the DEA he would refund to them their losses. This was an easy deal for Pablo to make because at the beginning no drugs were stopped. And it was incredibly profitable for him because the others were doing all the preparation work. So the Medellín cartel was an association by choice instead of a unified business. But the person at the top of this loose structure was Pablo, because he had started the business and had the best way of shipping the drugs and the most people loyal to him. The others have said that they were afraid of him. But they all made a lot of money with him.

The Medellín cartel was very different from the cartel running in the city of Cali, which got started around the same time. The Cali cartel was a much more traditional business structure, with four recognized leaders, and under them they had accountants, engineers, and attorneys, and then the workers.

The other independent drug operators who were recognized as the leaders of the Medellín cartel were Carlos Lehder Rivas, the Ochoa brothers, and José Rodríguez Gacha, who everyone knew as the Mexican. Each of these people built up their own business before joining the others. Carlos Lehder was a real smart guy who developed his ideas about smuggling coke into the United States while he was in prison there for smuggling marijuana. Carlos was probably the first to use his own small airplanes to fly the coke into America and was making millions of dollars even before working with Pablo. He was an excellent pilot, but I don't think he flew the loads himself. In 1978 he bought a big house on the island of Norman's Cay in the Bahamas for $190,000 and with the cooperation of the government authorities that he paid, he established his base there. Soon he controlled the whole island, which was like his kingdom. And from there he was in charge of the entire Caribbean. The stories were that he often had parties there that lasted for days, and always with lots of beautiful, mostly naked women. He built a protected runway and this island was used by everyone in the business as a place to transfer drugs from Colombia from big planes to small planes or to put them on speedboats for the two-hundred-mile trip to Florida. To use his island each person had to pay Carlos a percentage of the load.

Pablo and Carlos knew each other and they liked each other before they needed to work together. Eventually they would become close friends and Pablo would save his life, but they had very different thoughts; Pablo admired the United States but Carlos wanted to destroy it with drugs. Carlos called cocaine "the atomic bomb" that he was going to drop on America. This was because of his politics; his father was German so Adolf Hitler became Carlos's hero. And while Pablo only occasionally smoked marijuana, Carlos smoked all the time. A pilot for the cartel, Jimmy Arenas, once said about Lehder, "The three schools of thought he got was Hitler, Jesus Christ, and Marx. . . . When you mix that in one pot with marijuana it would be a big explosion."

Pablo and Carlos got together around 1979, when Lehder was kidnapped by the M-19 guerrillas. At that time M-19 was one of the four or five left-wing guerrilla groups operating in Colombia's jungles. Pablo knew some of the guerrilla chiefs because he paid them a percentage to protect the laboratories he built in the wild. If the guerrillas had wanted to destroy these laboratories they could have easily, instead they became the guards. All of the traffickers paid them. M-19 raised some of the money it needed to survive and grow by kidnapping wealthy people for millions of dollars' ransom. When they demanded $5 million for Lehder's freedom, another person in the drug business asked Pablo for assistance. Pablo's contacts found out that Carlos was being held in a farmhouse in Armenia and Pablo organized a team of six men to rescue him. When the guerrillas found out they were coming to battle them they escaped out the back, pushing Lehder into the trunk of their car. As they tried to race away Carlos was able to free himself, but while running away was shot in the leg. Two of the kidnappers were captured. And after that Pablo and Carlos became close friends and often worked together.

Like Pablo, Carlos had his own way of living. For instance, a few years later when the Bahamian government arrested several Colombian drug traffickers and put them in jail, he got so angry he flew a plane over Nassau and emptied boxes of cash over the capital city. He literally rained money. That was his way of reminding people how powerful he was, that he could do anything he wanted to do. That was Carlos.

José Rodríguez Gacha was the son of a poor pig farmer from the city of Pacho who also made more than a billion dollars in this cocaine business. Like Pablo, he was named one of the richest men in the world. While the Ochoas were educated people, Gacha had dropped out of grade school. Because he loved everything with Mexico—he owned the Bogotá soccer club the Millionarios and had a mariachi band to perform for the fans—and eventually established the routes through Mexico, he became known as El Mexicano, the Mexican. He made that name infamous. The Mexican was ruthless. Many of the terrible killings that Pablo has been blamed for were done by Gacha. But also like Pablo, he gave away much of his money to the poor people for health and education, to pay for farm equipment and seed to survive, and so the people of his region loved him.

The Mexican came up in the emerald business. Most people don't know that in Colombia there has always been more violence for the control of emeralds than there was for drugs. But killing in that business is very casual. Gacha became known in that business for having no fear of anyone and killing people to succeed. At one time he worked in a bar in Medellín that some members of Pablo's organization liked to go to. Even these people, very tough people, were impressed by the Mexican. He started doing small favors for them, and eventually came to run his own organization, opening new routes through Mexico to Houston and Los Angeles. It was the Mexican who first set up Tranquilandia, one of the largest and the best known of the jungle laboratories where more than two thousand people lived and worked making and packaging cocaine.

As poor as the Mexican was growing up, the three Ochoa brothers, Jorge, Juan David, and Fabio, came from a respected wealthy family. They had no needs that weren't satisfied. The main business of the Ochoa family was raising horses and there is a story I have heard told that early in the business they would send drugs to the United States in the vaginas of mares. The Ochoas were in the business in a small way for a long time. Like many others, they had no thought that this business would grow so big so quickly. And because the cocaine business was not considered a terrible crime in Colombia, Pablo met the Ochoas when he began being successful in the business. Pablo and Gustavo would often go to Bogotá for the auto races, where the Ochoas owned a popular restaurant, and met them there. Pablo and Jorge became friends. "I met him in the business. Medellín is a small town," Jorge said once. "And everybody knows each other." Later on Jorge became one of Pablo's closest friends. In the early times there was no competition between the dealers because the American market was so big each person could sell all the merchandise they could smuggle into the country. So rather than fighting over territory they helped each other. The Ochoa brothers eventually headed operations in Western Europe.

There were others who were part of the business, like Kiko Moncada, Pablo Correa, Albeiro Areiza, and Fernando Galeano, but they were not the main people. What brought all of them together into what became known to others—but never to them—as the Medellín cartel was the kidnapping in 1981 of Martha Nieves Ochoa, the sister of the Ochoa brothers, by M-19. The guerrillas had begun kidnapping the drug dealers and their families because they were rich and could not go to the police for help. After Martha was kidnapped Pablo called a meeting of all of the drug people at his grand home, Hacienda Napoles. More than two hundred people agreed with his idea and contributed to the forming of an army to fight the kidnappers, an army that was called Muerta a Secuestradores, MAS, Death to the Kidnappers. Because Pablo was known to have the toughest men working in his organization, everyone agreed that he should be the head of it. Nothing was going to stop Pablo from dealing with the kidnappers. While Pablo had been working with some of the M-19 people, he told them that this was a war and he would destroy them. Pablo told a newspaper reporter, "If there was not an immediate and strong response, the M-19 were going to continue screwing our own families. . . . We paid law enforcement 80 million pesos for the information they had at this moment and the next day they began to fall. My soldiers took them to our secret houses, our secret ranches and people from law enforcement went there and hung them up and began to bust them up."

Many of the M-19 were killed in the Colombian way of La Violencia, the most painful way imaginable, with limbs cut off, and within weeks Martha Ochoa was let free without harm. The success of this effort made the drug traffickers realize how much stronger they were working together than independently. And that was when the Medellín cartel came into existence, with Pablo the leader. From that time forward each of them would continue to run their own operations, but they would share their abilities to manufacture and distribute cocaine around the world. But, as I said, while they would meet for business and pleasure, there was no formal structure like Cali.

That also was not the end of the kidnappings. In Colombia kidnapping remained a profitable crime. Pablo's participation didn't even make our family safe. In 1985 our father was taken by a group of policemen. Some police were known to be kidnappers, they would use their powers to stop people on the roads and then take them away. Our father was on his way to visit one of Pablo's farms in Antioquia when six men in a jeep stopped him. They tied up the workingmen with him and then took him away. Our mother was frantic, yelling and praying. The kidnappers demanded $50 million. Pablo spread the word that the kidnappers should be told: "If I find my father with one bruise the money they are asking for won't be enough to pay for their own burial."

Pablo did not often show his emotions openly. In the best or the worst situations he was always in control, he always appeared calm. I remember when someone would show up at an office and tell Pablo they had good news and bad news, and asked which he wanted to hear first, he would tell them, "Any one, it's the same. We're going to have to deal with all the situations, so just give me the news." Calm. I have a temper and at times I get very angry, very upset. Even during this kidnapping, when our father's life was at stake, Pablo remained steady, giving orders and creating the plan to capture those responsible.

Our father had recently had a heart operation and needed special medicine. There were more than two hundred drugstores in Medellín, many of them with security cameras. Pablo made certain that those that did not have these hidden cameras got them installed.

Then he offered a good reward for photographs of any people buying that heart medicine. In that way he was able to identify two of the kidnappers. We also knew that the kidnappers were calling our mother's home from public phones. So Pablo gave out hundreds of radio transmitters to our friends and workers and instructed them to listen to a well-known radio station. Every time the kidnappers called my mother's home the announcer on the station said, "This song is dedicated to Luz Marina [a code name that was used]; it's called 'Sonaron Cuatro Balazos' and is sung by Antonio Aguilar," those people were to check nearby pay phones to see if they were being used. In fact, Pablo used television and radio codes to communicate several different times, especially when we were trying to negotiate a peace treaty with the government.

It was my job to negotiate with the kidnappers. I was to try to keep them on the telephone as long as possible, to allow our people to locate the area the call was coming from. They demanded a $50 million ransom. I began by offering them $10 million, but this they did not accept. They knew they had the father of Pablo Escobar and believed he would pay his whole fortune to free him. I negotiated with them for eighteen days while we gathered information. Our mother was absolutely frantic. Finally the kidnappers agreed to accept one million dollars. We put the money into green duffel bags—but in addition to the cash Pablo put electronic tracking devices into those bags. After the kidnappers had picked up the money, they were tracked to a farm near the town of Liborina, about 150 kilometers from Medellín. When the kidnappers returned there with the ransom people working for Pablo attacked the house from several sides. The kidnappers tried to escape but three of them were captured. Our father was unhurt.

Pablo passed sentence on them.

Within a few years the violence for which Pablo was blamed would start. I won't say Pablo was right in the things that he did, but he believed he was protecting himself and his family and his business. And he also knew that the people of Colombia profited from the success of the drug traffickers. Many thousands of Colombians were employed in the business, from the workers in the jungle to the police. And many others benefited from the public works each of the traffickers did. Eventually Pablo was forced to go to war with the government of Colombia, the Cali cartel, the national police, and special groups formed specifically to kill him. But at this time there was very little violence within the business. Instead it was just making money, making more money than any man in history had ever made from crime before.

Three

THE MOST FAMOUS AMERICAN INVESTIGATIVE REPORTER of the time, Jack Anderson, once wrote, "The Colombian-based cartel, which does $18 billion worth of business every year in the United States, is a greater menace to America than the Soviet Union."

Eighteen billion dollars? Maybe, but perhaps more. It is impossible to know. I know that Pablo was earning so much cash that each year we would simply write off approximately 10 percent of our money because the rats would eat it or it would be damaged beyond use by water and dampness.

There was never any shortage of customers for our merchandise. The market was always bigger than we were able to supply. Each step of the operation, getting the paste from Peru to our labs in Colombia where it was processed into cocaine, smuggling it into the United States and having it distributed throughout the country, while all the time being smarter than the law enforcement agencies, required the cooperation of many people. And a lot of money. Each person who dealt with the merchandise got his nice cut. At one point, for example, because so many people had to be paid, the minimum amount we could transport on each flight was three hundred kilos, anything less would result in a loss.

To supply the cocaine to the rest of the world Pablo and his partners in Medellín built many laboratories hidden in the primitive areas of the Colombian jungle, places that nobody went unless they intended to go there. Some of these places grew to become small cities with only one purpose, to produce drugs for the world. These cities had their own dining areas, a school for their children, medical attention, and even rooms to watch satellite television. One of Pablo's biggest and best hidden laboratories was built in the desolate area on the Venezuelan border called Los Llanos Orientales. Pablo bought a huge farm there, I'm guessing it was about 37,000 acres. What we built there was my concept. In addition to the central areas we constructed seventy very small houses. Really they were only one room with a bed, electricity but no plumbing. What made them different from anything that ever existed before was that they were built on wooden wheels and stationed directly on top of the longest of the seven runways on the farm. This runway was used for large aircraft. These houses had wooden walls and straw roofs; on the outside of one wall we attached a metal bar with a hook. From the sky the only thing that could be seen were two long rows of these small houses; it was not possible to see the runway. The rule was that one person had to remain in the house at all times. When a plane was arriving to deliver paste and then take away product it would signal its arrival and the owner of the house would then have three minutes to roll it off the runway. Most of the houses were so small they could be pushed by one person; it was no more difficult than pushing a stalled car. But for the others we had five small trucks that would attach themselves to the metal hooks on the house and pull them off the runway. Clearing the whole runway could take as much as one hour. At the end of the runway was a canopy of trees. The planes would land and immediately taxi under the trees, where the paste they brought would be unloaded and finished merchandise put aboard. The planes would also be refueled from gasoline stored in underground tanks. The turnaround could take less than a half hour, and when the planes departed the homes would be rolled back into place on the runway.

Eventually about seventy couples, including their children, as many as two hundred people, lived there. A few of them actually worked as farmers, but the others worked in the laboratory manufacturing, packaging, and transporting the cocaine. The children went to the school, Pablo hired two teachers. The laboratory was located about fifteen minutes away from the runway; it was above ground but hidden completely by the trees. Almost all of the workers were recruited from the poorest neighborhoods of Medellín; they received a salary as well as shelter, food, and medical care. Basically, we could produce and ship ten thousand kilos every fifteen days.

Getting those drugs from Colombia into the United States always required forward thinking. We had to stay ahead of the DEA. So Pablo was always searching for new methods of smuggling drugs into the U.S. Through the years Pablo created so many different systems: He bought hundreds of cheap refrigerators and Sony TVs from Panama, emptied out the insides, and filled them with the same weight in drugs, usually about forty kilos, then shipped it as regular freight. One of Peru's biggest exports is dried fish, which is sent on freighters all over the world; so Pablo mixed his product with the dried fish, a method that was very successful. In one shipment he sent 23,000 kilos, which until much later was the biggest single shipment he ever made.

The chemists discovered that cocaine could be chemically blended into products made of plastic, metals, and liquids, and when it reached the destination other chemists would reverse the chemical process and purify the cocaine to its original state. It was a chemical circle: paste to cocaine to liquid form, delivery, then liquid to paste to cocaine for sales. So from Guatemala he mixed the coke with fruit pulp, in Ecuador he mixed it with cocoa. The chemists discovered how to liquefy it and Pablo then added it to tons of Chilean wine—in this process only pure cocaine could be used or telltale particles would float on the surface, and even then about 10 percent of the drugs would be absorbed. After the success of this method was proved it was used to create products in almost every country in South America—liquid cocaine was added to everything from the most expensive liqueurs to the cheapest bottles of beer. Pablo's chemists mixed it with flowers, chemically soaked it into Colombian lumber exports, with soft drinks; the cooks even soaked clothes like blue jeans in the liquid and when they arrived at the destination the coke would be washed out of the fabric. There was one person in Florida we called Blue Jeans whose only job was to receive these pants and collect the product. The chemists also figured out how to make cocaine black, which was mixed with black paint. We used a method of chemically blending it into plastic and forming it into many different items, including PVC pipe, religious statues, and when we started shipping to Europe by ship, the fiberglass shells of small boats. About 30 percent of the cocaine was lost in this transition. The big advantage to this method was that when we shipped product by this means we no longer had to pay a percentage of the value to the transporter.

Pablo was always employing new chemists to create methods of smuggling the product. I remember the day in the warehouse the chemists showed us this method of embedding cocaine in plastic. They created a sheet of plastic about one meter long with cocaine inside to prove to us how easily it could be done. It could be made of anything imaginable of plastic or fiberglass. Like the DEA, we had drug-sniffing dogs of our own that were used to test methods of hiding. One beautiful dog was named Marquessa, and we walked the dog right past the fiberglass and it did not detect it. "This is good,"

Pablo said, with very little emotion. "This will work." Pablo was all business, always.

What started as a few kilos hidden in the fender of his Renault had become a very sophisticated operation. Pablo—and his other partners too—had some of the smartest chemists from Europe and America creating these methods for the business. Any product you could think of that was transported from South America to the United States and Europe, they would almost always find a means to include cocaine in it.

Pablo was always looking for unsuspected means to send thousands of kilos in each shipment. Someone, I don't remember who, came up with the idea to ship the drugs inside huge electric industrial transformers, which normally weighed more than eight thousand pounds. Pablo bought the transformers in Colombia and shipped them to Venezuela, where the inside machinery was removed and four thousand kilos were installed in its place. The transformers were sent to America. After the drugs were unloaded the Americans complained the transformers had technology problems—of course they did, there was nothing inside—and shipped them back to Colombia where the process was repeated. But then he had a problem; while the drugs were being loaded in Venezuela the men responsible for transporting a transformer to the docks were drinking. They got drunk and on their way to their port they made too much noise and got stopped by the Venezuelan police—who were both surprised and happy to discover four thousand kilos of cocaine. That was the end of that method.

But the primary method of transport was by airplane. After the system of used tires was abandoned Pablo decided to open other routes from Central America to America, building support systems in Panama—with the assistance of Panamanian police—and Jamaica, as well as using Carlos Lehder's services at Norman's Cay. Pablo's first airplane was the one for which he always kept the most affection, so much so that when he built the grand house Hacienda Napoles, he mounted this plane over the front gate. It was Pablo's way of suggesting that this plane was responsible for the riches at Napoles that the visitor was about to enjoy. The plane was a Piper Cub–type, powered by a single propeller. When he bought the plane from a friend it was already well used, but he had it completely redone. With the exception of the pilot's chair all the seats were removed and the floor was reinforced, leaving a compartment hidden under it for suitcases and extra fuel that allowed the plane to fly much further than was common. This plane was used almost exclusively to fly between Colombia and Panama. Pablo used Panama as a key point to drop off drugs to then be shipped to the United States and pick up cash being sent from America. The small size of the plane and the ability to safely fly low to the ground made it able to avoid radar detection.

Pablo didn't just pack the plane with drugs. Instead, he would buy thousands of dollars' worth of gold from the Indians in Chocó and put the gold on the floor of the plane—with the drugs stored beneath it. Then the plane would fly to Panama. In Panama the gold would be sold for a profit and the drugs would be unloaded for the next stage of their journey to the United States. Getting cash back from America to Colombia was as difficult as getting the drugs into that country. Maybe even more difficult because cash took more space than kilos of coke and there was so much more of it. Suitcases packed with cash from America would be put into the compartment and televisions and stereos would be packed on top of them. If the police had discovered the money, supposedly it was the profit from the sale of the gold. While the gold cost Pablo thousands of dollars, the plane could carry as much as $10 million in cash. Pablo used to say that the plane had brought more than $70 million back to Colombia.

Within two years Pablo would replace that one plane with fifteen larger planes, including his own Learjet, plus six helicopters. Each of these planes could carry as much as 1,200 kilos per trip. In addition, the other leaders of the Medellín organization had their own airplanes; even the Ochoas had their own fleet of planes. With Gustavo's supervision, Pablo continued to buy new and larger airplanes, eventually purchasing DC-3s. But no matter how big the planes, it was never enough. One plan that Pablo never had the chance to turn into reality was to hide the cocaine in the wing of a DC-6. The idea was to take the top of both wings off and hide the merchandise in a huge fuel cell, then make a bypass to an extra fuel system, and finally put the wing back on. The thinking was it was possible to put thousands of kilos in each wing. When the plane arrived in the United States the top of the wing would be taken off and the drugs removed. The DEA or Customs would never find it. There was no reason it would not have worked. Pablo just ran out of time.

Of course the business could not operate on a regular schedule like an airline. Each flight had to be carefully planned and arranged. There were about eight different routes that were regularly used and each of them was named. And at times parts of two or more routes were combined for a flight or even new routes attempted. People had to be notified a shipment was going to be made from wherever the drugs were loaded to wherever they landed. Pilots had to be hired for the trip; some of them were Vietnam veterans and they were paid by the kilos they carried. At the beginning there were maybe two or three flights a week, but by the end airplanes were almost continually taking off and returning with cash.

There were generally between four hundred and five hundred kilos shipped on each flight. Each load was made up from drugs belonging to several different members of the organization. Pablo would decide how much each person was permitted to send. For example, on a flight Pablo might have two hundred kilos, Gustavo might get two hundred, others the rest of the available space. Everyone paid Pablo a percentage for this transportation. Each group would put its own brand on the cocaine, the brands were called names like Coca-Cola, Yen, USA, and Centaito, there were many names. When the shipment arrived the kilos were separated by these markings and distributed to the people designated by the owner of the brand. The pilot carried with him a list of what brands each person was to receive.

Arranging for secure landings became a difficult problem after the DEA finally realized how many drug planes were coming to America every day and instituted new strategies. We used different methods to outsmart the government. At first the planes landed in Jamaica, where there were enough people on the payroll to ensure they would not be bothered, and then raced to Miami on sleek speedboats, or cigarette boats. The planes also dropped the merchandise packed into green military duffel bags by parachute, sometimes onto farmlands owned by friendly people or other times just off the beaches of Miami—this method was known as *El Bombardeo*, the bombardment, where they would be picked out of the sea by people waiting for them in speedboats, then brought to shore.

There were also small landing strips hidden all over Florida. One that was used often was in the Everglades near the city of Naples. There was an area called Golden Glades that was going to become a large housing development. The streets were paved and sewage systems were installed before environmentalists got the project stopped. There was nobody living nearby—so at night we used the empty streets as runways. It was almost our own airport.

It would be impossible to even guess how many people were on the Medellín payroll, including airport managers, ground crews, truck drivers, security patrols, even Customs agents. American Customs agents began using AWACS aircraft, airborne warning and control system, which were surveillance planes used to detect all incoming aircraft. Their radar couldn't be avoided. So instead, Pablo paid a Customs agent for providing the schedule the AWACS would be flying, the region they would be patrolling, the range of their radios, and the radio frequencies on which they communicated so our pilots could listen to them. So we knew when and where they would be in the air and could avoid those times and areas. Pablo often purchased this type of information. People could make more money in one day than from years of their salary. The agent was paid approximately $250,000 for information about the flights, but still he was greedy. He wanted even more money. It was refused—and the next flight was intercepted. Often two planes flew together, one to carry the merchandise and the other to fly high and watch over that plane as well as conceal its presence from ground control radar. This time the AWACS caught the drug plane on radar. The pilot in the cover plane warned the drug pilot that Customs had got him, so the drug pilot turned around and dropped his merchandise of about five hundred kilos over Cuba. When the plane finally landed in the U.S. and was captured one pilot confessed and was sentenced to forty years in prison. The second pilot kept quiet and eventually walked away free.

It was this danger of being caught and going to jail that kept the commissions so high. But if someone was arrested and kept quiet Pablo would continue to take care of him. The Lion, who would later help run New York and Madrid, remembers that when he was in jail in Colombia he continued to get messages from Pablo. "Don't worry," he was told by a guard on the payroll, "Pablo said be cool. He'll get you out of jail." Pablo arranged for him to be transferred to an easier prison. And every week a guard would hand money to him and say, "This is from the patrón," from the boss. After six months he was set free. There was always someone willing to take our money. In some situations prisoners were permitted to stay in hotels and return regularly to the jail. In most countries we purchased the cooperation of authorities. In the Bahamas, for example, we had someone who worked closely with the government officials. "I took several people out of prison," this person remembers. "For $50,000, or for $75,000,

I would just walk them right out. The American government knew about it, but there was nothing they could do."

After Customs began using AWACS, Pablo decided to change routes again and began bringing merchandise into the U.S. through Mexico. Pablo helped establish the Mexican cartel, telling people he knew there, "I'm going to bring my nine planes to Mexico and from there you take over." The Mexicans established their own routes into America. Pablo's planes brought about one thousand kilos each flight into Mexico, and from there the Mexicans smuggled it into Miami, New York, and Los Angeles. When it reached those cities, individual dealers would take it and distribute it to the smaller cities. In this way it spread through the United States.

We also depended greatly on ships. Of course we used the traditional methods of sending the drugs on freight ships, especially for those drugs embedded in other products—like lumber and wine—usually sent by the sea. But we also had our own ideas. We attached small containers—PVC tubes that could hold as much as fifty kilos—to the hull of the ship and filled them with merchandise; when the ships reached their port our divers would open them and retrieve the drugs. When the DEA learned about that method Pablo instituted a system in which the tubes would be held against the hull by an electromagnet. Before the ship reached port the magnet would be turned off and the tubes would fall harmlessly to the bottom, where they would be retrieved by waiting scuba divers.

In addition to the freight ships we had a small navy of speedboats, cigarette boats that would carry loads from Jamaica to Florida, or pick up loads at sea and race them to the Florida shore. Sometimes, like in the movies, they would land them on the beaches at night, but often we used the docks of friends who owned homes on the water. We also had many fishing boats working for us, bringing paste from Peru to Colombia, then proceeding to Mexico with as much as 15,000 kilos mixed with Ecuadoran fish flour.

There had been many drug traffickers before Pablo, but no one before had ever had the organization this size or was able to find so many new ways of smuggling the product into the United States. For comparison, a big load for the most famous drug organization before Pablo, the French Connection, was about one hundred kilos of heroin. We were bringing in tons of cocaine every week. Perhaps the most unusual method we employed came from a James Bond movie. Pablo loved the James Bond movies and watched them over and over. Sometimes while we were watching one of these movies and Bond or the villains would use an ingenious method, Pablo would say suddenly, "Oh, maybe we could do something like that for the business." That was where his idea to transport product by submarine came from. When I think about it now, it seems too much to believe—a submarine? Who could buy a submarine? But in our business anything was possible. So when Pablo said we should transport by submarine, no one thought it wasn't possible. No one questioned him. Instead we decided it was a wonderful idea and then had to figure out how to get a submarine.

In fact two submarines. Certainly we couldn't purchase a used submarine without drawing attention so we knew we had to manufacture them. It didn't matter how much it might cost, money was never a bar to anything Pablo wanted done. We hired a Russian and an English engineer to design this for us. From my education I was involved in the creation of the electrical systems. Two were built in the quiet back of a shipyard near the coastal city of Cupica. For certain reasons, in the past we always explained that these vessels were operated by remote control, but in fact they had pilots on board. They were small and they weren't very pretty inside, but every two or three weeks each of the two submarines could carry 1,000 to 1,200 kilos. The submarines couldn't come too close to the shore, so divers would meet the boats and transport their loads to the beach.

Pablo invented this method, but it remained so effective that in

August 2008 the U.S. Coast Guard still intercepted a submarine of drugs coming from Colombia worth $187 million. A month later they caught a second sub with cocaine worth $350 million.

Pablo never ceased trying to expand the business. He usually had between twenty and thirty different regular routes through all regions of South and Central America, but besides Gustavo very few people knew about all of them. He changed these routes frequently. To build these routes he made deals with many different countries to cross through their airspace or land planes there. In 1984 he made a deal with the Sandinista government in Nicaragua to build a laboratory on an island off the coast. That was never built, but like Norman's Cay, the island was used as a place to refuel planes and transfer drugs from small planes to bigger planes. For that right each member of the Medellín group paid a great amount of money.

The general we worked with in Panama had control over everything we needed. But this general would charge for everything. Every helicopter that arrived or departed, every connection, he charged for every single thing. Plus he received a percentage of every kilo passing through his country. For a while this general was a good partner. When Pablo would tell him, "I need to talk to you in two days," he would immediately come to Colombia. But we learned this general was loyal only to himself. Once Pablo paid him $1.5 million for a large shipment to pass through the country, but it was intercepted by the Panamanian army. Drugs were confiscated, a laboratory was raided, and a young employee named John Lada was arrested and placed in jail.

Pablo was angry at this betrayal. He told our general: "We don't need these headaches. You have to clean up the issue." The general corrected this mistake, perhaps paying a judge to close his eyes to the situation. The drugs eventually were returned.

In Haiti another powerful general worked with Pablo to make certain our flights to his country would not be bothered. He was paid $200,000 for each plane that landed and took off without difficulty.

I remember particularly when Vladimiro Montesinos, the chief of Peru's intelligence service, visited Pablo. His first night with us Pablo entertained him with five beautiful young Brazilian dancing girls. The following day they raced Jet Skis and finally Pablo got down to business. "We need places in Peru where our planes can land and take off," he told him. "Places that won't be bothered by the Peruvian air force." Pablo agreed to pay $300 for each package of cocaine, which would amount to about $100,000 for each plane that landed in the Peruvian jungle. All the transactions had to be done in cash. Montesinos would keep 40 percent for his share and the rest would be distributed to the military.

The main thing that Pablo demanded from anyone who took his money was total loyalty. Many people made their fortune working for him, but they knew that the penalty for betrayal was harsh. When one of Pablo's main security people, Dendany Muñoz Mosquera, known as La Kika, was put on trial in the United States, prosecutor Beth Wilkinson said about Pablo: "He let everyone in the organization know that if they cooperated with the government, if they stole money or merchandise from him, there would be one simple punishment: death to the employee and his family. To make that organization work, the threat had to be carried out when someone violated the rules, so he hired bodyguards, killers, and hit men from throughout Medellín . . . and his hit men killed and terrorized those who did not follow his orders." Much of that statement is true. During that time no member could snitch or steal from Pablo without their life being in jeopardy.

There have been many stories told about Pablo, especially after his death, that I do not believe are true. When people were on trial they offered these tales to help themselves, knowing people would accept anything about Pablo and there would be no retribution. The bigger the stories they told, the better it might be for them. For example, a pilot the DEA captured agreed to testify in an American trial to reduce his own sentence. He told the prosecutor that after a shipment had been intercepted he said to Pablo, "It's strange. Every time Flaco [who was a trusted worker for my brother] has something to do with things, the government comes in and they take it, or they were there taking pictures. You need to find out what the deal is with Flaco."

A few weeks later this pilot asked Pablo what he had learned about Flaco. As he told a courtroom: "He said, 'It's been taken care of.' One of Pablo's *sicarios* [hit men] had three color photographs, Polaroids, and he handed them to Mr. Escobar and Mr. Escobar handed them to me. He pointed to one of them. He said that was Flaco.

"There were three men. One of them was a heavyset man, one was tall and slim like Flaco, and the other one was a short fellow. They had all been skinned alive. Their testicles had been cut off and their throats had been cut."

The only way the pilot knew for sure it was Flaco was because Pablo identified him. "I asked him what kind of person would do this to another human being. He looked at the sicario. The sicario looked back at him and smiled and that was the end of it."

This was his testimony. It would have taken a brave man to sit at Pablo's table and insult him like that. But stories like this one have been told, and have helped build the outlaw legend.

The markets for the Medellín cartel expanded as fast as a shadow sweeping over an ocean. New York was a very important territory, and it was opened to Pablo by a friend known as the Champion. Champion had been sent to New York from Medellín in the 1970s by his mother, who was concerned because he was spending his time on the streets. He was learning from the wrong people. So she sent him to live in America with his successful older brother, intending that he would go to college. Champion lived in New York for five years while becoming an engineer for air-conditioning systems. It was while Champion was studying in New York that Pablo established his presence in the business in Colombia. When Champion returned to Colombia he hooked up with the same rough friends—and started fixing air conditioners. When he learned about Pablo Escobar he decided, I'm going to make some money with that guy.

Pablo agreed that Champion would handle his business in New York, taking charge of the distribution when the merchandise arrived and collecting the payments. One of Pablo's strong senses was his ability to know who would work well for him, and to put them in the right position to be successful. To assist him in New York, with Pablo's permission Champion brought his own cousin the Lion into the business. Lion had been living in New York City for a few years, working as a busboy at the fancy French restaurant La Grenouille. At that famous restaurant he had poured water and cleaned up for the rich and celebrated people of the city, among them former mayor John Lindsay, the actor George Sanders, Jacqueline Kennedy Onassis, and Peter Lawford. He would tell us that one night Mrs. Onassis ordered a large steak but ate only the carrots. Later in the kitchen he ate Jacqueline Kennedy Onassis's untouched steak. In that job he was an invisible man, providing service to the most famous and wealthiest people in New York. But within a couple of years he was storing $25 million in cash in an apartment. We sometimes wondered how some of those famous people would feel if they knew their busboy was now richer than many of them—and was supplying the cocaine that many of them enjoyed.

The most important person for the cartel in New York was Champion's older brother, who we knew as Jimmy Boy. Jimmy Boy was well educated; he was a professional economist, an elegant, calm man who worked on Wall Street. He was a respected member of an important country club. His friends ran major corporations—which is why he became so necessary.

Champion and the Lion ran the business on the streets. They were in charge of shipments, distribution, and collection of the money. The biggest problem they had was how to handle the money. At times they would have more than $20 million in cash in the apartment they kept two blocks from the United Nations. They had whole rooms with cash stacked in boxes; they were running out of space. Jimmy Boy was the man who laundered most of that money. He began using some of the cash to buy stocks in companies, always under a false American name—nobody was going to find Pablo Escobar in the stock market. Soon Jimmy Boy began making straight investments in the companies of the big people he knew. He would tell them, "I've got a friend who wants to invest $3 million in your company." There were some people who wouldn't accept cash, but enough people would, especially owners of factories. Jimmy Boy also was dealing with the managers of banks. Banks like money. Jimmy Boy was able to open up lots of accounts under many names. So the money came through the American financial system and got cleaned.

After New York was in business, in 1982 the Lion went to Pablo and told him, "Champion has New York. Miami is taken care of. I have a girlfriend in Madrid, I have family there, so let me open Europe." Pablo agreed. Spain was to open the door to the rest of Europe.

A friend of the Lion's from Medellín had become a popular bullfighter in Spain. "I've known you for thirty years," the Lion said. "Now would you like to make some good money?" The bullfighter knew people of stature in Madrid: the executives, the promoters of the bullfights, the businessmen, the rich people who loved the nightlife, the actors, the high-class people and, maybe most important, the beautiful women. The men always followed the beautiful women. The bullfighter held parties and dinners and opened the connections for the Lion. In the beginning, before the routes were established, cocaine was so expensive that only the rich and celebrated people could afford it. But when the celebrated people of Madrid, the people known to live the most exciting lives, began using the product and talking about it, the regular people wanted it. The Lion began supplying the street people with product to sell. It took some time, but eventually Madrid became like Miami. Spain was open. From Spain, Portugal and the other countries followed. The continent of Europe was open.

I know cocaine is bad. I understand the damage, now. But then, it was different. Pablo had no feelings of guilt about it ever. "This is a business," he would say. "Whoever wants to use it, fine. You use it when you want to feel good, you get high, you have a good time. But alcohol and cigarettes kill more people than cocaine on the average."

Some territories took longer than others to open. But at the top of the business there were basically fifteen countries that were receiving regular shipments, and from those places other nations became involved. The United States was huge, Mexico was huge, even in Cuba there was some business being done until Fidel Castro found out that some of his colonels and generals were involved and killed three of them.

Only in Canada did the business not take root. Champion tried to open Canada for us, but it didn't work. Pablo sent Champion and the Lion to Montreal and Toronto to meet some people, but after making these connections they just didn't sense it was right to go forward. There was no more explanation than that something felt weird. Champion and the Lion had problems with the Canadian police. They didn't get arrested but they believed the police knew they were there. It was playing with trouble, they decided. Finally they told Pablo, "It's too risky. We don't need this."

Pablo told them to go back to New York.

Canada wasn't necessary. We were earning hundreds of millions of dollars. In the history of crime there had never been a business like this one. The biggest problem we had with the money was that there was too much of it. It was as difficult to launder the money—make it look as if it had been earned from a legitimate source—or simply transport it home to Colombia as it was to smuggle the drugs into America and Europe. Pablo used so many different methods of cleaning the money. The important thing was there were always people ready to make deals for cash. So in addition to investing in companies, putting it in banks and real estate and allowing it to flow through the money systems of countries like Panama, Pablo bought magnificent art, which included paintings by Picasso, Dali, Botero, and other famous artists, antique furniture, and other very desirable items that could be sold easily for cleaned money with no questions asked.

There were some creative methods that were used with great success. For example, Colombia is the world leader in the mining and exporting of emeralds, supplying as much as 60 percent of the world market. The emerald trade between Colombia and other countries is hundreds of millions of dollars annually. The way this cleaning system worked was that a legitimate buyer in America or particularly Spain would place an order for a few million dollars of Colombian emeralds. It would be a legal contract. But instead of sending real emeralds worth that price, what was shipped were bad emeralds that had been injected with oil to make them shine bright. These emeralds would stay shiny for three months, after that forget it. But only experts can detect when an emerald has been injected. So the emeralds would pass inspection and the legal payment would be sent to Colombia. Millions of dollars were cleared this way.

Laundering money could be very expensive, costing as much as 50 percent or 60 percent of the total value. So there were always people willing to do deals. It wasn't just Pablo who had to launder money; it was everyone working in this business. We all knew the people who would make deals. Among the groups well known for cleaning money were the Jewish people with the black hats, long curled sideburns, and black coats. One of our pilots used their services regularly—because they only charged 6 percent. They wouldn't get involved with drugs, so to work with them you had to have a convincing story of where the money came from. "For each transaction," this pilot explained, "my name was Peterson, his name was made up. He always wore a red carnation; I always wore a red carnation. We'd go to a room I'd reserved under a totally different name. I usually had a few million dollars in cash in a suitcase, which was guarded by two very well armed men. He'd ask, 'Where are the funds?' I'd point to the suitcase. I tried to speak as little as possible. He'd pick up the bills and instead of counting them, he'd fan them like a deck of cards. The guy was a human counting machine. Then he'd use the phone and call whoever and say, 'The transaction is satisfactory. You can go ahead to the next level.' Then he'd say to me, 'Five minutes.'

"We'd wait five minutes, then I'd pick up the same phone and ask, 'Can I tell him to have a nice day?' He would nod. I'd say that and the transaction was complete. What happened then was that someone in Europe deposited an equal amount of money minus the 6 percent in a numbered Swiss account. At that point the money in the suitcase belonged to him. I had two huge guys there with handguns and this little guy would take that suitcase with millions of dollars in cash by himself and wheel it through the streets of New York.

"It was a great way of doing business. The money never had to be moved physically across any borders. And my money was always there in the account."

But most of our money came back to Medellín as straight cash in suitcases and green duffel bags. Truckloads of cash. A mountain of U.S. dollars and Colombian pesos, the currencies in which we worked. So much cash that we would spend as much as $2,500 monthly on rubber bands to hold the money together. Cash was brought home by people on commercial planes and in stuffed suitcases and duffel bags; it came by airplanes and helicopters, by speedboat. One of our associates owned a Chevrolet dealership in Colombia and the Chevy Blazers he imported from the United States would arrive with millions of dollars stuffed into door panels and tires, everywhere you could hide it.

The good problem we had was finding enough places to keep it secure. We put a great amount of our money into banks under accounts opened under the names of our employees and relatives. Until 1991 there were no laws in Colombia that allowed the government to check bank accounts. For several years this method was sufficient; no matter what the legal authorities really believed, they publicly accepted the story that we were successful real estate people and our fortune came from business. We paid those people who needed to be paid to assist us or protect us. In fact, so many *paisas*—as people from our region are called—were employed by the business that it was said, "When Pablo sneezes, Medellín shakes."

In those early years there was very little violence associated with the business and what there was affected only those people involved in it. The violence was not arbitrary. One of the first people to be killed, maybe even the first, was named José. It isn't necessary to say his family name. José had an automobile body shop and he used to make the hidden compartments in the cars for Pablo to transport drugs and money. One of the cars for which he had made the hidden stash compartment was robbed and fifty kilos were stolen from it. Later fifty kilos would have no meaning, but this was when Pablo was establishing his business and losing fifty kilos was a serious blow. But what was strange was that the thieves knew exactly where to look in the car. Only José, Pablo, and a few other people knew about this hiding place. Pablo faced José, but he denied being part of the robbery. "No," he said. "I swear it wasn't me. I wouldn't do that to you, Pablo."

Pablo began his own investigation. With the people he knew on the streets of Medellín it was not difficult to find the person who had bought the stolen drugs—and that person identified José as the person who had sold them to him. There was no question that Pablo had been betrayed. Now, within only a few years violent death would become a common part of the business, but not yet. Not yet. People don't believe that's true; it is. José had to pay the full price; the big question was how to do that so the police would not follow the tracks back to Pablo. What happened was that Pablo made a plan in which a fight would start in a café between a few mechanics who were with José and some locals. When that fight ended José was dead on the floor. He had been shot several times. The police believed he had been killed in the brawl. The killing was explained that way.

But at the beginning that violence was unusual. For most of the time, many Colombians were making good amounts of money and no innocents were being touched. There was every reason for the government to stay out of our business. So the biggest headache was hiding the money.

But when the government and our other enemies began coming closer we needed other places to keep the money, places we could reach easily that were out of the legal reach of the government. I created the system of caletas, small hiding places inside the walls of houses and apartments, which we used very effectively. These weren't steel safes; they were just regular walls of normal houses, except that there was Styrofoam between the sheetrock to protect the cash. There easily could be as much as $5 million in cash stored in a single caleta, sometimes much more. We kept the money in at least a hundred different places, most of them houses or apartments that we owned under different people's names and paid those people to live in them. Many of the people who lived there knew that there was money in their house, and their job was to make sure that the money was not touched, but those people only knew about that one location. That way if the police showed up they wouldn't be able to say

anything about the other places. Only Pablo and I knew the locations of all the caletas. This information was never written down; it
was all in our memory. While some transactions took place in banks,
when cash arrived I would decide where it should be directed, to a
bank or to a caleta.

In addition to these caletas we built other hiding places. For example, we bought a beautiful house in the rich neighborhood called
El Poblado. We let people live there to protect the house, that was
their only job. They didn't know about the caleta hidden beneath
their feet. When we bought the house it had a swimming pool, but
I had the idea to build a second pool for the children. This pool was
fiberglass, half below ground, half above ground. It was surrounded
by a wood deck. What people did not know was that this kids' pool
was build on hydraulic lifts, and underneath were six large spaces.
The base of these spaces was cement, the spaces contained wooden
cases wrapped in Styrofoam to keep the storage chest dry. Inside
these chests we kept millions of dollars. We also put coffee in each
caleta because after a long time cash starts to smell, especially when
it's in a damp place, and we learned that coffee kills the smell of the
bills. A fortune was hidden under the pool and Pablo and I were the
only ones who knew the combination to bring it up.

We tried to change the money in these caletas at least every six
months, sometimes more frequently. When it was time I would call
the people living there and tell them, "I'm going to bring my girlfriend there to spend the day. I don't want my wife to know, so please
leave." They would go away for a day or two and we would exchange
the hidden bills for fresh cash. But eventually it got to the point that
there was so much money and we were so busy with political problems that we couldn't change the money that often and the humidity
would damage the cash beyond use. I have no idea how much money
we lost this way, but for business purposes we would estimate 10
percent each year. That was considered acceptable.

We also put cash in places we could reach quickly if necessary. At Napoles, Pablo's favorite house, we kept cash inside the old tires of a big truck. On different farms we buried money in plastic garbage cans that nobody knew about. When we surrendered and went to prison we buried more than $10 million in plastic cans inside the prison in different places. The more pressure that was applied to us the more important it was that the money be available. It wasn't just Pablo who had this problem, it was all of us. Toward the end, when we were escaping from our enemies, our cousin Gustavo went to the home of another cousin, who had nothing to do with the business, and said, "Cousin, I have a million dollars and I need to hide it. I want to have that for my family." That cousin turned her couch upside down and put the money inside. They wrapped the money in aluminum foil. Every few days Gustavo would have more cash delivered to the house inside television sets that I prepared for him until finally the couch sagged badly. It was not made to hide three or four million dollars. Fortunately for our cousin, Gustavo took out the money and a new couch was bought just days before the special elite task force chasing Pablo arrived to search the house.

To keep control of the money we had ten offices all around Medellín with accountants working in each of them. Again, the locations were known only to Pablo and myself. The offices were in buildings and in private homes. In buildings they were disguised as real estate offices with different names for cover. In the houses we didn't need to do that. Each office had a special purpose. At one office we would meet the people who hid money, in another office we would meet our friends, and another was for the banks. When we had to meet with people we would always do it at the one place they knew, instead of allowing them to know the location of the different offices.

My favorite office was also in El Poblado. It was an old house on a very large property. We even had a big lake there and sometimes we would catch fish and have an employee prepare it for lunch. That house also had a soccer field, small, but sometimes in the afternoons we would go outside and play. In my personal room there I had a beautiful big desk and a white polar bear fur rug on the floor. We acted inside the office like any other business. I know people think we always had to operate in secret with danger waiting for us, but for many years, except for the fact that our product was cocaine, our offices seemed no different from an insurance office or an importing company. We ran the organization as a business. In the accounting part of it, there was no difference.

I hired the ten accountants. Some of them were relatives; others were friends or strongly recommended professionals. Two of them were young and we paid their costs to go through school to study accounting and then we put them to work. People wonder how it was possible to keep track of everything that was going on. With ten very organized people working full-time we were able to do so. Each of those people had responsibility for only a part of the business. It was my place to review the numbers, to make certain everything was entered. These accountants were very well paid. We didn't offer benefits, but we gave great salaries. All of our accountants, all of them, were millionaires. They had farms, their kids went to the best private schools. Their lives were very good—until the wars against us started. Seven of the ten of them, including one of the two young people that we put through college, were murdered by the groups pledged to kill Pablo.

The question I am asked most often is how much money did Pablo have. The answer is billions. The exact number is impossible to know because so much of his money was involved with possessions whose value changed continuously. He owned property all over the world, he owned as many as four hundred farms in Colombia and buildings in Medellín, he owned an $8 million apartment complex in Florida, he owned property in Spain, he owned famous paintings and a very valuable collection of antique cars. But certainly many billions. More than any man could ever spend in his lifetime. In 1989 *Forbes* magazine noted Pablo was the seventh richest man in the world, saying that the Medellín cartel earned as much as $30 billion a year.

There was so much money that even those times we lost millions of dollars we slept soundly. And there were times we lost a lot of money. Once, for example, we were shipping home $7 million in cash from America hidden in refrigerators. Someone put them on a ship that was unloaded in Panama. Can you imagine the guy who opened the refrigerator door? The money disappeared. We couldn't get it back. When I told Pablo I expected some angry reaction, but instead he said, "Son, what can we do? Sometimes we win, sometimes we lose."

Another time an airplane flying $15 million in cash from Panama to Colombia crashed in the jungle and exploded: $15 million. We sent people to the site but the plane had burned. The money was gone forever. We also accepted that busts were part of the business. Sometimes we won, sometimes law enforcement won, but mostly we won. We lost tons of cocaine when police raided a warehouse in Los Angeles. The rule was that the people who were responsible for the losses had the opportunity of paying it back. In this situation Pablo sent more drugs to give them a chance of recovering what was lost. If they were not able to pay for their mistakes, they disappeared. This was the accepted way of doing business.

I know this is something few people will believe. But sometimes Pablo would pardon people who lost money, even people who cheated him. Others, especially Gustavo, would not. With Gustavo there was no forgiveness, no second chance. There was a girl who worked for Pablo known as "the girl with the pretty legs," and she remembers the story of Memo. Memo grew up with us and was trusted by Pablo. His job was to carry money to the places Pablo directed. But instead, several times he took the money to the casinos to gamble.

His plan was that he would keep the money he won, deliver the principal to the destination, and no one would know. Instead, he lost. So the next time he carried money he tried to make up those losses. He returned to the casino—and lost again. Finally Pablo found out that his childhood friend Memo was stealing from him. That could have been a death sentence. The girl with the pretty legs was there when Pablo confronted him. Instead of retribution, she remembers, Pablo told him he was fired and let him leave unharmed.

When Pablo learned about the *Forbes* magazine list he was surprised, but he didn't say much about it. Pablo never fell in love with the money. He knew well that in Colombia, where corruption was accepted, money was the best road to power. It was the way he used this power and his wealth that made the poor people of our country love him. Even now, so many years after his death, the greatest majority of the poor continue to love him. Today, go into many houses in Medellín and Pablo's picture is hanging there or there is a small shrine dedicated to him. Only a few years ago a cousin of Pablo's was hired to sing mass in a small home. This is a Colombian tradition. These people did not know she was related to Pablo. While she was there she found these people had many pictures of Pablo hanging and asked why. The woman explained, "When we were hungry the boss came here and helped us. He gave us food, he gave us a lot of things. My son used to work for him."

When the cousin asked where the son was, the woman said, "This mass you are singing is for my son." She said her son died for his patrón, his boss, but she had no blame for Pablo. "It was the circumstances."

Yes, Pablo used his money for his own pleasure and for his family, but he also used it to improve the lives of many people. In the town of Quibdó, one of many examples, he established a private social security system. People without a job went to an office to apply for help and Pablo covered some of their expenses for a certain period of time, two or three months. During that period other men who worked for Pablo would search for jobs for these people. But the agreement was that once you got a job you were finished with the program and you had to work for at least a year.

Once in 1982 Pablo and his cousin Jaime were with some friends of the organization at a soccer game when they heard the news that there was a fire in the dump called Morabita. It was a mountain of garbage in the northern part of the city, and the poorest people in Medellín lived there in dirty shacks, surviving by picking through that garbage for items to sell. In the fire many of these huts were burned down, leaving families without even a roof for shelter. Pablo and his people went there immediately. Many politicians were already there, making the usual promises of help that were usually forgotten. When they asked Pablo what he was doing there, he said he had come to help these people who lived in the mud with rats and cockroaches.

Pablo told Jaime to organize a committee and work with these other people to develop a viable solution. "Give me the budget," he said. "Find the terrain and let's start building." This program was known as *Medellín sin Tugurios*, Medellín Without Slums. Eventually more than four hundred small nice houses were built in the new neighborhood, Barrio Pablo Escobar, and given to these people who needed them most of all.

Where the poor were involved, Pablo became the man of getting things done. He bought a much larger house in the middle of Medellín that became known as the Chocó Embassy because he would bring the very poorest people from Chocó to the city to get them medical care and clothes, to put their lives in shape. Usually there were about sixty people living there and they stayed for several weeks, then others took their place.

Pablo did so much for people. He paid the expenses for those who couldn't afford the medical treatment they needed; one employee's only job was making sure the twenty or thirty people a month who asked him to pay for cancer and AIDS treatments truly were sick. He paid for the college education of young people. When the rivers rose during the winter there were many floods and Pablo and Jaime would go around our country replacing everything washed away by the waters, bringing mattresses, cooking utensils, furniture, and the things people needed for living. And then they would bring engineers to find ways to prevent more flooding. Pablo would supply the materials to the villagers so they could help reconstruct the affected areas. Our mother, Hermilda, had been a teacher and she went all over Colombia to work with teachers and build schools and buy supplies for schools. Pablo built hospitals and equipped them, he built roads for small towns that before had been unreachable by car. He built hundreds of soccer fields with bleachers and lights and supplied equipment for the games—and he would often attend the opening of these fields and give a speech to the people. The girl with the pretty legs was charged with buying gifts for children on holidays, and each year at Christmas and Halloween she would go to local stores and order five thousand toys for Christmas. There was no limit. He fed the hungry, he provided medical aid for the poor, he gave shelter to the homeless, jobs to the unemployed, and education to those who couldn't afford it and they loved him for it.

He became just like the Godfather. People would line up for hours outside his office to ask for his help. And if they truly needed that help, Pablo would provide it for them. When others write about all the good things he did they always give Pablo a sinister reason for doing so: He was trying to make them ignore his real business. He was buying loyalty so no one would report him to the law. They tell endless stories. But the absolute truth is that this goodness was part of Pablo Escobar, as much a part of him as the person who was able to take the violent actions. I'm defending him because it is the right thing to do. The houses he built still stand, the people he paid to educate still have good jobs, many of the people whose medical expenses he paid are healthy. All the good things he did should be remembered. If Pablo had not been so successful as a drug trafficker that he attracted the attention of the world he would have continued his good works. He might have even achieved his goal and become the president of Colombia. And without any question the lives of countless thousands of people would have been made much better. But none of that happened.

I have also been asked what Pablo bought for himself with his money. And I smile and respond: everything. Pablo and all of us lived very nicely. If we wanted something we took the money and bought it. Pablo and I had no salaries, we just took money as we needed it. We took from the bank accounts as well as the caletas. When I wanted to buy something expensive I would tell Pablo, "I'm going to buy this apartment. This is how much it's going to cost." He never objected.

It was important to Pablo that our family be taken care of. In one of the deals Pablo made, instead of receiving cash he was offered the deed to a new house. This wasn't common, but it wasn't too unusual; most of the time the value of the transaction was far greater than a house. One day Pablo took our mother on an appointment, I don't remember where, maybe a doctor. On the way he told her, "You know what, I've got to check this property because I'm doing a business deal and I might take a house in return." She accepted this; as far as she was concerned, Pablo was a real estate man. When Hermilda saw this house she fell in love with it.

Our mother was part of a singing group with her older women friends called the Golden Ladies of Antioquia. All of them were teachers. After finalizing the deal for the house, including all the furniture, Pablo invited our mother and the ladies to the house for a mass in celebration of this new house. Our priest was there to bless it. After the singing was over Pablo handed the keys to Hermilda.

"This is yours, Mother," he said. She cried with her friends out of happiness.

That's the way Pablo gave things away to our family. At Christmas in 1981 he bought an entire block and built houses for members of the Gavíria family, about forty houses total. He wanted the family living close together. He gave our family many presents, including nice cars. Not Porsches or BMWs, but regular cars for safe transportation. The children in the family had their education supported. For Maria Victoria, his own wife, he would give anything. Whatever she wanted he would have for her—beautiful clothes, jewelry, paintings, and many houses.

For himself, Pablo was not that interested in fancy clothes. He wore jeans and white sneakers pretty much every day, although he always had new sneakers. But Pablo bought pleasure. He had a lot of beautiful cars and so many farms and houses and we had many people to serve us at all times of day and night. We ate food prepared for royalty. And when possible we traveled; Pablo loved to travel with his family and friends. In 1982 we went all over Europe and then to Hong Kong. It was in 1983, when it was still safe for us to travel, that we made our second visit to the United States—and that was when we went to Disney World and the White House and Las Vegas where we made friends with Frank Sinatra.

This was years before Pablo became infamous in America. Pablo, Gustavo, and I took all our families, including our wives and children, our sisters and cousins, nieces and nephews, and our mother to Florida. We visited Disney World and other tourist places, and we had some business meetings too. One night we almost got killed. Pablo, Gustavo, and I and a couple of the guys went to a monster truck rally. We were sitting there happily right in the front row, in the best seats we could buy, watching these huge trucks smashing cars, when I got the feeling that we should move. "Come on," I told him. "We need to move now." Pablo thought I was silly, but he moved. We all moved.

A few seconds later a monster truck smashed into the place we had been sitting. If we hadn't moved we would have been killed. Pablo just looked at me with wonder, and said, "Are you a magician or what?" How did I know to move? There was no answer, I just felt that we had to.

Another night in Miami we almost got arrested. Pablo and I and our two bodyguards, Otto and Pinina, went to a nightclub to meet some associates. I always carried cash with me wherever we went. That night I had at least $50,000, hidden at the bottom of a camera bag under a nice camera and souvenir T-shirts for the kids. When we left the club we got into a large van. While we were waiting for the remainder of our friends the driver fell asleep or skidded, and the van went crashing into several other expensive cars. The event was bigger than the damage, but people got scared and started yelling. The police came racing toward us. Pablo said to me, "We don't need this, let's get out of here."

We ran away, not wanting to answer questions about the cash we were carrying. Maybe running wasn't such a good idea. The police stopped us half a block away. "Somebody told us you were involved in the accident," they said. They frisked us, but just casually. They didn't find the money. Pablo denied we had been in the van. He explained innocently that we were just plain tourists from Colombia. The police locked us in the back of their police car and returned to the scene. This was a dangerous situation for us. The police did not know who we were and definitely we did not want them to check our identities. We didn't know what the government had on file about us. We had to get out of there.

The police made the mistake of leaving a nightstick in their car. We were able to use that to reach into the front and open the locks. We opened the door and got out of the patrol car. We ran. We took a taxi back to the hotel and got out of there with our belongings, spending the night at the home of a friend. Otto and Pinina stayed at the accident and paid the owner about $10,000 cash, much more than the cost of repairs. But to be careful we left Florida the next morning.

We went to Washington, D.C., and did the tour of the FBI Building, we visited President Kennedy's grave, and we had our pictures taken in front of the White House. I remember that Pablo was fascinated by the FBI museum, particularly the guns belonging to the famous criminals like Al Capone and Pretty Boy Floyd. From there we went to Memphis to see Elvis Presley's house, Graceland. Pablo Escobar and Elvis Presley, the two kings! Pablo loved Elvis's music. He played his tapes all the time and used to try to dance like him. "Look at me, Colombian Elvis!" While we were there he bought the entire collection of Elvis's music—and years later when we submitted ourselves to arrest that collection was one of the things he took into the prison with him. When we left prison we couldn't take it with us, which Pablo always regretted. Somebody stole it.

Our families went home and Gustavo, Pablo, and I went to Las Vegas. We had arranged for more than $1 million in cash to be waiting there for us. We stayed at Caesars Palace for five days, and I actually won $150,000 playing blackjack. We had an American friend who made all the arrangements for us, and he was the one who introduced us to Frank Sinatra, who was singing at the hotel. Supposedly our friend, who did big real estate deals, told him that we were important real estate investors from Colombia. It quickly became obvious that Sinatra thought we were involved in the Mafia, but I don't know if he knew of our involvement in the drug business. I have absolutely no knowledge if Pablo and Sinatra did any business. There are stories, but I don't know the facts.

I know that we had dinner one night with Sinatra and our translators in a private room in the back of a restaurant. It was an honor for us. When I met him I actually had goose bumps, but I had to be cool to maintain my position. During dinner Pablo told Sinatra that we were going to make a helicopter tour the next day and Sinatra asked to come with us. The next day Frank Sinatra became our guide as we spent about an hour and a half flying all over the area. This is the Colorado River, this is the Grand Canyon. He showed us all the scenery.

We got some of his albums signed by him—and lost those too when we escaped from the prison.

Supposedly, after Pablo became infamous our friend who had arranged this got a phone call from Sinatra. "I've been watching TV," he said. "Is that Pablo Escobar the guy we met in Las Vegas?" I don't know what happened after that, but I guess Sinatra said very firmly that he didn't want to be associated with Pablo. And until now he never has.

It was a great life we were leading. We had to be careful with our actions, but nothing like what it would soon become. Although none of us knew it at the time, the wars had actually begun in 1979, when the United States and Colombia signed a treaty that declared drug trafficking a crime against the United States and permitted Colombian traffickers to be extradited to the U.S. It was that law that changed everything.

Four

I KNOW THAT AS THE PRESSURE ON PABLO INCREASED, as people who had profited from him betrayed him, to protect himself and his family and the business, Pablo became vengeful against those who deceived him or his organization. But for as many people who will tell you that Pablo killed someone himself there are as many who say that he only gave the orders. Pablo wouldn't kill anybody himself, and of that I am sure. The Lion remembers being there when Pablo made his decisions. "When Pablo talked it was an order. Everybody knew that what he said was going to happen. So he would say, 'You have to kill this guy,' like it was nothing. He would say it as if he was asking for more water. But I never saw Pablo doing anything himself. None of the executives ever saw that."

There are people who tell stories about things they supposedly saw at the Hacienda Napoles. George Jung, the original partner of Carlos Lehder, said that he was at Napoles when a man was brought there by two bodyguards. Later Jung was told the man had been caught providing information for the police. This man believed that if he had escaped his whole family would have been killed so instead he gave himself up. Jung claims that as he watched, Pablo got up from the table, walked over to the man, and from a few feet away shot him in the chest.

This is typical of the stories told about Pablo, but like most of them I don't believe it to be true. I know what the world believes about my brother and I know his legend has been built on tales of brutality like this one. People have their reasons for telling these stories. And I know that when I protest against them people think that I am protecting my brother. But I am telling the truth as I know it to be.

The violence was always part of it, but it was never the soul of Napoles. Napoles was Pablo's favorite home, it was his finest possession, it was loved by the family and all our friends, and it was a place unlike any that had ever been built in Colombia.

Hacienda Napoles was a drive of several hours or a brief flight from Medellín. Far enough away from the problems, and the people, of the city. Pablo and Gustavo bought the land and began building their dream kingdom in the late 1970s. It was ready in 1980, almost 7,500 acres of beautiful land, with a river running through the property. The land was spread over two departments, or political regions. Eventually it would contain several houses in addition to the large main house, a complete zoo opened for free to the people, as well as some runways for airplanes to do business. For someone who had been raised as simply as he had, Pablo somehow understood and appreciated great quality in all parts of his life. And Napoles was the fulfillment of all his material passions.

There are two things that everyone who was ever there remembers: Above the entrance gate he had mounted that first Piper airplane that he used in the business. He believed that airplane had started his fortune. After passing through the strong security at the gate, people would drive on a winding road past fields of lime trees, lemon trees, and all sorts of tropical fruit past the open meadow with several thousand grazing purebred Braham cattle, for almost two miles until they reached the zoo. The zoo was another crazy dream of Pablo's that came true. Who builds a zoo at his house?

This was a real zoo with many big animals, including hippopotamuses, rhinoceroses, giraffes and ostriches and elephants, emus, a pink dolphin, zebras, monkeys, and a kangaroo that liked to kick soccer balls. There were also many types of exotic birds. Pablo loved birds, especially parrots, and wanted to have a male and a female of every species. He had a favorite parrot, Chinchón, who could name most of the great soccer players of Colombia. However, Chinchón also liked to sip whiskey and would fall asleep. Unfortunately, one evening she fell asleep on a table and one of the cats ate her. After that Pablo prohibited cats from Napoles—even big cats like lions and tigers.

Pablo bought the animals from the circuses that performed in Colombia as well as from the United States. It was legal to buy them in America, but not legal to import them into Colombia without a special license. Bringing those animals in from America was a big problem, a very big problem. How do you smuggle a rhinoceros? Pablo was careful, and a veterinarian traveled with each animal to advise our keepers about the proper care of the animal. Usually they were landed on our business runways and transported by our disguised trucks to Napoles. One time, though, a rhino arrived illegally in Medellín but it was too late to drive it to Napoles. The journey would take them through guerrilla territory and they did not want to make that trip at night. That left Pablo with a great problem—how do you hide a rhino overnight? Even in Medellín where people have become used to some unusual sights that was hard to do. It was suggested they put it in a private car garage and so that's what they did. The truck put the cage inside this garage and a keeper stayed with it. The family kept its car on the street that night, although they could not explain to anyone that it was necessary to do so because there was a rhinoceros in their garage. The next morning it was put on a truck and driven to Napoles where it joined the herd. There was a whispered saying that came from that: "If he is willing to hide an illegal rhinoceros there is no question he would hide cocaine anywhere."

The only animals that I kept at Napoles were my horses, my beautiful horses. From the time I was a boy I have loved riding and when it became possible I started buying horses to ride and to breed. Pablo didn't share my passion for them, he never bought one for himself, only for the ranch. But he would often joke with me, "Oh, what a beautiful horse. You spend all your money on these expensive horses. That's a crazy thing to do."

I would respond to him, "You know, Pablo, at least I enjoy riding my horses, but you and all those animals . . . You don't enjoy the animals. Try to ride a hippo and see what happens."

Pablo did keep some horses at Napoles. He had four horses that pulled a silver carriage slowly around the property, and he also had miniature ponies to entertain the children who visited.

The zoo at Napoles was open for the public to enjoy. Pablo explained to a Medellín newspaper, "Napoles zoo belongs to the Colombian people. We built it so that children and adults, rich and poor, can enjoy it, and owners cannot pay for what is already theirs."

One day three years after the zoo had been open an official document from the Institute of Renewable Resources arrived and told Pablo he possessed eighty-five animals and he did not have the proper license: "This is all illegal. You have these animals without permits. What are you going to do about it?"

Pablo was polite. "Please, if you want, take them," he said casually. "But you know the government doesn't have the money to feed them all and take care of them. So you should sign this paper and I'll take care of them." The government fined Pablo about $4,500 but left the animals at Napoles.

In addition to his real animals, Pablo had five full-size cement prehistoric animals, including a T. rex and a woolly mammoth, all constructed for the children to play on them.

Beyond the zoo were the houses. There was intense security on every part of the property, some of it easily seen, but more of it concealed. No one could get through the gates to the house unless they were cleared personally by Pablo. If you didn't have an invitation the armed guards turned you away. Even if people did have invitations the guards faxed them to the house for Pablo to check. Near the house was a lighted runway for the transportation planes to land. By the runway was Pablo's collection of cars, and among them was an old bullet-holed car that he told everyone had belonged to Bonnie and Clyde and an old Pontiac that supposedly had belonged to Al Capone. The Bonnie and Clyde car had been sold to him by our friend in the United States who introduced us to Frank Sinatra. Frank Sinatra was real, I wasn't so certain about those cars.

By the main house were the lighted tennis courts, swimming pool, and basketball courts, the outdoor dining areas, and the game room. Everything for pleasure that could be wanted was there. The river on which we often held races with wave runners, spaces to play soccer, and long open pastures for my horseback riding and hiking. There were stables where the riding horses were kept, even a bullring where visiting matadors entertained our guests. For transportation and to race we had cars and motorcycles, some of them with sidecars for passengers, we had Jet Skis, boats, even hovercraft.

The houses offered even more pleasures, swimming pools, Jacuzzis, large dining rooms, a theater for watching recently released movies, even a discotheque for parties. The professional kitchen was always open and if we wanted a special meal in the middle of the night it was prepared for us. The meals were so nicely prepared that for each meal there was a menu. During the meals Pablo would move among the tables, sitting with his workers, his guests, his bodyguards, and the family. He would stand up and recite poems, which he loved, or even sing tango music from Argentina to the music that seemed to be always playing, just like he always loved to sing opera in the shower.

Every member of the family had their own bedroom and bathroom on the first floor, which were named for the letters of the alphabet. The second floor was the private floor where Pablo and Gustavo lived. There was always noise and life going on in the house. It was always fun. Pablo liked to have people around. He would sit with Gustavo or the Mexican relaxing and sometimes they would bet a lot of money. They would bet 50 or 100, but that meant thousands of dollars and they would not bet on the usual winning or losing, but instead it would be $100,000 if at 1:27 of the first half Nacional had the ball. The money meant nothing to any of them. There was more than they could spend.

The parties were like those of Hollywood or even better. The performers would be the best singing groups from Colombia as well as all over South America. The most beautiful women were at these parties, the beauty contest winners. People from business. Artists. And, always, the people he worked with in the business. There was no better place for the politicians of Colombia to raise money for their campaigns. But remember, at that time Pablo's true business was still hidden and he was accepted by the public as a successful real estate investor.

There was also business done at Napoles. When those public crowds were gone, Pablo quietly entertained important people for the business. This included Colombian politicians, government leaders from nearby countries, people on the upper levels of the operation. This was one place where everyone could relax in complete privacy and safety. Flights to transit points took off from the runways. One incident I remember well was the afternoon an old friend named Walter came to visit. When Pablo was just starting out in contraband he had earned $10,000. This was right at the very beginning. "Do me a favor," he had told Walter in 1973. "Hold this money for me. I'll ask you for it in a couple of weeks."

When Pablo needed the money he reached out for Walter—who

had taken the money and moved to the United States. He had disappeared. Ten years later Pablo was informed that Walter had returned to Medellín. Pablo said to a friend who knew them both, "Tell Walter you're going to invite him to a nice farm for the weekend. Tell him it's going to be a great party. But don't tell him it's me."

Walter came to Napoles. When he learned he was on the ranch of Pablo Escobar he was shaking worse than leaves in a hurricane. They brought him to the dining room, which easily sat fifty people. But only Pablo, myself, Walter, and the person who brought him there, our cousin Jaime, and an aunt and two daughters were there in the big room. "Long time no see," Pablo said. "How are you?"

We were laughing to ourselves to see this guy shaking. He'd stolen money from the wrong person.

Walter could barely speak. "I'm sorry for the $10,000. I'll find a way to pay you back. Just give me time, please."

"No, no, don't worry about it," Pablo said casually; his whole attitude was not angry. Then Pablo asked one of the bodyguards, "Hey, please bring me my gun." Pablo's favorite gun was a big Sig Sauer. When the bodyguard returned Pablo stuck the gun in the waistband of his jeans.

Walter's eyes popped open. "Are you going to kill me?"

Pablo's exact words were, "No, listen. I don't kill anybody for money, and especially you because you were my friend when we were kids."

They ate lunch, but naturally Walter didn't eat too much. After, Pablo offered to show him around the ranch. "That's okay," Walter said. "I already saw around."

"Come," Pablo said.

"I don't want to go, Pablo." He was afraid to leave the dining room.

Pablo insisted, and when they stood up Pablo touched his gun. We thought Walter was going to jump through the ceiling. Pablo showed him his collection of beautiful cars, but still sometimes touching his gun. When they finished Pablo said, "Come to my bedroom upstairs. I want to show you something."

Walter was convinced that was where he was going to be killed. As they walked up the stairs Pablo asked him what he was doing. "I have a taxi in Medellín that I drive. I just bought a house. I promise, Pablo, I'll pay you the money little by little."

Instead, when they reached the bedroom Pablo opened up a suitcase filled with cash. He reached and took a pack of bills. I don't know how much it was, but a lot. "Here," he said, handing it to Walter. "But listen to me. Don't ever ever steal anything from me again, because I won't take it."

Walter was crying, but he wanted to get out of there. He couldn't believe Pablo would let him go. He did a kind of walk that was really running, and went back to Medellín with the money Pablo gave him. We never heard a word about him again.

What made our lives change forever was Pablo's decision to run for the Congress of Colombia. This was to be the beginning of his campaign to become the president of our country. At no time did he believe his business would prevent him from having a political career. The tradition of corruption was very strong in Colombian politics, many of the country's elected officials had accepted his money without complaint, and he also knew from experience that the leaders of other Central and South American countries were doing business. Even in America it was well known that the father of the beloved JFK had made a fortune from the sale of illegal alcohol. What all of these men had in common was that they had power before they were elected, military or financial. Pablo had the financial power. He believed that once he had the political power his career in the drug business could be put away. The whole idea of getting involved in politics seemed very bad to both me and Gustavo. We were very much against it. In the business we were in, the last thing you want is attention; in politics, attention is first and necessary. I predicted it would cause us great problems. "Don't do this, Pablo," I told him. "That's the biggest mistake you are going to make. We should stay calm and quiet."

Gustavo also argued this with him, but Pablo was firm. "I'm going to be the president of Colombia," he still insisted. "We already have money. I don't have to worry about my family having a place to sleep or getting food. We've been established, Roberto. I want to help people the legal way. And I'm going to stay away from this."

I believe that was true. He was always talking about one day being president. He felt certain it would happen. And he promised that he would be the president of the poor people, he would work for them. Colombia had been ruled for so long by the same class, "the Men of Always," as they were called at that time. Maybe the faces of the leaders changed, but their policies were always against the poor.

Now, other people say that his real reason for joining politics was that he was worried about the laws passed by America and Colombia allowing drug dealers to be extradited to the United States. I agree that was also true. Pablo often said he would rather lie dead in Colombian dirt than be alive in an American prison. By Colombian law, as a member of Congress he would be immune from prosecution. Also, he believed that by being an elected representative he could begin his campaign to make it illegal for Colombia to extradite people in the drug business to the United States.

The first race he would make, he decided, would be for representative. The system in Colombia works a little different from that of the United States. Our representatives in Congress are elected with alternates, so if they are sick or absent the alternate will take their place. Pablo ran for office as an alternate for the municipality of Envigado. It's probably true that Pablo supported much of the primary candidate's positions. Pablo could have been the main candidate, but this was better. It attracted less attention. To start, he was to be a candidate for alternate for the New Liberal Party, a people's movement against the traditional ruling class. But the leader of that party, Luis Carlos Galán, insisted he knew where Pablo's fortune had been made. Galán had heard the rumors. When Pablo refused to reply, he and his running mate were cut out from the party. Instead they became candidates of the Liberal Party. Pablo didn't lose his temper, but I know inside he was angry at all the politicians who were happy to take his money but then ran away from him.

Pablo's strongest supporters were always the poor people. During his campaign Pablo held most of his rallies in the poorest towns in the election district. His campaign slogan was "Pablo Escobar: A Man of the People. A Man of Action! A Man of His Word!" Many thousands came to these events, and sometimes after the speeches money was handed out to the people. To begin these appearances our little niece and nephew, María and Luis Lucho, would sing the campaign song that had been written by our mother, Hermilda: *A human person has just been born, a very human person. As very good Pablito citizens we are here to show our support. The new politician. The people run and run and run and jump and jump and jump. They run to go and vote. Everyone is so happy they can go and vote for Pablo Escobar!*

Pablo liked to campaign. He would always dress as a man of the people, in his jeans and sneakers, but well groomed of course. Nothing fancy. During those times when he was speaking to the people, I believe in his mind he was able to move himself into another world, a world away from the business. He could see his future. "I'm tired of the powerful people running this country," he would tell them. "This is a fight between those powerful people and the poor and the weak people, we have to start with that. Being powerful doesn't mean you can abuse the poor."

After giving his speech Pablo had his bodyguards around the stage and he opened some cases with money. People came close to the stage and Pablo had his bodyguards handing money person to person. He told the bodyguards to give money to everyone but especially to old people and young people. The people loved him. They would kiss his hands. Pablo didn't like that touching, but he would put his hands on the person's back and hug them, saying, "Do well."

It was funny. Some politicians find secret ways of buying votes. Pablo just handed out money to the poor people, but not demanding anything in return. Sometimes instead of rallies he would have his airplanes fly over small towns dropping flyers, "Vote for Pablo!" And money. Of course the people loved him.

Also like every politician at these rallies he would make promises about what he was going to do. "I'm going to put good lights on the football field . . . I'm going to paint the church . . . Provide books for the schools . . . I'm going to do this and that for you . . ." He said the things he would do—but what was different from other politicians is that within a few days his men would begin doing what Pablo had promised.

At these rallies Pablo often spoke out strongly against extradition. "This is our country," he would say. "Why do we let the Americans make policy for us? We don't need American judges to be in charge of Colombian law. Colombians should be free to take care of Colombia's problems. As a Colombian every person who makes a mistake against the law should be judged in Colombia, nowhere else!" The fact that President Ronald Reagan in 1982 declared trafficking in drugs a threat to American national security was understood in Colombia to mean that people in the business would be considered the same as terrorists. If they were allowed to be extradited they would be treated very harshly, they would spend their life in an American prison.

One of the principals who helped Pablo throughout his campaign was Alberto Santofimio, a Colombian politician with experience. He had been a minister and a senator and he very much wanted to be president. I remember he used to promise Pablo that when he became president he would eliminate all extradition, and he suggested that if Pablo helped him become president, after his term ended Pablo should become the president. That was exactly what Pablo wanted to believe. Now it seems easy to see that it was never possible, but during that time it really did seem like it might happen. Politics in Colombia was always dirty, and many times before the voters had forgiven the past.

In 2007, in Colombia, Santofimio was convicted of being the mastermind behind the killing of New Liberal Party presidential candidate Luis Galán during the campaign of 1988. During the trial it was testified that Santofimio was always telling Pablo that he had to kill people to move ahead. But that would come much later, and was nothing that Pablo ever spoke of to me.

One big issue of the campaign of 1982 was called "hot money." That meant money given to politicians by drug organizations. All of the different drug groups supported candidates who were sympathetic to them. The New Liberal Party, the group that had broken away from the traditional Liberal Party, particularly accused Pablo and his running mate, Jairo Ortega, of being supported by the "drug mafia," as these organizations were called in Colombia. The word "cartel" wasn't heard for a few more years. This was the first time that Pablo was accused publicly of being connected to the cocaine organizations.

The media was pretty fair to Pablo, sometimes calling him "a real Robin Hood." They wrote about him as a philanthropist, a man who easily gave away his money to people who needed it. They also wondered where his fortune had been made, but most of the media didn't write about the drug business. The people didn't care how Pablo got rich. He came from them and had become the equal of the wealthy class, and didn't forget them, so they loved him for it. On election day I rented buses for my three hundred employees to drive them to the voting station so they could vote for Pablo. But truthfully, I didn't vote for my brother. He knew that I thought this was a big mistake and I couldn't personally support it. So I didn't vote at all.

No matter of importance. Pablo easily was elected as a deputy/ alternate representative to the Chamber of Representatives of the Colombian Congress. The Congress is in Bogotá. On the first day he was to take office I was there with him, but I was to leave the country to go do business for my bicycle company, my right business. I don't remember Pablo being excited; as with his anger he kept his joy inside. I know he was proud and believed this was his new beginning. I dropped Pablo at the Congress and went to the airport, so I didn't know what was erupting there.

One thing, Pablo never wore a tie. He was wearing an expensive respectable suit, but no tie. The rules said that all members of Colombia's Congress must wear a tie. So the guard refused to allow him to enter the chamber. Pablo was upset by that. He said, "Here in Colombia the people know that members of the Congress wear nice suits and expensive ties and then they go and steal money. What does appearance have anything to do with the work?"

The radio reporters told their listeners that a congressman was stopped at the door because he didn't want to wear a tie. It became a big story. Meantime, because of traffic I missed my plane. That was okay, I decided, if I miss this trip it is because it is no good for me. So I returned to the hotel to see this mess going on with Pablo. His very first day and he was attracting attention.

Finally a guard said to him, "Mr. Pablo, Mr. Escobar, here is my tie. Just use it."

Pablo put on the tie and entered the Congress. Then when he sat down he took off the tie. Basically he was telling everyone that the tie wasn't essential, I'm here and I don't want to wear this tie and it has nothing to do with the job that we are supposed to do. That was Pablo's introduction to government.

One of his first official duties was to travel to Madrid with others from the Congress for the inauguration of Spain's prime minister, Felipe González. He met the new prime minister at an official meeting. At that time the operation was opening up Europe, so Pablo also met some important businessmen and politicians knowing that they might become sympathetic. It's accurate to say that some of the most successful people in the legal business world in Spain today made their first fortune with Pablo. From Madrid, Pablo visited other countries in Europe, including the small principality of Monaco. Monaco impressed Pablo, with its freedom and fun. So eventually when he decided to build a lovely modern building for himself in Medellín, he named it Monaco.

Under the law of my country, our president must give several cabinet posts to members of the opposition parties. President Belisario Betancur awarded the Ministry of Justice to the New Liberals, who named Senator Rodrigo Lara Bonilla to the position in 1983. Lara was one of the strongest speakers in the government against the influence of the drug mafias, against the hot money.

During the political debate about hot money in August 1983, Jairo Ortega held up for everyone to see a photocopy of a check for one million pesos, about $12,000, to the campaign for the Senate of Lara Bonilla signed by the chief of a drug group in Leticia, the capital of the Colombian Amazon, who was known for bringing in paste and other chemicals from Peru. He had once served a sentence in Peru for smuggling. Pablo knew this drug chief and some people accused him of getting this copy of the check. It is possible that this money had been donated to Lara's campaign with this accusation in mind. It was an amazing moment—Lara was being accused of taking hot money!

In response, he denounced the drug chief and Pablo. This was the first time that Pablo had been accused in public of being a drug trafficker. A few days later a newspaper in Bogotá reported, also for the first time, that Pablo Escobar had been arrested for smuggling thirty-nine kilos in 1976. Pablo told me he was not surprised at any of this. "The people running this country don't want me to succeed. I'm a threat to the same politics. They're going to be against me because they're used to robbing and I'm going to transform the system. Everybody in Medellín knows that I have real estate businesses and that's how I get my money for politics. I love my country, and we want to make this country beautiful. I admire the United States, but I don't agree with the way they are doing politics here in Colombia."

Lara, the justice minister, told the newspapers that the United States had made charges against Pablo accusing him of being a drug trafficker. Pablo had a response for everything. "That's not true," he replied. "As a matter of fact, here is the visa I got three days ago from the American embassy."

Within a few days, however, the U.S. canceled that visa. Two months later Lara requested that the Congress take back Pablo's immunity from extradition. Pablo never returned to the Congress. His political career was over.

At first President Betancur was against extradition. This was a very controversial issue. Many agreed with Pablo and the other leaders of the cartel that our country should not allow the Americans to enforce their law on our territory.

Pablo remained calm throughout and denied all of Lara's charges, continuing to proclaim that he was a real estate man. But this was what Gustavo and myself had most feared. The attention being paid to Pablo Escobar had shone a bright light on the business. Now people were asking hard questions and the police were looking around.

For many of the Colombian people the facts were simple: Pablo and the other business leaders provided more to them than did the government. Even if they believed the stories, the drugs were not hurting them as much as ending the drug trade would hurt them. Later, when we were trying to make peace with the government, an important drug trafficker of Medellín explained this to a representative: "This is a business like any other business. The cocaine that leaves from Colombia is not being used in Colombia. The cocaine that leaves is giving many peasants a source of work. People who have no other means to survive. Right now there are more than 200,000 people in the plantation."

So naturally there was very mixed reaction to Lara Bonilla's call. But the justice minister continued his campaign mainly against the drug traffickers. He named thirty politicians he claimed had accepted hot money. He insisted that Aerocivil, the government's aviation agency, take back the licenses for three hundred small planes owned by the leaders of the Medellín cartel, and eventually the deputy director of this department went to jail for assisting the traffickers. Lara even proclaimed that the drug mafias were helping control six of Colombia's nine professional soccer teams. No question he was making an impact. In Colombia, our secret had finally become public knowledge.

Until that moment we were doing business pretty easily. The operation was smooth. We were well established in the U.S.—just like in Colombia, in Florida and New York we owned many stash houses and apartments. Usually we got old couples that no one would suspect to live normally in them, except that in their closet was three hundred or four hundred or even five hundred kilos of cocaine. It was stored there until the time and place for distribution. The market just couldn't stop growing. Sometimes we worked in cooperation with other cartels like of that of Pereira in Colombia, and those of Peru and Bolivia to fill the needs. All of our employees were making incredible sums. A pilot could earn $3 million for a single trip. Tito Domínguez, who was one of our main transporters, had a fleet of thirty airplanes, including a 707; he owned one of the largest exotic car dealerships in the world, which had Clark Gable's $6 million Duesenberg on his lot; and he owned entirely a new housing development of more than one hundred houses. Domínguez owned personally four Lamborghinis in different colors and each day he would drive the color that matched the shirt he was wearing. Another pilot when he was arrested admitted he owned thirty cars, three houses, some warehouses, twelve airplanes, and millions of dollars in cash.

Until this time the problems had been pretty simple to deal with. They weren't exactly the normal problems, for example the operation was consistently losing product that was dropped into the water to be picked up by the fast boats, because no matter how well it was packed some of it got wet. And definitely we did not have the benefit of other businesses of firing employees who stole supplies. But Lara brought other problems to the organization.

The biggest thing Lara accomplished was the raid on Tranquilandia, which was one of the largest jungle laboratories. It was owned mostly by Gacha, but all the others of Medellín contributed to it. About 180 people lived there full-time, making cocaine. Deep in the Colombian jungle, Tranquilandia was 250 miles from the nearest road. Its advantage was it was the bridge between Colombia, Bolivia, and Peru, the place where all the chemicals and raw product from those countries met to become cocaine, and could easily be flown out. The chemists at Tranquilandia could turn out as much as twenty tons of cocaine each month. In only two years it had produced $12 billion worth of product. The existence of this place was well known, even to the authorities, but they had not been able to locate it in the canopied jungle until March 1984, when two helicopters carrying forty-two armed men landed and destroyed it completely.

It was only many years later that I learned how Tranquilandia was located by the authorities. One of the chemicals necessary to make cocaine is ether. Seventeen liters of ether are required to produce one kilo of coke. At this time the supply of ether in the world was limited. Only five companies in America and seven others around the world produced it. The U.S. government and the Colombians, using turncoats, wiretaps, and inside agents, learned that a company in Phillipsburg, New Jersey, supplied most of the ether for the cartel. Eventually they sold ninety-five drums of ether to the American representative of the owners of Tranquilandia. What nobody knew was that inside two of those drums were transponders to signal their location.

In March, while Lara continued his campaign, the transponder signals came from a ranch. Two days later the signal had moved to the jungle. Tranquilandia. The raiders followed the signal and arrived in force. They burned down the entire camp, destroying almost twelve thousand drums of chemicals and fifteen tons of cocaine. At that time it was the largest seizure of cocaine in history. The impact on the marketplace was severe. For the first time in three years, the price of cocaine in Miami went up.

There are many pieces of the business that Pablo kept from me. I was the front man to the world for Pablo and so as much as possible he kept me away from certain parts of the business. In his mind, I believe, he thought he was protecting me. And, in fact, he did. When we surrendered finally to go into our own prison we had to invent a crime for me to plead guilty to. My real crime, as I told them then, was that Pablo Escobar's blood ran in my body.

So to tell the whole story of Pablo I sometimes have to refer to information provided by other people. Such as the assassination of Lara Bonilla. Wherever there are great amounts of money there are always people who want to take some of it for themselves. In Colombia, in addition to the normal greed we have struggled with kidnappings. So from the beginning the organization had to have people able to protect the money and protect the leaders. These were the security people, the bodyguards, the people able to do whatever jobs were necessary to protect the organization. They were people capable of violence. Men with ready guns who took nicknames like Chopo, Arete, El Mugre, Peinina, La Yuca, La Kika and his brother

Tyson, named for the American boxer. Sadly, it was not difficult to find young people to do these jobs. They wanted these jobs. As the Lion once described the process: "These were mostly the poor people from Medellín, people who lived in the mountains. Recruiting them was simple because they had nothing to lose in life: 'You have no money. Your mom is broke. Your sister is pregnant and she doesn't even know who the father is. There's nothing to eat. Tomorrow I'm going to give you a motorcycle and I'm going to give you some money and help you find a clean apartment, but today you're going to work for me.' Who is going to say no? They said, 'Okay, patrón.'"

When you live in poverty in Colombia or Peru or anywhere in our region there is no time to be a child. You survive, that's all it is. The men and sometimes the teenagers who protected the organization became known later as sicarios, assassins, or in Mafia talk, hit men. They could be very young, and too many of them did not survive to become old. In the poor parts of Colombia many children have their own guns by age eleven. They get them where they get them. Guns are easily available in my country. Sometimes these are machine guns.

It wasn't only Pablo who had these young guns working for him. All the organizations needed the protection and fear that they offered. So long as they kept their work within the business the police would leave them alone—and as long as the police continued to be paid their fees. The police in Medellín were paid $400,000 monthly to cooperate and offer some protection.

One of these young sicarios told the American court trying La Kika how he got into this world. "I was working at a garage making 300 pesos a week, approximately one dollar. So I quit to hang out at El Baliska, the pool hall where the hit men from the Antioquian neighborhood fell out." Someone there gave him an assignment to locate a gunman who had betrayed the organization, and paid him about $300 to do so. When this gunman was found, he contacted

La Kika, and told him, "I have already located him. And he told me he didn't need him alive. That he should be killed. I went over and I looked for two hit men I knew so they would kill him. I hired Tribi and Paleo to kill him. Tribi and Paleo were more or less thirteen to fourteen years old. I told them where he was and they went over and killed him. I was a few blocks away and I heard the shot and went over to see what happened. The gunman was lying on the floor. I was paid 1,500,000 pesos, I kept 500,000, which was between $3,000 and $4,000 then, and paid the rest to them."

There were always people near Pablo ready to do whatever he told them to do. When he said something needed to be done, no one questioned, they did it. Pablo never told me a word about the assassination of Lara Bonilla. It was not something I wanted to know too much about. And I was still living with my family in the city of Manizales and was not with him every day. But Lara's murder changed the lives of all Colombians. There are many stories how it went down. During the trial of Alberto Santofimio in 2007, one of the people testifying claimed that Santofimio had taken part in the planning.

It was on the night of April 30, 1984. In the weeks before there had been many threats made on Lara for him to back off. He had many enemies. So for his safety, earlier that day he had been told that he was to be Colombia's ambassador to Czechoslovakia and would be moving there with his family.

There was a new method of assassination that was becoming common in Colombia. It was to become known as *parrillero*: A man with a machine gun riding on the back of a motorcycle sprayed his victim— usually in a cart—with bullets. The safety helmets gave the assassins a good disguise and the bike provided the best way of escape after the shooting. Eventually this method became so common in Colombia that the government passed a law *against* people on motorcycles wearing helmets, so they could be identified. The new law never made any difference, as no witness would testify against cartel assassins.

This is the way Lara was killed that night. He carried a bullet-proof vest in his car with him, but he wasn't wearing it. The justice minister had been assassinated, and because of that many thousands of others would die.

As a tribute to Lara Bonilla, President Betancur agreed to sign the extradition papers, allowing for the first time Colombians to be arrested and sent to the United States for prosecution. The name on the top of the list was Carlos Lehder, who was in hiding. I know I should remember all the details of those days, but there were so many moments when each decision determined our fate that they slip through my mind. I remember pieces of days, more than the events. After knowing that Lara had been killed I remember the feeling that I had, that the structure of our lives had been undone. I had a feeling of emptiness, I had the sense that something was coming toward us, but not knowing what it was.

About six on the morning of May 4, 1984, I left my house in Manizales to go to a hotel I owned, the Hotel Arizona. My wife, Dora, and my young son, José Roberto, remained at home with Hernán García, who would drive my son to school. The Hotel Arizona had been built completely with clean money from my bicycle stores and factory. It was top-of-the-line; the rooms were as big as apartments. They had full kitchens, cable television from the United States, large beds, some rooms with waterbeds, many mirrors. The amateur bullfighters stayed there during the Feria de Manizales, the annual carnival held the first days of January. Wealthy people stayed there and sometimes the expensive prostitutes with their dates stayed there. The hotel was a successful business and I worked hard to make it profitable.

We had heard rumors that the government believed Pablo was involved in the assassination, but there had been no action taken. But at seven that morning the police showed up at my house. They wanted to do a search but they had no legal authorization. When my wife asked for their papers they arrested her. They came into the house and basically destroyed it. When my four-year-old son started crying one of the police hit him, almost breaking his nose. He was bleeding. Hernán García told them to leave the boy alone, and the police said, "Stay quiet, we do what we want," and then they started hitting him hard. They hurt him.

They were searching for guns or drugs, anything to attach me to the business. During those days everyone believed my work was in real estate. There was nothing to be found there, so they put some guns they had brought with them down on a table and they threw an army uniform on the floor, then they took pictures. Those pictures were published in the newspapers. They wrote that those pictures showed that I was trying to help the guerrillas by giving them guns and uniforms, which was totally untrue.

They stole some paintings from my house by Colombian and Latin American artists and took away my wife.

At the same time the police were searching my home other police squads were coming to the Hotel Arizona as well as Gustavo's house in Medellín. It was all coordinated. When I saw them approaching the hotel I called my wife; when no one answered I knew something was wrong and escaped from the back. The police burst into the hotel, they knocked down doors of people sleeping and having sex, and everybody was screaming and had to go into the street without their clothes. It was terrible. Again, they searched for guns, uniforms, drugs, anything that might associate me with the organization. They found nothing, for there was nothing there for them to find.

They put yellow police tape around the hotel and it was closed for a year.

I hadn't committed any crime, yet they were looking all over for me, including going to my bicycle factory. They went to Gustavo's house, pushing people around, making threats, setting up phony pictures and arresting his wife. Gustavo also managed to leave. The two wives were put in jail.

From my hotel I went to a farm that I owned just outside Manizales. I thought I would be safe there and have time to decide what to do. But soon after I got there the police showed up. This time to escape I tossed two car tires into the nearby river and floated safely downstream to the house of a friend. We made some phone calls so I could find out what was happening. My wife was taken to prison, my son had been hurt. I would never again have even a little trust in the police. I borrowed this friend's car and drove to Medellín to speak directly to Pablo. What was happening? Gustavo was already there. My mind was in a terrible condition. When I found Pablo I was very upset: "I don't understand what's going on. We've got to get my wife out of jail. What's going to happen?"

Pablo was calm. Pablo was always calm. "Okay," he said. "I want you two guys to go to this farm and hide there for now. Let me see what I can do."

This farm was not known to many people. It was just outside the city. Pablo had kept it as a good place to hide when he might need one. Gustavo and I got to the farm. We had to be careful but we were desperate for information. Both of us were worried terribly about our families. Gustavo wanted to call an attorney he trusted one hundred percent to try to get his wife out of jail. "Don't do anything," I said. "Nobody knows about this place. Let's give Pablo some time."

But Gustavo insisted. He gave the attorney directions to our location. We spoke with him at length and he decided, "Let me study the case. I'll come back tomorrow."

That night the little priest visited my dreams again. He told me we were in danger. The next morning I told Gustavo, "You know what, man, you made the biggest mistake. I don't trust this guy. I think they're going to come for us."

A few hours later one of the bodyguards came into my bedroom. "Mr. Escobar, somebody called me from the town to say they saw a lot of police and army guys coming toward us."

"See?" I told Gustavo. "See? I told you, man. Let's go." We ran. The sewer and water pipes from under the city ran near the farm to the river. These are huge round pipes that you can stand inside. We had no choice but to escape through this system. It was nasty, dirty, and disgusting. I had on shorts; Gustavo was wearing jeans but no shoes. We knew there were rats but we didn't see them. We walked for a long time. Any connection with my old life, that life as a bicycle champion, El Osito, ended as we hurried through the filth.

We walked for a long time until we finally came into the streets. The police were looking for us, but as we were at that moment no one could recognize us. Our faces and our clothes were mud-covered, I had lost my shoes, we smelled bad—and we needed help. We decided to go to the home of one of my employees, who I trusted to help us. "Listen," I told Gustavo. "We have to pretend that we're crazy while we're going there." Crazy people could be as filthy as us. People would move away instead of looking to see who we were. So we acted crazy, hiding our faces with leaves from trees. People shouted at us from their cars, "Move, you crazy jerks, get out of the street."

It was a very painful experience. One that lives with me now.

When we reached the home of my employee he first tried to get us to go away. Then he realized who I was and brought us inside. We took showers there, one of the nicest showers of my life, and put on loose clothes that we borrowed. For the first time in my life I was running from the police. It was a strange feeling, but in the years to come I would get used to it.

The question was what we were going to do at that moment. I didn't know what the police had learned about Lara's killing. But I knew they had created evidence against me and could assume they wanted to connect me to it. I was innocent, but at that moment I didn't know exactly what Pablo's involvement had been. When we got in contact with Pablo, he told us that he decided the whole family had to leave the country quickly and go into hiding. Some of Pablo's

Pablo's mug shot.

With my sons, Jose Roberto (left) and Nicholas,
in a photo taken at the maximum security Itagui Prison in 1994.

Proposing a toast, sometime in the mid-1980s.

Pablo at his happiest, speaking to the people during a political campaign.

Unlike other politicians, when Pablo gave his word to the people, he kept it:
He always brought in his people to supply or build exactly what he'd promised.

Pablo with some of our cousins.

At the clinic for Christmas 1996, we made these candles by hand, to be given away to the poor; this helped me earn time off my sentence.

Pablo during the good times, riding a watercraft on Peñol Lake in 1986.

Our sister Marina at a costume party.

Pablo's many good deeds have not been forgotten in my country.
This town organized a parade to show its appreciation for
a new soccer stadium.

At my daughter Laura's First Communion, with my mother (left)
and my brother-in-law and sister Marina.

Pablo fought against Colombia's policy of bowing to the United States and allowing drug cartel leaders to be extradited to America for trial.
Here he is at a protest rally.

Pablo was never afraid to speak to reporters—in fact he died because he was answering questions for a German magazine. Here he is in 1984, while serving in congress, giving a TV interview.

A family picture taken inside the Cathedral in 1992; I am hugging my daughter Laura. We never wore any prison uniforms, just our regular clothes.

Pablo at the Cathedral in 1992, with his son, Juan Pablo, and our sister Gloria.

Although the government and our enemies were looking hard for us, Pablo threw a twelfth birthday party for his son, Juan Pablo (left), at Napoles in 1989. He is seen holding his daughter, Manuela, and our mother.

Me and Pablo's wife, María Victoria, in 1987. It's difficult to believe the good life we could still lead while the government hunted us.

At a gathering in 1986. The man with the mustache is our cousin Gustavo, who started the entire business with Pablo and ran it alongside him.

Tito Domínguez with his famous pet mountain lion, T.C., for "Top Cat."

With the trophy I won for the mountain segment of the 1966
Colombian Mountain Tour.

In this 1965 race, I'm running second to my friend Jose Momeñe.

Here I am as a seventeen-year-old in 1965, working on a bike
with world champion Martin Cochise Rodriguez.

At the finish line of the 1967 Halaixt Colombian Tour.

Pablo probably contributed to the construction of more than
800 soccer fields, including equipment and lights.
This is at the dedication of a field in La Paz.

As I look today.

partners who were being pursued had made the same decision and would go with us. Even some leaders of the Cali cartel were making plans to leave the country. We would go to Panama, Pablo said. He had worked out an arrangement with an important general to give us his protection. Each group in the organization agreed to pay him $1 million to stay there, a total of $5 million.

Pablo went to Panama first to get our situation established. We stayed hidden, the lawyers working to get our wives out of jail. My wife was locked up for fifteen days and was treated badly. They didn't want to give her food or clean clothing and made her time there as difficult as possible. There was no reason for that. She had done nothing against the law.

Pablo made all the arrangements for us to join him in Panama. I was in charge of bringing his wife, María Victoria, who was pregnant, as well as my family. The helicopter that was coming to pick us up was late and we began to get afraid something had happened to it. I watched the area around us carefully, wondering if the police would suddenly show up. María Victoria was having a bad time. Finally, though, it arrived and we all scrambled aboard. For the first time I was able to relax.

And then the helicopter started making strange sounds. "We have a problem," the pilot said. "Hold on." We went spinning down too quickly. We thought we were going to die, but we landed safely near a small town in Chocó. We were surprised to still be alive. Within hours a second helicopter picked us up and took us to safety in Panama.

Life as we had enjoyed it was over. The existence of the Medellín cartel was now known all over Colombia. Pablo and the other leaders of the cartel were being blamed for Lara's assassination. The United States was putting great pressure on our government to stop the flow of drugs and in the States the face they put on cocaine was Pablo's. So instead of just being a fugitive from Colombian authorities, Pablo became known in America and Europe as the man behind the cocaine epidemic. They wrote as if all of the drugs reaching those places were because of Pablo.

We settled into Panama. We had no idea how long we would stay or what we would do next, where we would go. Obviously money was not a big problem. Pablo began meeting with Colombian government representatives to try to agree how we could return home safely without being extradited.

We were on the run and we wouldn't stop for another seven years. And Pablo, my brother, who I loved, was becoming the legendary great desperado of the world.

Five

IN PANAMA, OUR FUGITIVE LIFE WAS VERY NICE. We were there with the acceptance of Panama's dictator, General Manuel Noriega. We stayed at a house owned by a high government official near a golf club, but it was like being in a hotel. They gave us cars and provided what we needed. There was not much we could do there but wait while we tried to negotiate some change in the extradition policy in Colombia, so we spent our time playing soccer, going to the gym, sitting at the pool, using all the facilities. We went often to the club for meals and the people there looked at us like we were rich Colombian businessmen. They had no idea that at that moment we were the most wanted outlaws in the world.

I can remember Pablo doing push-ups every morning while Gacha, wearing bright green sweatpants, would try to work out while smoking a big cigar. I remember Gustavo and Carlos Lehder playing tennis all afternoon. Carlos loved to read the newspapers. And I spent much of the time riding bicycles to try to stay in shape and clear my mind of the problems. It was unusual, we were living near the golf course and Pablo didn't play golf. But what we would do was early in the morning or later in the afternoon we would turn over our T-shirts and play soccer on the golf course.

After staying awhile in the high official's beautiful house Pablo and I each rented our own homes with our families near the country club. Panama was so nice that I asked Pablo if we should buy a property in there. He told me, "No. I don't trust Noriega. If anything happens he'll take possession of our properties. Better to rent than buy."

While we were in Panama Pablo and various associates held meetings with representatives of Colombia's government to try to work out an arrangement for all of us to go home safely and without charges against us. These were secret meetings, as the Betancur government wanted no one to know they were negotiating with the traffickers. In return for being granted amnesty and canceling the extradition treaty, Pablo and his associates offered to stop the business, give aid to a program that would develop substitute crops to replace income from marijuana and cocaine—and pay off the total national debt of Colombia. I don't remember exactly how many billions that was, I know it was more than $9 billion, but it would have been necessary for all of the drug cartels in Colombia to participate in exchange for the end of extradition. Even with everyone involved it would have been difficult, but possible, to raise those funds. The threat was that if there was no deal the cartel would have to fight back.

Would Pablo have actually gotten out of the business? I believe it was possible. He already had enough money for the rest of his life and this deal would have let him live completely free. But no one will ever know for sure, because when the supporters of Lara Bonilla in the government learned of the negotiations they insisted the government reject any such agreement out of respect for the justice minister's life. They even built a monument to Lara. For a short time we had hope that we could go home and live our lives, but the rejection made it clear that was never going to happen.

To make certain that we had no surprises from the Panamanian government, Pablo was paying a couple of colonels on our general's staff to provide us with inside information. So we knew every move that Noriega was going to make. It was one of these colonels who informed Pablo that Noriega had said that he was going to speak with the North American government, especially to the DEA. He said, "They are looking at him and he is trying to negotiate his freedom. His deal was that if he gave them you, he would be clean."

Probably to show his serious intentions to the Americans, Noriega ordered his military to capture 16,000 barrels of ether that were supposed to go to the new laboratory being built in Panama with his approval, organized by some of Pablo's associates.

Pablo knew that there was nothing he could do as long as we were guests in Noriega's country. In secret he gave the order that everybody had to leave Panama right away. He had a couple of airplanes and helicopters sent to him. Several members of the family went back to Medellín, others to Europe, and we were to go to Nicaragua.

There were only a few places we could safely go. Finally we requested asylum from the Sandinista government in Nicaragua, and there we settled for some time. Pablo brought with him 1100 kilos, which could be turned into cash.

Some of Pablo's friends went to Brazil and others to Spain. Most of the leaders were going their own way.

It's hard to describe the strange thoughts I had in my mind. Only months earlier I could go anywhere in Colombia and be greeted with respect as an athlete and a successful businessman. Now I could no longer walk down any street in in my own country without the fear of arrest. I had been forced to flee. To become a hunted man and be powerless to do anything about it shakes your soul. To watch your family suffering and not be able to stop that is the most terrible feeling. And I was a fugitive without committing any crimes: I was pursued by Belisario Betancur's government just for being Pablo's brother. But that's where we were, at the mercy of my brother and his ability to solve his problems.

In Bogotá the Betancur government began the new policy of extradition to the United States. One of the first four Colombians to be delivered to the Americans was Hernán Botero Moreno, the owner of the Nacional soccer team, the most popular team in Medellín. Botero came from a wealthy family who owned a great hotel in the city and he was accused of laundering $57 million for the drug traffickers. The fact that he was arrested was unfair because at that moment there wasn't a law against transporting money. Even though he had been arrested he didn't believe he could be extradited for committing an act that wasn't a crime under Colombian law. In addition to Botero, extradition papers were signed against Carlos Lehder in case he was caught. And the word we got was that they were looking hard for evidence against Pablo in order to sign the papers on him.

While we were in Nicaragua Pablo spent time trying to establish a new foundation for the business. He split the 1100 kilos he had brought with him into two shipments. Pablo hired a pilot named Barry Seal, who normally worked for other leaders, to deliver six hundred kilos to the United States. Barry Seal previously had delivered more than one hundred loads' worth, valued at between $3 and $5 billion. But this load got seized when he landed in Florida. Then it was discovered that Seal was a former CIA man who was collaborating with the American DEA. He presented dark, hazy photographs to the DEA that he said showed Pablo and others loading the drugs onto his plane. President Reagan showed one of those pictures on television to prove Pablo was sending drugs from Central America. Pablo said loudly that it could not be him in the picture, because one thing he never did was load drugs himself.

The public naming of Pablo Escobar as a drug kingpin was very painful to our mother. She told me that the first time she heard Pablo called "Most Wanted" on television she wanted to die. Pablo calmed her: "Your son is on TV but don't believe everything that's said. I'm not going to tell you, Mommy, that I'm a saint, but I'm not the devil either. I have to protect myself, I have to fight back. Mommy, you need to understand that they made me like this. I was in the business helping people, but they made me like this."

Supposedly this Nicaragua story was revealed to the newspapers by Colonel Oliver North, who was working in the basement of the White House to help the Nicaraguan rebel contras overturn the Sandinista government. This story served his purpose well. But this also gave the American government evidence that Pablo was a drug trafficker and allowed them to get an indictment against him and Gacha so that they could be put on the extradition list. Barry Seal was to be the important witness in the U.S. trial against a friend of Pablo's if this person could be extradited to America. Two years afterward Seal was assassinated in Baton Rouge, Louisiana, and naturally Pablo and the Medellín cartel got blamed for it. Like always, it made headlines and was useful to political people. Except that afterward three Colombians eventually were convicted of this assassination and when questioned they said they were instructed in the operation by an anonymous military officer, who they believed was a colonel.

Eventually Pablo decided that the safest place for him was Colombia, where he had control of the people around him. Things had cooled down enough for him to return, although no longer with a public profile. But he still believed it was possible to reach an agreement with the government to take off the pressure. "I'm going to go home," he told me. "I'll make arrangements for everyone."

I traveled briefly to Brazil and finally landed in Madrid, Spain, where we were in operation. I spent time there with a Medellín cartel boss. We were in Madrid only for a short time before I started getting my warning feelings again. It felt like someone was following me when I walked or drove in the city. Then my wife told me the same thing, that when she went shopping she had the feeling people were following her. I also knew that Cali's cartel bosses were also living in Madrid. Finally I decided, "You know what, I know some people here, but my life is in Colombia. I need to go back."

The depth in which my country was held in my heart was surprising even to me. Colombia is a beautiful nation and even with all the dangers waiting for us I wanted to be there. I left my family in Spain until I knew it was safe for them to return and then I started my journey home.

I arrived by helicopter to one of our farms called the Circle at five in the afternoon, just as Pablo brought together a meeting of the most important drug traffickers in the country, some very prestigious people—even some priests—and owners and presidents of the country's soccer teams. There were about seventy people there and they brought at least two hundred bodyguards with them. We have a saying in Colombia, "with all the toys," meaning with all the weapons, all types of guns. Believe me, these bodyguards came with all the toys. This was a major getting together of some of the most important people in the country, and Pablo had made arrangements with the commander of the police, so that he could be informed of any actions against the drug dealers. He had guaranteed to all the people who attended that they would be safe.

Pablo was trying to find a peaceful way to respond to the extradition of Botero. It was at this meeting that he said his famous words, "I would rather have a grave in Colombia than a jail cell in the United States."

"Gentlemen," Pablo said to them, "this extradition law is not only for me. It's going to be for all of you. That's why we have to be together to stop it now." Then he proposed his plan: First, the soccer teams would strike in protest. They would refuse to play the championship until the extradition was canceled. The people would say, "What's going on?" and tell their leaders to stop the extradition.

In addition, Pablo wanted to organize a collective security force made up of the sicarios. He already had his own group of bodyguards but he wanted everyone to work together to create a larger group that would be distributed throughout Medellín. His plan was to divide the city into five or six zones and each group would have charge of one zone. In this way all of the people in the business would be protected from extradition.

Only a few of the people at this meeting agreed immediately to support the plan, while most of the others wanted more time to think about it. Right then Pablo was one of the few traffickers whose names were known to the public. It was his problem, they believed. They thought they could continue to live as they had been for the last few years, having no idea what was coming. They were very selfish. After they had all left a few hours later I was able to breathe the air of my country for the first time in months. Not for too long though. After midnight a Mercedes came to the farmhouse and a nicely dressed lady knocked on our door. "I have flowers for Dr. Hernández," she said, naming a person we didn't know. She claimed she was delivering wedding flowers and had been given this address.

"This is not the place," I told her, and she apologized and left.

I watched her drive away and I had my uneasy feeling. "That's strange," I said to Pablo. "Something's wrong. I've never seen someone deliver flowers in a Mercedes-Benz."

Pablo thought I was nervous because I'd just come home. "Maybe it's the owner's car," he said.

"It doesn't make sense," I told him. "We're far away from the city. Something is wrong." Pablo dismissed that, but I warned the bodyguards: "If you see something weird just start shooting into the air." Pablo and I sat talking for a few hours, catching up with our lives of the last few weeks. It was two in the morning; Pablo was drinking coffee and eating some cake when we heard three shots fired.

"I told you," I said. "I told you. Now we gotta run." We went out the back way and started running, really running. Some of the bodyguards came with us. Suddenly whoever was coming, we figured it was the police or the military or both, started firing at us. One of the gun shots struck a small stone wall and pieces of the brick hit me in the face. I started bleeding badly. I thought I was mortally wounded. But I was able to keep moving. Another gun shot grazed my leg. There was confusion all around as we ran through the night, people were shouting orders. I was looking for my brother, but in the mess I couldn't find him. Then I saw him walking calmly. "You guys are gonna kill yourself running where you can't see," he said. I couldn't believe how calm he remained. Some of our people had been sleeping and had fled without getting dressed.

We managed to get to a road down below, where we had some luck. One of the bodyguards had been praying at a nearby cemetery and was coming back in a car. Pablo and I and Gustavo jumped into his car and escaped, others went through the woods, but eight of our people were captured. My wounds were slight and needed only a Band-Aid. But for me this was a major escalation. Because of my position as the accountant I had been far from any kind of violence. Now people were shooting at me. Although I had known the stakes of the business before, the coldness of it had never been so close to me. It was more than just leaving the country, or having to hide, it was living every day with the possibility of instant death.

The question was, How did they find us? What happened to the protection Pablo had paid for? When something went wrong there were always questions Pablo wanted answered. We learned two weeks later that a drug trafficker from Cali had gone from the meeting at the Circle and called someone in the government, believing he could win a guarantee that he would never be extradited by informing on Pablo. And Pablo also discovered that the raid had been directed by Colonel Casadiego Torrado, who Pablo had considered a friend and had been paying $50,000 a month for cooperation and information. But maybe this colonel figured that by capturing or killing Pablo Escobar he could ensure his career. Pablo sent him a message: "Now you are against me and you know what I think about that."

For his own protection the colonel was transferred to another city and worked there. And eventually he was promoted to general and rose to a position of power in the Colombian police. Right at that time there wasn't too much we could do anyway, we were so busy. A few years after Pablo's death Torrado got killed near Cali, but I think that was because he got caught up in his own problems.

After this Pablo changed his way of doing business. Instead of keeping colonels and generals on the regular monthly payroll, he informed them he would pay them only for the information they provided.

On the night of the raid at the Circle, at exactly the same time in Madrid, police had arrested Jorge Ochoa, the Cali cartel's Gilberto Rodríguez Orejuela, and a third man who was a friend of theirs. When I had left I'd given the key to my apartment to Jorge and told him to use it if he needed it. But it was their own actions that attracted attention, so when Torrado informed on them the police knew where to find them.

They were put in prison. The United States requested that Spain extradite Jorge Ochoa to the United States for his participation in drug trafficking. Colombia also officially requested his extradition for the crime of smuggling fighting bulls into our country from Spain. This created a serious problem for the Spanish government about where to send him. If Ochoa was sent to the U.S.—where he had been indicted three times—he would spend the remainder of his life in jail there; if he went to Colombia the penalty would be much less. The Ochoa family hired lawyers in Spain and America and spent twenty months fighting extradition to the U.S. It was well known in Europe and South America that the decision to return Jorge to Colombia was made by Spanish Prime Minister Felipe González. Ochoa was sentenced to twenty months in prison in Colombia, but the power of the traffickers proved enough and eventually he put up a bond for $11,500 and walked free.

Pablo and I, the Ochoa brothers, Carlos Lehder, Gacha, the Mexican, we had all become wanted men. Now whenever we traveled precautions had to be taken. Bodyguards always were with us. Pablo, and I suppose the others, would not permit any photographs taken. In Medellín, Pablo owned more than twenty taxicabs to move around. In some of the places he stayed he had secret hiding places built into walls just in case he got trapped. When Jorge Ochoa finally got out of jail he also took elaborate steps to hide. One of the people involved in negotiations between the traffickers and the government described to the law how he was taken to meet with him.

"We drove twenty minutes around town," he said. "We went into the garage of a house. In the garage they asked me to change vehicles. I got into a taxi. The car drove me to what I believed was an industrial area—lots of warehouses, large double-trailer trucks—and the driver asked me to get out of the car. He went over to one of the trucks that were parked on the street. He got into the driver's seat and opened the door for me. After I was seated in the cabin, he asked me to pick up my feet and get my hands off the door. He activated some mechanism and the seat that I was sitting on moved backward, and at the same time, a door in the body of the truck opened up, and when I realized it I was already inside the body. There was a very nicely appointed office where Jorge Ochoa found himself. He said to me, 'I would like to know whether I can count on you in order to establish discussions that would be very confidential with the government in the sense of asking the government to cease their attacks on us to let us work.'"

The thought was still that we would be able to make an agreement with the government that would permit us to resume our regular lives. No one believed this could go on for long.

When Pablo failed to get the support he wanted to fight the extradition laws he started building up his own security forces. There were many young people in Medellín who wanted to work for Pablo. It was considered a job of honor. But what was happening now was different from anything ever before. In Colombia the smuggling businesses, the drug business, the emerald business, the coffee business, the flower business, and the mining business had all for many years been an accepted part of our economy. They employed many people, including police, military, and politicians. They brought money into the country. The violence in all these businesses—as I've mentioned, in the emeralds it has always been much worse than with drugs—was kept almost completely inside the business. So the government watched them, but didn't try hard to end them. Now the United States wanted Colombia to solve the Americans' drug problem—and our government had agreed to do so. This is when the violence that shocked the world began. It was this decision, a decision that would not be of great benefit to our country, that led to the deaths of so many people.

To fight back Pablo established offices in four areas in the city, where the sicarios waited. These offices were in pool halls, barbershops, places where men would hang out together. The sicarios originally were formed to be the police of the cartel. Much of the power of the cartel came from the threat of violence as much as actual violence. People heard stories about what happened to men who cheated or betrayed the drug traffickers, and so they took great care for themselves.

Until the extradition treaties, dealing with informers or thieves was the kind of job done by the sicarios. An airport manager who betrayed the cartel by informing to the government was not an innocent person; he was making his fortune from the business and knew the consequences of his actions. But the government's decision to change the understanding between the legal system and the traffickers by extraditing to the U.S. was considered a declaration of war on the drug traffickers. To respond Pablo and the others in Medellín formed the secret group, Los Extraditables, to fight the extraditions. At the head was Pablo, but members were all of those who were indicted in the U.S. or might be charged there with crimes. Because our government had refused to negotiate, the leaders of the cartel had nothing to lose. That's why the motto of the organization became Pablo's declaration: "Better a grave in Colombia than a jail cell in the United States." In 1986, for example, twenty-eight Colombians were extradited to the U.S. to stand trial under American law.

The first blow struck against the government came in November 1985, when Los Extraditables financed the M-19 guerrillas to stage a raid on the Palace of Justice, where the Supreme Court held its sessions. The friendship between Pablo and the M-19 went back to the peaceful resolution of the Marta Ochoa kidnapping. To solve that situation Pablo had met with Ivan Marino Ospina, the main leader of the rebels, at one of the farms he owned outside Medellín. The arrangement was made that the cartel's force, the MAS, would not attack the guerrillas and the M-19 would leave all of the traffickers alone. During these negotiations Pablo and the leaders of the guerrillas made a firm bond. To strengthen that bond Ospina told Pablo the recent history of the sword of the liberator Simón Bolívar, a great treasure of our country. It was known to all Colombians that the sword had been captured by the founder and commander of M-19, Jaime Bateman, from a museum in 1974, who announced it would not be returned until a peace agreement was reached between the guerrillas and the government. For the M-19 the sword was a symbol of their struggle. It had been passed among rebel leaders, eventually ending in the hands of Ivan Marino. It was given to Pablo to seal the treaty between the two groups.

The sword of Simón Bolívar hung on the wall of one of Pablo's homes until he gave it to our nephew Mario Henao, and told him to hide it in Medellín. Meanwhile, the whole country was searching for this symbol of freedom.

The sword remained in Pablo's possession until 1991, when the government agreed to peace with the rebels. As part of the agreement the government wanted the sword returned. So much had happened since he had received it that Pablo didn't automatically remember it was in his possession. Worse, Pablo wasn't sure where it was. We had thousands of hiding places in hundreds of apartments and houses all around the city. The search lasted for a long time. At that time we had voluntarily surrendered and were jailed in our own prison, the place called La Catedral. The sword of the liberator Simón Bolívar was smuggled into the prison—a deed we all believed was symbolic. We all held it, passing it around. I remember holding it in my hands and looking at it; it was both beautiful and dangerous, just like Colombia.

Pablo returned it to two M-19 leaders in Medellín and in 1991 it was given back to the government.

The evidence against the drug traffickers was kept inside the Palace of Justice. The best way to prevent extradition was to destroy all the files that they had collected. What happened in some ways was like what happened in America when the government attacked in Waco, Texas. As far as I know now it was never intended that so many people would die; the plan was just to destroy the records against the drug cartels. In fact, the traffickers offered to pay the rebels twice the millions of dollars for this if they were able to negotiate successfully with President Betancur. Some of the guerrillas got into the Justice Building the night before and waited there. They slept in the building. The next morning other guerrillas got to the building in a stolen truck and raced inside; a few security guards were killed at that time. The guerrillas took three hundred people hostage, including the members of the Supreme Court of Colombia and other judges. Almost two hundred of them were rescued within a few hours. But then the siege began.

Colombians were shocked by this attack on the government. The television covered it completely. I know Pablo watched it on television like everybody else, as I did. I don't know if he was in contact with the rebels during this time. Because Pablo rarely showed expressions of emotion, it was difficult to know what he was thinking. I know it was difficult for me to accept that we had reached this point.

The first thought of most Colombians was that this was only a rebel attack. The M-19 did have a recording delivered to a radio station, demanding that President Betancur come to the building to negotiate. Obviously that was impossible. Hours after the siege began, the fourth floor, where the files against the traffickers were kept, was on fire.

Supposedly inside the government the generals took over, telling the president to stay out of the way. The army circled the building with tanks. On the second day they attacked the rebels. More than a hundred people died in the battle, including justices of the Supreme Court, workers in the building, and guerrillas. No one knows all the details; some of the hostages died in the attack, but others were killed by the rebels. Even today no one knows the complete facts of what happened in those hours. No question that the rebels killed innocent members of the justice ministry, but it also is known that many people who left the building alive—the shopkeepers, shoeshine people, people who were safely away from the rebels—disappeared and were never seen again. Their bodies were never found. The military and the police remain suspect in those killings.

Even inside the organization some people were shocked at this attack and decided to leave the business. If they did so respectfully there was not a problem with that. For example, in Spain the Lion felt the business was getting too dangerous and he made his own decision that it was time to leave. That was when he quit. Some others made the same decision.

The attacks on the government continued. The girl with the beautiful legs was friendly with one of the prosecutors known to be trying to make a case against Pablo by the name of Miriam Belles. One morning soon after the violence started, the prosecutor was walking out of her house to the protected cars when the sicarios went by on a motorcycle and killed her. Without evidence, the girl believed Pablo had ordered this killing. "I had an emptiness in my soul and a pain in my heart," she remembers. "It was an action without any sense.

Pablo didn't need to kill a woman who had two children." While still sometimes she would do a task for Pablo, she explains, the feelings she had for him were gone. The Pablo Escobar she had cared for did not exist.

Whatever threads were holding together the Medellín cartel were finally ripped apart. Each organization was left to protect itself. By that time Carlos Lehder's organization had fallen apart completely. Like Pablo, Lehder had once dreamed of becoming president of Colombia; he even had started his own political party, the National Latin Movement. But his politics were much too hard-line; he remained an admirer of Hitler, so he never was very popular. Also, the stories of his grand life on Norman's Cay had become public. He had ruled that place completely. All the while the cocaine planes landed and unloaded and took off again, making Lehder a billionaire.

But his most powerful weapon was money, not fear. Eventually a report on television in the United States made public the corruption of Bahamian government leaders, including their beloved prime minister, Lynden Pindling—although nothing ever was proved against him. I don't know the truth of that specific accusation, although it was so easy to bribe officials that I wouldn't be surprised. But the result of that report was that Norman's Cay was closed as a transit point and Lehder could not return there. We began using other places in the Bahamas for landings, like the Berry Islands and Great Harbor, without much interruption.

Lehder spent most of his time in Colombia with Pablo. They were together at farms, and offices; they traveled through the country together. The bold Carlos that we had met a few years earlier was now gone. The government froze almost all his accounts and took over his properties and possessions. Once his fortune had been estimated at $2 billion, but now he was nearly bankrupt. While he was on the run he had to go into the jungle and there he got sick with fever. It was feared there was nothing that could be done to help him.

He was dying there. Pablo sent a helicopter for him and brought him back to Medellín where he received the proper treatment to save his life. Even then he was very weak.

When he finally recovered, Pablo gave him work to do. Basically he became a trusted bodyguard, although he was given the respect he had earned. Once he was recovered he decided to start making a second fortune at a farm. One of Lehder's new employees who was running the farm called the police, and Carlos was captured and extradited him to the United States. I was saddened, because I cared for him, because of his intelligence, and the great friendship he gave my brother Pablo. After his trial he was sentenced to life in prison without parole, plus 135 years, so all of us now knew how we would be treated if we permitted ourselves to be extradited to the United States. With the government refusing to negotiate, our choices were only to fight until the state canceled the treaty or die fighting. As far as is known to anyone, Carlos Lehder remains hidden somewhere in the American prison system, still making appeals of his sentence.

During that time we were careful about where we stayed, and we moved often, but we didn't feel under tremendous pressure. Pablo still returned to Napoles, although now he only remained there for brief periods of time. It was in this period that all the good deeds Pablo had done for the people began to pay off. The people who loved him refused to help the police or the military find him. In fact, many members of the police and the army remained on his payroll while they were searching for him.

We always had a great amount of security around us, whatever we did. In our family security, it was normal to have the men with the mustaches and the solid bodies, but we also had several beautiful women. In those days nobody in Colombia would think that a beautiful girl having a drink at the bar could actually be looking over the place to see if it was safe. One, I remember, was a tall blond girl with gorgeous blue eyes known as Lorena, and after working for me for two years we helped her become a model in Italy. Lorena, who later helped save my life, looked like a Barbie. She was very strong, very serious. To answer the unasked question, no, there was never a sexual relationship between the security and the principal.

The reason for using the women was that they could easily go to public places without raising any suspicion. When we had a meeting in a hotel or a restaurant they could check it out without bringing any attention. If we wanted to go to a nightclub we would always send two of these women with two nicely dressed male bodyguards an hour before we wanted to show up to check the place. They acted like couples, but they were watching carefully. Later, when it became very risky for us to go out we would send as many as ten different couples, who sat at different tables and let us know if there were any problems. One night I was going to a club and sent a few couples to look the place over. They called and told me, "Everything's cool. You can come ahead." But just to be sure, I decided to dress like a bodyguard without using any expensive jewelry or watch, unlike one of my own bodyguards, who always wore lavish clothes and accessories. I dressed more casually. So when we got to the club, the well-dressed bodyguard with the pretty girl was invited inside—and they wouldn't let me in! I had to go to the corner and called them inside, and everybody left.

To increase security we would also pay the club security $500 to make sure nobody with a gun got into the club. "If they show a permit," my people told them, "tell them to walk away." Remember, there were no cell phones then, but we had the big military phones and used them.

Although the fact that we were often on the move made it more difficult to manage the operations, our business didn't seem to suffer. Our organization had been well established and could continue to operate smoothly. We had secure routes, guaranteed transportation, and good distribution. And we had more customers than we could supply.

When the DEA began making more drug busts in the U.S. some

people thought that meant they were defeating the cartels. But the real reason they were successful in making more intercepts was because more drugs were being sent into America. It was said that Medellín was responsible for shipping 80 percent of the cocaine in the world. For example, the DEA found a Colombian cargo plane carrying one thousand kilos hidden in cut flowers and wood products and said its value on the street was $20 million. Twenty million dollars! That was one shipment. With that amount of profit the business could never be stopped, there would always be people ready to take their chances to earn their fortune, even risking a prison term.

The big problem we had then was that we could supply more than the demand, so the price went down. From $35,000 or $40,000 a kilo it went down to $9,000. The profit was almost nothing but still the flow didn't even slow down. So instead of paying the delivery men a fee for each kilo, it was better to give them ownership of part of the load. Transporter Tito Domínguez stockpiled his share when the cost was low. And when there was a big bust, like the cargo plane, the price went up quickly, and people like him would sell their product.

Pablo's people were always able to make moves ahead of the U.S. government. Sometimes there were as many as eight different agencies trying to stop the drugs; besides DEA there was Customs, the Coast Guard, the local city police department, the state police, and the military. When Domínguez was caught he was charged with crimes by seven different agencies. One thing that helped us was that these agencies got to keep the equipment they seized, so instead of working together they were all in competition with each other for the publicity and the materials they could seize and own. They had airplanes and speedboats and fishing boats and cars that sometimes they sold and used their profits. But Pablo's people continued to outsmart all of them.

Domínguez explained: "The government worked three men

minimum on a speedboat pretending to be fishing. When we had a shipment arriving we had eight or nine boats in the area. We would check out every boat in the area and if a boat didn't have any fishing equipment or looked suspicious they would radio, 'Tito, mother-in-law's in the driveway. How far out are you?' I would shut down and wait until I got the word that mother-in-law had left the area.

"We had real good intelligence. When the talk of the town became that the government was doing speedboat busts we switched to sport fishermen. When we found out they were focusing on the Miami coast we moved a few hundred miles up to places like Cocoa Beach.

"I had one big house in the north and one in the south, each of them on the water with a big dock. These were ports of entry, nothing else. The drugs would go in the back door and right out the front door. These houses were just a doorway to America. They were in expensive neighborhoods because the neighbors' houses were further away for privacy. The boats would deliver as much as one thousand kilos and be out of there in minutes. It was a system that was never stopped."

I'm not defending the violence that happened, I'm explaining it. But the leaders of the Medellín cartel believed they had to force the government to change the extradition law and this was the path they chose. Soon all the judges were under protection, but there always was someone willing to inform on them. Until finally in December of 1986 the new Supreme Court found that because of a technicality the extradition treaty could not be enforced; the reason given was that it had been signed only by a temporary president. It was a small victory because the new president, Virgilio Barco, signed it fast, but it proved the impact that the attacks had on the judges in the country.

One thing that is important to remember is that there were good police and bad police. These police were not like the regular police in the United States, who are trained to protect the public. Some of them were not innocent at all. The police sometimes acted more like attacking soldiers than men who upheld the law. There were police who searched houses for Pablo who acted as gentlemen; they would make their search and leave. But others did crazy things. They were hard with innocent people, they stole possessions, they broke things for no reason, and they left after making threats. Or the police would go to a house at random and knock down doors, terrorizing people, and steal their belongings. It was known that even having in your possession a photograph concerning Pablo—even if you weren't in it—had become a crime. If the soldiers or the police found such a picture in your house or your car, you could be arrested for cooperating with the criminals and your property would be taken. The girl with the beautiful legs remembers that her family burned every picture of Pablo. The searchers came to her house to search at least seven times. This was called *ayananie*, although they were always accompanied by a judge who made it legal. They stopped her many times in her car at roadblocks and they broke into her car while it was parked. But of course they never found anything to associate her or her family with Pablo. Their searches were so tough that when people wanted to get even with their neighbor for any reason they would call the police from public phones and tell them, "Pablo Escobar is living at this address."

And sometimes the police killed. Our cousin Hernando Gavíria was at his farm with his family for a vacation when the corrupt police arrived looking for Pablo. Hernando did not know where Pablo was, nor was he in contact with him. But still the police started thrashing him. They hung him upside down, and covered his eyes to torture him with electricity, and they also inserted needles in his testicles, all in front of his children and wife, while threatening the children and wife if they didn't tell them where Pablo was. He died in front of his family.

Even while this was going on, many of the police continued on our payroll. On Fridays the police would line up, some in uniform, and be given a salary. For that money they performed surveillance services.

For example, after the war started between Medellín and Cali in the late 1980s, some police in both of those cities worked for the traffickers who controlled those cities. So that when a car came into Medellín with a license plate from Cali, or when strangers would check into a Medellín hotel, the Medellín police would check them out. If they were from Cali sometimes they would take them into custody and if their intentions were innocent they would be released; but if it was suspected they were in the city for a crime, instead of being taken to the police commanding officer they would be handed over to the cartel.

Pablo's war against the police started with the murder of Diego Mapas, a friend who was one of our associates. He got the nickname Mapas, map, because he was incredible with directions. If you gave him an address, he would find it better than a map.

One afternoon Diego Mapas and two other bodyguards rented a taxi in Medellín to go to Bogotá to make a drug deal. What they didn't know was that they had been followed from Medellín. The police pulled them over, and took Mapas, his bodyguards, and the taxi driver to a farm near Bogotá, where they were tortured the same way as our cousin Hernando, and disappeared never to be found again. And all these tortures were in order to find out where Pablo was hiding. The Colombian government offered $10 million for both Pablo and myself—dead or alive, but preferably dead.

Pablo learned what had happened from a member of the police force named Lieutenant Porras who would supply information to Pablo, because Porras did not agree with the way the police were carrying out their corrupt methods. Pablo encouraged him to denounce all the crooked cops, so Porras did go to the district attorney, and surprisingly for Porras the DA put him in jail. After a few weeks he supposedly escaped from the prison and then was killed by the police in a barricade near Boyacá. It's not correct to think of the police in those days just as people keeping the law. Many of them were corrupt—something we know for sure.

Pablo fought the police hard. They were trying to kill him, so he killed them. They put a price on his head; he put a price on their heads. The total war started about 1988. In Medellín the police had hundreds of small stations for about three or four men called CAIs, for Centro de Atención Inmediata, and they were put in intersections all over the city. They were like guard posts or checkpoints, and they would stop traffic. The sicarios would attack these posts with machine guns or sometimes bombs. There would be money paid for the death of each policeman. The amount of payment was figured by the rank of the policeman. A regular policeman was between $1,000 and $2,500.

There were many poor people in Medellín trying to collect that money. It was a big business and sometimes different people made claims about the same shootings. So a system was set up that before the event the assassin would need to inform the head sicario where he would attack, and afterward he would have to present a newspaper story about the attack to receive his pay.

There are many, many guesses about how many policemen were killed, from about two hundred to two thousand. I don't know the exact number. One reason for that difference was that there was violence done from so many different places. Pablo was the easiest to blame for all the deaths, but many of these assassinations were done by other police trying to get paid, as well as other people wanting to get even.

The police fought back with their own assassins. The secret police death squads would go in black cars into the poor neighborhoods, the barrios, at night. Most regular people would stay off the streets after work, so the police decided anyone on the corner was a bad guy, and that they worked for Pablo. Their secret squads with machine guns would drive around shooting young people for just standing on the corner, or they would take them away and later people would find their bodies. This was every night.

Another attack by the corrupt cops against innocent people was the following: One night they went to a nightclub called Oporto in Medellín; there they took about twenty young men from eighteen to thirty years old outside the parking lot to look for Pablo's son. All these young men were sons of Medellín´s wealthy including some politicians. Right there on the spot they were told to lie face down, and they were massacred. The government kept quiet, and this way the police had more confidence to do their slayings. And another night at a Medellín street corner in the humble Castilla neighborhood another massacre occurred where twelve young men ranging from twelve years old to twenty-four were killed when they stood outside. All this was done by the secret police unit. The deaths kept piling up.

In a neighborhood called Aranjuez in Medellín the killing secret police unit went to a house where there were eight young men. The police took these young men in unmarked SUVs with tinted windows to the police's Carlos Holgüin School. There these police tortured these teenagers to find out where Pablo was hiding—without success, of course, because how would they know? The next day most of these kids were found murdered, but a couple did manage to escape to tell the story.

Pablo actually wrote letters to President Cesár Gavíria and the attorney general to make public the truth that the police were killing innocent people. But the government didn't do anything with the names of the corrupt police. I don't know how much really they could have done to stop it, but Pablo wanted the people to know the truth. The bodies kept piling up in the streets of Medellín's poor neighborhoods, especially over the weekends.

What was amazing was that Pablo's mood never changed. He accepted what was happening and never panicked. He understood his fate. I remember hearing him say several times, "No drug dealer ever died of old age." The fact is that no matter how much pressure he was feeling, no matter what had happened during the night, no matter where we were, he always acted the same and positively. He would usually get up sometime past noon, while Gustavo loved the early mornings. Pablo never saw him. So between Gustavo and Pablo they covered the entire day. Once Pablo got up he would spend his usual half hour or more brushing his teeth. That was his obsession, brushing his teeth, which were perfect. Then he would put on a new shirt; he wore a new shirt every day 365 days a year. After he wore a shirt he would donate it to someone, there was always a person who wanted a shirt of Pablo Escobar's. When possible he would enjoy his favorite breakfast, arepas, it's like a corn patty with scrambled eggs, chopped onions and tomatoes, and nice Colombian coffee. Pablo loved to sing and sometime in the day he would be singing songs he loved. If he wasn't able to speak to María Victoria or his two children, his son Juan Pablo, and his daughter, Manuela, because it was too difficult or too dangerous for them, he would write poems for his little daughter and send them to her or record tapes for her to hear. I think of all the things that he lost while we were running, the only thing that truly affected him was not being with his family. He missed his family every single day.

It was while this was happening that the legend of Pablo Escobar was being built. All of the other drug traffickers had used violence in the business, all of them, but all of the publicity was focused on Pablo. In the United States and the rest of the world his name was put on the entire drug business coming from Colombia. This was good news for all the others. The concentrating on Pablo took much of the attention off the other cartels.

The media of the world made it seem like catching Pablo would end the drug trade from Colombia. Maybe what made Pablo so interesting and exciting to everyone was the fact that he couldn't be caught. He was one of the richest men in the world, he was running a major drug organization, he was fighting wars with the government—and he was like a ghost. He was everywhere, but he was nowhere. When he was in the city the few people who knew about his presence never gave him away. The main reason for this was that the poor people of Medellín loved him and protected him. Some people were afraid of him, that's true, but for the people with nothing he was their hero. The government had done nothing for them, the gifts of money and houses he had given them before were repaid with their loyalty.

Six

FOR MANY YEARS WE WERE CONTINUALLY ON THE MOVE, always watching the movements around us. It began with just the Colombian police and military searching for us, but eventually we were at war with the Cali cartel, with very specialized units of Colombian police created just to scour the earth for Pablo, with representatives of America's Delta Force, and even with the Colombian paramilitaries. And yet Pablo was able to fight them all and survive.

For much of this time we stayed on farms Pablo owned, some of them on mountains with views of the city he loved, but other times we lived deep in the safety of the jungle. Only the closest friends knew where we were. When Pablo needed to see someone, a lawyer or a politician or a friend, that person was brought to him blindfolded, often by an unusual route. Even our mother did not know where we were; when Pablo wanted to see her she would be brought to a named point. I would meet her there and make her wear a pair of blackened glasses and then take her in another car to the meeting point. Once, I remember, I handed her these glasses and told her to put them on. When she did she began making faces. "What's wrong with these glasses," she asked. "They're very expensive, but I can't see anything."

I explained, "Mommy, these aren't for fashion. They're for security."

Security was always first. Pablo always bought farms on the roads miles away from our location and put his people living there. If necessary he would build houses for them. When an enemy force went by that place day or night we would be notified immediately to get ready to leave. Only once, I can remember, did the police come upon us completely unannounced—and these people never knew who they had found.

Pablo and I were staying at a farm on a road near Amagá, which is about forty miles outside Medellín. This was toward the end of our time on the run, after Pablo had decided we should be without bodyguards. The price on us was $10 million each. As Pablo said, we paid the bodyguards very well but not $10 million. For that kind of money we knew the only people we could trust were each other. Our agreement was that we would watch out for each other; we slept at different times so one of was always alert.

It was a beautiful house surrounded by orange and apple trees and flowers; it had a swimming pool, a place of great calm. We often had barbecues outside, where we would sit and play dominoes. I became a master of that game while we stayed there for about eight months. When Pablo was buying this farm a dog bit him, so Pablo insisted the dog stay with the farm. He named it Hussein, and eventually the animal calmed down.

We were living in the house with an older married couple we had known for many years, Albertino and Ilda. The farm had been bought in their name. They were both artists, painters. In addition to living in the house, they were given a salary and all their expenses were paid. For our protection Albertino would begin a painting but leave it unfinished. The picture that was there at the moment was a beautiful farm with a small cow. The only thing to be finished was the green grass, which I could paint to look real if necessary. Pablo would wear the painter's cap and in the morning both of us would put paint on our hands and our clothes in case the police showed up. Pablo had grown a beard and when he was splattered with paint he would look authentic, like he did his work there.

The importance of this farm was that it was near enough to Medellín for Pablo to be in contact with the attorneys negotiating a compromise with the government to do away with the extradition laws. These meetings usually took place late at night, sometimes at one A.M. When Pablo had to go to places he would wear his artist disguise and Albertino would drive. The negotiations took a long time because Pablo knew exactly what we wanted, which was for the government to change the constitution. Meanwhile, we hid.

Very early one morning the police suddenly came to the farm. It was not a raid; there was only one patrol car with two men, so I figured they were not looking for Pablo Escobar. I opened the door for them. Albertino and Ilda were having breakfast and when Ilda saw the police she slipped away to wake Pablo. In this house we had built secret stashes to hide money as well as hideouts for ourselves. Pablo moved into one of them. When the police came to the door I welcomed them. I was pretending to be a painter with the cap and the artist's glasses. I began reaching out to shake hands, but stopped politely because, as I indicated, I did not want to get paint on them. They explained their presence. "We're doing a search in the neighborhood because we found a body at the side of the road." In fact, he said, they had found a head on one side of the road and a body on the other. He continued, "It happened last night. We were wondering if you saw anything weird or heard something unusual."

"No," I said, and that was truthful. That corpse had nothing to do with us. "I was up very late working on my painting." I invited the police inside and served them a cup of coffee. They admired the house and left. When they had driven away I used our knock code to tell Pablo it was safe to come out. Later we learned from the people in town that the body was that of a husband who had been killed by his wife and her young lover.

Wherever we stayed we made certain there were places for us to hide quickly if necessary. It was this way with all the hunted men from the drug organizations. One time the police got a call that a major leader was hiding in an apartment. The exact address and apartment number were given. When the police went into the apartment there was warm food still on the table. They searched this apartment for hours but found nothing. The man had disappeared. The police were used to being given false information—people were always calling them to say they had seen Pablo Escobar in a store or walking into a building, for example—and this seemed no different.

A month or more later this same person again called the police and insisted the leader was at that address. From the outside the police saw a candle burning. The army knocked down the door. The candle was still burning, the bed was warm—but the apartment was empty. This time they had the answer to the mystery. They stuck the point of a pen into a tiny hole that no one could find unless they had been told it was there. The wall opened up. This man was there. He had prepared for a stay of hours—with him was a canister of oxygen. He was captured and eventually extradited to the United States.

The hideouts we built were not fancy, but effective. They allowed us to fade into the walls in an instant. One that Pablo built, I remember, could be opened only by turning a hot water faucet to one side. The difficulty with being inside one of these hideouts was that the person could not know what was taking place outside. That made it necessary to have some type of secret code, a code that said it was safe to appear.

But the best hiding place was the jungle. And eventually even we got comfortable there. With the protection of our bodyguards we could disappear into the jungle and the police and military would not risk tracking us in dangerous territory. In the jungle they were the invaders.

There also was the time that we were staying at the farm called the Parrot. We had been there for several months along with Gacha, Pablo's brother-in-law Mario Henao, Jorge Ochoa and his wife, and some of our people. There had been no worries. Usually I would go to bed early in the evening and rise in the morning by 3:30. But one afternoon about six as everyone was watching the news on television I felt very tired and took a nap. As I slept the small priest visited me again, warning me: "You guys gotta go. The police are going to show up."

It was a powerful dream but I was too embarrassed to tell it to anyone. I thought they would laugh at me. So instead I shared with them, "I feel very strange. I've just got a feeling the police are going to show up tomorrow."

"How come?" Pablo asked. "Did you get any phone calls?"

"No, I just got the feeling."

They didn't pay any attention and of course I didn't blame them. But I went to our employees and told them to get some food ready, pack some clothes, and put the seats on the mules: "Just in case we have to leave this place quickly." The farm was right next to the beautiful Cocorná River, which is so clean you can see the fish below, so I also had them make certain there was fuel and supplies on our boat. I went to sleep that night at the usual time, but this bad feeling I had didn't go away.

One of the radios Pablo had given to all our neighbors made a noise about 6 A.M. It was from one of the people who lived on a nearby farm by the name of José Posada. He was one of the people who would call frequently to say everything is good, everything is quiet. But this time he said, "Leave. The police are here. We've seen trucks and heard helicopters. Go now!"

Within a few seconds we heard the helicopters coming at us. The "damn mosquitoes," Pablo used to call them. And then he would make a movement to slap them away like they were nothing at all to him. Not this time, though, they came too fast. There was no time to go for the mules or the boats. As they approached they started shooting from the air. We ran, firing back as much as possible. Some of us ran to the river, others into the jungle with just the clothes we had on our backs. Pablo was in his sleeping clothes without even a shirt or shoes. He left all his papers behind. Fortunately, Pablo had planted some pointed trees and bushes, which made it impossible for the helicopters to land. But they continued shooting at us from the air. Bullets hit the ground and the trees and whizzed by my ear. I ran, faster than I had ever run in training. This time there was no stopping until we got free of there.

Long ago we had made a blood pact that we would shoot ourselves behind the ear rather than be extradited. Jorge Ochoa thought it looked like this might be that time. They were all around us. Jorge took his .38 revolver and was ready to commit suicide, but Pablo stopped him. "It's not the time," he said. If it were, he vowed, he would do the same. Somehow we managed to get loose of the raiders. But it was close.

It was later I found out that those damn mosquitoes had killed Pablo's brother-in-law Mario Henao, our brother in our souls, as he tried to get to the river. Pablo saw him get shot. I didn't. Pablo was shooting back as he ran. Maybe he hit one of the choppers with a machine gun; it was said he did but I didn't see that either. But the loss of Mario was a terrible pain to all of us. When we were safe in the woods we received the confirmation that he died and that was the only time I ever saw Pablo cry. In addition to several dead, they had captured fourteen of our people, but none of the leaders were among them.

We had many close escapes while we were negotiating. Once we were staying on a farm we call the Cake, near the top of a hill in the wealthy area of el Poblado. While there was a very old, very large house, with fourteen bedrooms, on the land, Pablo built for himself and his close friends Otto and Pinina a Swiss chalet–type.

The house was typically well defended. We lived there with 120 bodyguards. The perimeter was established by two rows of barbed-wire fences, and the gaps between those rows was patrolled by vicious dogs. There were also twenty raised watchtowers that were manned twenty-four hours each day, and a motion-detector lighting system that warned of any intruder. There was also a battery-operated bell system that would alert us if the police had shut down the power, as well as radio scanners to hear the approach of an enemy, and surveillance cameras all around to cover the perimeter. I had supervised the installation and kept checking it to be sure each piece operated successfully.

One day Pablo called me urgently on a secure line to tell me our radio communications frequency was blocked. "It's got to be the police," I said. "Get prepared." A minute later I was told that truckloads of soldiers were coming up the hill. Twenty minutes later bells were off from four places, meaning the soldiers had practically surrounded the perimeter. Pablo remained calm, as always. He noted that the bells had not run from the southwestern portion of the property, so we went in that direction. Pablo picked up a submachine gun, Pinina and Otto took their weapons, and we started walking among the pine and eucalyptus trees.

When we reached the towers 13 through 16, where the bells had not rung, Pablo took armbands with the insignia of the DAS from his pocket and we all put them on our arms and kept walking. Pablo was wearing a military cap and dark glasses, and he was dressed in the civilian way, as the DAS agents always wore. The helicopters were now flying over the house. One of the guards from the watchtowers had a rope, and as planned Pablo tied the watchmen's hands with it. Then they began walking down the hill, as if these men were Pablo's prisoners.

Soon we spotted several soldiers. "Hey!" Pablo yelled to them. "Come help us with these guys we caught from Pablo's command post." Pablo handed the four men to these soldiers and told them not to mistreat them, and that he and his men were going to go after two others from the house they had seen running. Pablo took with him one of the soldiers who carried a water canteen. As they walked, Pablo asked him where the other soldiers were posted, and this young soldiers provided that information. Once Pablo learned where the other soldiers were, Pablo told him to wait right where they were standing, that his people were going to look around and would return. He was left standing there.

Eventually we arrived at a modest farm. The farmer and his wife understood who we were and took us inside. They fed us and let us stay there safely. Eventually they loaned Pablo their car—their son even rode ahead on his motorcycle to make certain the road was open. The escape was complete.

Ten days later Pablo returned to this small farm. He admitted he loved the property, because it was secluded in the mountains and looked on to a waterfall. He offered the farmer a great amount of money for it. His offer was accepted, and Pablo had another safe house set up for himself.

Each time we were attacked we would move to another place that had been prepared. While this was happening the business continued. Pablo remained convinced that in return for an end to all the violence eventually the government would agree to his terms: There would be no extradition to the United States and if we went to jail in Colombia it would be for a reasonable time and in a situation safe for us. The search for Pablo divided much of our country; while the poor people supported Pablo, others did not. For me, like Pablo, the most difficult part of it was being separated from my life. We all had to believe our families were being watched and people were listening to their phones, so it took careful plans to be able to be in contact with them. It was painful for me, for example, to watch my second marriage fall apart and be helpless to do anything to stop it. Even in the middle of this worldwide hunt our personal lives continued.

My second wife went with our ten-year-old son, José Roberto, to the beautiful vacation city of Cartagena. We owned a home there and a boat. Many members of our family were there, so my wife gave the house to some of them and stayed at a nearby hotel. One morning she said she wasn't feeling well because she had a fever and sent José Roberto with his aunts to cruise on the boat. José Roberto was a fine boy and didn't want to leave his mother alone, so when they reached the boat he started crying and complaining he wanted to go home. His aunts were insistent but finally he ran back to the hotel. He knocked hard on the door to her room but nobody opened it. He called down to the reception and made everybody worry: "I'm the son of Roberto Escobar and my mother is in this room and she isn't answering. This morning she had a fever and I'm worried she is dying." Deep inside, though, he wanted to find out the truth of a feeling he had.

When the security received no response to knocking they opened the door with the master key. Nobody was there. José Roberto told them that his aunt was staying in another room and thought, "Maybe my mother is there."

And again, they knocked, and again no answer. They opened the door and my wife was in the Jacuzzi with another man. José Roberto was stunned. She said to him, "Please don't say anything to your father. You don't understand."

José Roberto was a pretty smart kid, and kept quiet. But instead he sent me a letter telling me this whole story. I was hurt terribly when I received this letter but there was nothing I could do about it. Nothing. I thought women were just like money; neither can truly belong to you. If I said anything against her she might call the police and tell them where we were staying. She had access to much of the money. She knew the bank accounts, she knew the safe combinations. She had our son with her. So I had to lie there at night wondering what was going on and being able to do nothing about it. She was a beautiful woman, but the love and compassion I had for her quickly disappeared. Still, though, to this day, it remains unclear to me why she did that. I was a formidable husband to her, she had love, money, and everything necessary for happiness.

This was part of our lives as fugitives. There were so many feelings about being out of touch with the rest of the world and helpless to change our situation. We got our news from the television or during phone calls with our families. Our relatives would read the newspapers to us, which sometimes told us where the government thought we were staying, or where they were searching for us. Every day, every minute, our lives were up for grabs. Every time we heard an airplane approach we stopped and waited. We lived our lives ready to leave instantly.

About three months after this escape we were staying in an old house at the top of a mountain. And it happened once again. I lay down to sleep and the small priest visited me. This time I told Pablo, "I got that strange feeling again. I think they are going to be here tomorrow."

After our last experience Pablo believed my warning. He ordered our people to pack the mules with food and water, the guns were made ready, and we all slept lightly. In the morning we got a call from a contact in the police. "The police know where you are," he said. "They are going to come up there." We got up on the mules and climbed into the mountains. Several of our employees stayed behind and were there when the police arrived shooting. The police killed the groundskeepers and the farmers.

I am not usually a person who believes in the mystical world, but I have experienced the warnings of this priest. I don't know why he comes to me. He doesn't come each time my life is in danger. There have been very bad situations that have happened with no warning.

But when he does come danger follows him. So I've learned to listen to his warnings.

Our most difficult escape took place in 1990. This time I got the greatest warning of all from the priest that danger was coming. We were at a farm called Aquitania with about forty people. It was about a hundred miles from Medellín, in the jungle. About four in the morning we got notice from the outer security that the police were about six miles away and coming fast. Because there were so many of us, instead of a hideout, we had built a house underground about two miles away, deeper in the jungle.

An employee of Pablo's named Godoy lived in the jungle and people believed he sold wood to earn his living, but for his real job he would build hiding places for us and guide us through the jungle. The underground house he had built was amazing. People could hide there for days if needed. The moment we got the word we ran for this shelter. Godoy took us there. We could hear the helicopters behind us shooting at the place we had abandoned. At those times you never stop to wonder how they could find you, but it was clear we had a traitor in the organization. With the rewards for Pablo and myself it's not surprising. We reached the underground house and secreted ourselves there for the rest of the night. The next afternoon Pablo sent Godoy to his own house, which was not too far from our hiding spot, to find out as much as possible. Godoy looked like a simple workingman so he could move about without being suspect. The police had passed the whole day searching the area without finding much. About 6 P.M. the police showed up at Godoy's farm and asked him questions. "I live here with my family," he told them. "I work with wood. I produce a little coffee to sell to the city." The police looked around for an hour but left when he told them he wanted to have dinner with his wife and his kids. He was not suspected.

As soon as the police cleared the area Godoy called me on the radio. "They left my place ten minutes ago. Be careful. They are very close." Even though the hiding place was not visible from the ground, because we did not know who had betrayed us we didn't know how much information the police had gotten. Only a very few people knew about this underground house, but if one of them had talked to the police we would be trapped with no way to run. We knew that it was better to have a chance to get away than to be trapped underground. We moved outside and gathered our supplies. While Pablo was deciding when to go we heard a helicopter flying nearby and looked up at it through the trees. There we saw a terrible sight.

One of our security people, El Negro, was hanging by his feet out the door of the helicopter. When we saw El Negro flying from his feet we knew we had to run, because he had helped Godoy build the hideout. Later we found out what had happened. El Negro had been captured by the police at a farm about a mile below us. They tied his legs and took him up in the helicopter and hung him outside, telling him, "If you don't tell us where Pablo is we will drop you right now, motherfucker."

El Negro screamed that he would talk and they saved him. He wasn't a traitor but they were going to kill him. When they landed on the ground he started walking with them toward the underground place. But there was a miscommunication between the police walking with El Negro and the army searching for us. The army in the helicopters started shooting at the police on the ground, because they thought it was Pablo and his crew. The police on the ground started firing back. Everybody was shooting at everybody, and we took advantage of the gunfight and fled to the deepness of the jungle. El Negro also escaped, and made it to a nearby town where no one knew who he was, and the town's priest hid him in his residence so he wouldn't get murdered. It was twenty days later that El Negro made it back to Medellín.

Godoy led our escape. Among the forty people who ran with us were our loyal and trusted friend Otto, our cook named Gordo, and a very good soccer player we gave the name of a great Argentine soccer player. We didn't follow an established path because, as Godoy told us, "The police won't come this way." It was tougher, though, climbing up a mountain covered with trees and bushes. We walked for about five hours in the night until we got into guerrilla territory. That first night about twenty of our people got separated and lost, so we arrived at a small house with the remaining twenty fighting people. We believed some of the others would find us there. A few did as the hours went by. This house was lived in by an older woman whose son was a guerrilla. At first they got scared because they thought we were the police, but when they were introduced to Pablo they relaxed. The message was simple: Many Colombians had great reason to fear the police more than drug traffickers.

Our clothes had been ripped badly by the underbrush we'd run through. This woman gave me a uniform from her son, who must have been at least six and a half feet tall. It was so big over me that I had to tie it at the ankles and use rope around the waist to hold it up.

I was carrying with me as much as $500,000 cash. I always carried money, knowing that in many situations it is much more valuable than weapons. As we sat eating the soup made for us a campesino showed up. We paid him $100,000 to lead us out of the jungle. But when we finally got ready to go Pablo realized that Otto, our loyal trusted friend, was still lost. In our escape Otto had been next to Pablo much of the time, ready to protect him, but had disappeared in the night jungle. "I know there are a lot of guys missing," Pablo said. "But I won't leave this jungle without Otto." Pablo didn't care if the police were coming; he wasn't going to leave Otto behind. So Pablo and I, one other person, and the campesino agreed to go back and search for him. We took gas lamps with us and walked in a straight line, one behind the other. In the distance we could hear the helicopters shooting blindly into the jungle. The bullets zipping through the leaves made a snapping sound. Every few minutes we would yell for Otto. Finally we heard him answer back, saying he was hurt. I was learning the jungle; I found out that sound travels so well it's hard to know where it is coming from. The peasant told us to be silent and led the search. It took almost an hour to climb through the vines to find Otto. He'd tripped and fallen into a deep hole. His face was cut up and we thought his arm was broken. It took us all working together another hour to cut him free from the grip of the jungle.

We left the farmhouse the next night. I left the people $50,000. They had never seen American dollars before and I had to explain to them what they were. I warned them to wait a couple of months, then go to town and exchange it a little at a time. I explained that if they exchanged too much they would attract attention, and if the police found out where they got the money they could be killed. Before leaving, we had radioed ahead to one of our people to meet us at a place with the supplies we would need. He told us that the army and the police were everywhere, it was a major search, and it would be better to stay hiding in the jungle for a while. We were led through the jungle for several days to a dirt road, then handed a map that would take us to a bridge that crossed over the River Samaná to a safe place.

At that road our people met us with those supplies we needed to stay safely in the jungle—food, clothing, sleeping bags, and medicine, all those tools of survival. Then we started walking again. My life on the bicycle had given me strong legs and good energy, but it was a hard walk. Some of our people struggled keeping up with us. In two days we found another small house and approached it. A man and a woman lived there with their two grown sons. Pablo told those people we were part of the guerrillas. No, the man said, "I know who you guys are because they're talking about you everywhere." These people didn't have electricity; they had only a battery-run radio, and no TV. On their radio they heard the news that Pablo Escobar and his brother were in the jungle and that the government was offering a $10 million reward for each of us. "Don't worry," they told us. "We're not interested in anything to do with the government." They invited us to stay at their house and the woman cooked a meal for all of us on wood. We agreed to spend the night there.

I woke about four in the morning and watched silently as one of the sons left and walked into the jungle. I woke Pablo and told him. "Don't worry," he said. "Wait until a more normal hour and we'll ask where he went."

Before everybody woke up I felt restless. I couldn't wait. An hour later I got up and started making noise, waking everyone. I said casually to the couple, "Oh, where's your other son?"

The father said that he'd gone to the nearest neighbor to get an ax to chop the wood needed for cooking. "We want to make you a nice lunch so we need more wood to cook for all of you."

In the position we were in we couldn't trust people we didn't know. There was a lake close by and we went there to wash up. As we went back toward the house I saw a big pile of cut wood stacked up high. So I knew then that this man was lying.

Pablo said to me, "Don't show worry." To everyone else he said nonchalantly, "Let's have something to eat. Then we can move." That was typical Pablo calm. But while we were eating a plane flew high up above us, way off the usual route. I believed it was from the army but Pablo questioned that. "It's so high, how can you think that?"

But I did. "You know me, man. Sometimes I feel things." This was different. But still I had that bad feeling. A little bit later there was a helicopter flying nearby. We heard it, but didn't see it. When I asked the father about the son, he said he would return that night. That was curious, I thought. Before he said that the son would be back with an ax to make lunch and now he's saying he'll come back at night? I told Pablo, "We gotta go. I don't want to make a big deal, but I think the son left and went to the next town to talk to the people who are looking for us."

I was ready to go but still Pablo preferred to wait. I decided to start walking with the few people who wanted to walk with me. Pablo stayed and we agreed to keep close contact on the radios. We had been walking about an hour when we saw another helicopter coming near us. We hid. This was an army helicopter and it was flying so low I could see the people inside—and one of them was the son. I called Pablo and told him to get out right away. "I saw the son riding in the helicopter. They're coming."

Pablo and our men ran into the jungle. The helicopter approached but didn't see them. The police helicopters would randomly shoot all the time at anything, but the army only fired at targets they could see. We met up with Pablo and the rest of the group at the River Samaná bridge. There were twelve of us. As we were about to go over it we saw army guys coming from the other side. They didn't see us so we moved away quietly. We couldn't use the bridge so we had to swim across the river about a mile away. It was very difficult to get across carrying all our supplies. The river was wild. It carried us along for about three miles. One of our men with the nickname Ears, because he had big ears, almost drowned. Pablo was a very good swimmer and went to save him. Ears grabbed Pablo around his neck and almost dragged him under, but Pablo was able to save himself and Ears, but just.

We were soaked and very exhausted but we knew we had to keep moving. This was on the run like never before. Helicopters were in the sky looking for us. We kept going into the safety of the night. Finally we put up the tents and covered them with brush to make them invisible in the light. Just so things could be worse, it started to rain hard. It was so cold, so cold. We had to sleep next to each other to keep our bodies warm. I was still carrying the suitcase full of money and that night I used it as a hard pillow. The smell of the damp money under my head was terrible. It was then I thought that money made such little difference in life. I had hundreds of thousands of dollars in my hands but there was nowhere I could get the small things we needed most, dry blankets and warm food. I was ready to burn the money to keep us warm.

The days of Napoles and the great parties seemed very far behind us. Now it was just surviving.

Late in the night suddenly we heard a huge explosion. We all got up and were ready to move quickly. I said to Pablo, "Oh man, I think they're bombing us!" Pablo and one of our people went to look for the damage. It wasn't a bomb. A giant rock had been loosened in the rain and tumbled down the mountain. It bounded on a ledge and flew right over us, crashing into the trees and knocking them down all the way to the river. I said we should move our base, but Pablo decided that one rock had gone over us; chances of another rock following that path were small. But if we moved we might move right into the path of another rock. No one slept soundly that night.

In the morning we began walking. We were moving through thick jungle. A couple of times we saw poisonous snakes, frogs, and other wild animals that added to the danger. But they kept their distance. We walked for two days, taking water from the lakes but all we had to eat was some chocolate and peanuts, because we were running out of supplies, and some of the others guys were way behind. Our blankets and tents had been made useless. We were very uncomfortable. Eventually we walked right into territory controlled by the guerrilla group FARC 47. We didn't encounter any of the guerrillas, but we did discover a small supply area with hammocks, food and water, and some guns. I believe that discovery saved our lives. We ate like crazy and took turns sleeping in the hammocks. While Otto was sleeping a tarantula walked on him and settled on his chest. Otto still slept. Pablo saw it and put a piece of wood in front of Otto's face, and when the giant spider walked on it Pablo tossed it away.

We were new again, and we walked some more, reaching the very small town of Santa Isabelle. It was full of guerrillas and they welcomed us. We slept there, shaved, and ate bread, eggs, and pasta, especially lots of pasta. The guerrillas hid us in their houses. Because they didn't want to risk anybody calling the police they took us to another small town, St. Carlos, where our employees José Fernando and Guayabita were waiting in a truck to take us to El Peñol, where Pablo owned a farm. Finally we settled there.

The thirty-day walk had made some of us badly sick with coughing and fevers. My own fever was very high and I didn't know where I was. They took me to a hospital under a made-up name. For three days I was unconscious with the fever. They would give me cold showers to cool me down. Sometimes I would wake up screaming, demanding to see Pablo. Fortunately, no one knew the Pablo I was calling for was the most wanted man in the world.

Pablo also was sick but he stayed at the farm. For security there Pablo hired a gang from Medellín to protect the people while they recovered.

We had lost some of our men during our journey but again we had escaped the wave of police and soldiers searching for us. After we got better Pablo and I and a few of the top men like Otto moved back into the comforts of Medellín.

Not too long after the walk through the jungle Pablo decided to change his whole security situation from a big number to only a few. Rather than moving with as many as thirty people, he used only two, which made it much easier to travel around and kept us more discreet. Sometimes we stayed at the homes of regular people that we trusted, couples with no children in the house. When we moved around in the city we often wore different costumes. Some people said that Pablo dressed as a woman, but that was false. We wore fake mustaches, sometimes wigs, always different types of clothing. We would pretend to be a doctor or a laborer fixing roads; sometimes we drove our own cabs. Very few people knew where we were staying. When we had meetings with government representatives or our lawyers to try to work out a good arrangement, usually they were at farms and houses outside the city. The people who went there were always taken with their eyes covered.

One night I will never forget for my whole life was December 1, 1990, Pablo's birthday. We were staying in a nice home and the bodyguards with us were Otto and El Gordo, the fat one. It was nice to be calm after everything we'd been through. There were few days when we were free to be happy. At breakfast everybody was saying "Happy Birthday" to Pablo. He was happy that day, feeling confident that the government would soon be ready to make a deal. He said to me, "I'm going to have a party tonight and I'm going to bring in an orchestra. I want live music."

Naturally I believed he was kidding. It would be impossible to bring musicians to the house. Once they left the first thing would be to call the police, to collect the reward. The police were not interested in putting us in jail, they wanted us dead. I was concerned. "With all respect, Pablo," I asked, "how are you going to bring this group?"

Pablo was smiling. "Don't worry. Just trust me. It'll be okay."

Pablo and I never argued. But this made no sense to me. Sometimes Pablo thought he couldn't be captured, but this was like giving the canary to the cat. We were watching television in the afternoon when Pablo called El Gordo and told him to get the group. "Cut it out, Pablo," I told him. "It's not funny anymore." But he insisted, sending El Gordo.

The people of the house were really worried. I went upstairs to prepare my clothes to leave. I tried once again to talk Pablo out of this crazy idea. I told him, "You're my baby brother and I love you, but I don't understand this. I'm staying with you until the group shows up. I'm going to listen to a couple of songs and then I'm going to be out of here. I'm already packed. I have a suitcase with money and I have another place to go. But I'm not going to stay with you."

We spoke for about an hour. It was a very sentimental talk, and

Pablo told me, "I love you too, brother. You have been with me in all my problems, it's not fair that you leave on my birthday." And then he smiled mischievously. In my mind this was the time we were going to go apart. Pablo went downstairs and I could hear everyone laughing and having a good time. I took a shower and came downstairs with my suitcase and it was then I saw the six blind men playing their guitars.

All of them, blind. They could not know who they were playing for. I didn't know whether to laugh or be sad or be angry. But that was so Pablo. Everybody was having a blast, and no one thought that Pablo could pull something like this. It was so astute. For the meal he had ordered all kinds of seafood, lobster and octopus and four bottles of the Portuguese wine, port. He invited the musicians to join us, and he was very happy to share his birthday with this group.

At the end of this party the musicians were ready to sing "Happy Birthday" but they asked to know the name of the man celebrating his birthday. Suddenly everyone was silent. But Pablo stood up and said, "All right, I don't want you to be afraid, but you are singing to Pablo Escobar." The musicians didn't believe this, but nonetheless they sang to Pablo.

When they were finished singing, Pablo told me to give them each $20,000. I handed them the cash. Now they believed it was Pablo. I remember watching them feeling the bills, but they couldn't figure out what they were because they were so used to the size of Colombian money. "That's U.S. money," Pablo explained, and then he gave them the same warning given to anyone he paid: Be careful, don't bring the whole amount to one place. Go with somebody you trust, cash the money in small amounts, and don't mention my name. Otherwise you're going to get in real trouble.

There was no danger with these people. El Gordo and Otto returned them home. Even if they told that they had played for Pablo

Escobar, they didn't know where they were taken. Of course not, they were blind.

Amazingly, through all this time the business continued. Nothing stopped the business from growing. The biggest problem remained smuggling even more and more product into the United States. In 1989 Pablo and pilot Jimmy Ellard purchased an old DC-3, which could make the flight from Colombia all the way to Nova Scotia in Canada. The plan was that from Nova Scotia the product would be driven over the U.S. border to New York City. But on the airplane's test flight an employee did not pay some dollars to a local radar guy and the plane became visible to Colombian air force radar. As the DC-3 landed, military jets raced out of the sky and shot it into pieces with tracer bullets. For a stupid $20,000. Through the years the organization had used every type of airplane, from the Piper plane on top of the gate at Napoles to multi-engine jets, to planes specially built by Domínguez out of parts of other airplanes for the drug flights. Pablo's "air force" had more planes flying than most countries. But then Ellard began searching for a stealth airplane that could not be seen on any radar. The dream was a plane with only a little metal; they made a deal to buy a Rutan Defiant, a special plane constructed almost completely of plastic. They also were going to replace the metal propellers with plastic propellers and cover it with radar-absorbent paint. But during the first flight the top of the canopy popped open and material flew out hitting the back propeller and making such tremendous damage the plane was no longer usable.

But the profits remained so large even losses like these were easily accepted.

No matter what we did or where we went during these years, we lived constantly with the possibility of death coming around the next corner. That was true for all the leaders from Medellín. Pablo was forced to feel that in December of 1989. Pablo and the Mexican, Gacha, had remained in good contact with each other, maybe because there was nobody else with the equal of their power. The government had made the two men, Escobar and Gacha, the biggest targets of its war on the drug traffickers. Everyone agreed that they couldn't stop the river of cocaine flooding into America, but they could make people think they were having success by getting these two leaders. The United States had given the Colombian government more than $60 million and helped build up the army to catch them, mostly leaving the Cali cartel and other groups from Bogotá and the northern regions of the country alone. Our president, Virgilio Barco, was also criticized a lot by the U.S. for not doing more to stop the drug smuggling. Colombia was taking houses and bank accounts and cars, but the leaders were not being caught. So the U.S. applied more pressure on Colombia to give them big names to put in their headlines.

The Mexican and Pablo had each built their security armies for protection and fighting back against their enemies. So everyone who came near them was watched closely, everywhere they moved was searched. But the one weak spot that Pablo had, that Gacha had also, was for their families. They would do anything for their families. This was the place that the government knew they could be touched. In the end this was the lesson that Pablo never learned.

The story told by the police was that Gacha's seventeen-year-old son, Fredy, had been captured in a raid in September. The biggest charge against him was being the son of a man they wanted desperately. But the legal charge they made against him was for possessing illegal weapons. After two months they secretly released him, but from then on they followed him until he went to his father at a small ranch in Tolu, about an hour south of Cartagena. And then they sent an army against Gacha. The way the Mexican died is still a question. Was he killed by gunfire from the army or by his own hand? Did he die fighting or escaping? Also killed was his son and fifteen soldiers of his security force.

After Gacha was killed by the police, 15,000 ordinary people crowded the streets of Gacha's town of Pacho to pay tribute to him as he was buried. They surrounded the cemetery to keep out the curious, and allowed the family to have its privacy from the media. Pablo was hurt by Gacha's death. He had warned him that there was a snitch in the organization, but Gacha did not believe him. Pablo felt sure the informant was a friend and partner. There are stories that this was the real way the Mexican was found.

By this time Pablo had seen a lot of killing and so he accepted it without much emotion. Did he see in it his own fate? Pablo had always understood the penalties for his actions, and nothing he ever said or did made me believe he was afraid of his own death. I think if this battle did anything it made him positive that he had to continue inflicting such terrible damage on the government that they would agree to find a means to stop the violence. The government would have to change the constitution to prevent extradition, and Pablo would serve time in prison, pay a huge fine—and then be free. We had several lawyers and priests negotiating with the government for us. In this way the negotiations went on and on for several months.

The war was expanded on January 13, 1987. Pablo had built for himself and his family the most beautiful home in the richest and most secure area of Medellín. It was the five-story building that he had named Monaco. One floor was a dining room, one floor was the master bedroom, one floor was the penthouse. Inside were sculptures and paintings from Picasso, Botero, the Ecuadoran painter Guayasamín and other well-known artists worth many millions of dollars. The floors were of imported marble. Everything was made from the best materials.

Monaco was very secure. It was built from reinforced steel. It had the first security camera system in Colombia and there were monitors all over the building. We had told the architects and engineers to include some safe rooms for members of the family to hide in case killers got into the building. Pablo used to call Monaco his castle.

On this particular night Pablo had eaten dinner with his family. After putting his children to sleep he went secretly to a farm about ten miles away. At 5:30 in the morning a bomb was exploded, destroying Monaco. It was a huge bomb and woke up half the city. This was the first bomb of the war that was to shake Colombia. I was staying about two miles away. After the explosion awakened me I went immediately to the building in which my mother lived. The police there told me, "Nobody knows exactly what's going on. Everything here is fine, but people are saying it's a bomb." We had all seen bombs on TV, but the experience for us was new. From there I went right to Monaco. A policeman stopped me a few blocks away and told me a bomb had exploded at Pablo Escobar's building. I was stunned. A bomb? That was not the way the government worked.

When I got to the building it was destroyed. I started helping the police move broken doors and windows and debris. We found María and the two children, all of them safe, but crying and afraid. The ceiling had collapsed around the baby crib in which Manuela was sleeping, and it took rescuers some time to reach her. I called the bodyguards and they took the family to safety.

I went to see Pablo. "I'm going to tell you something," I said. "But don't worry, everything is fine."

"I already know everything," he said. How so quickly, I wondered. And then he told me, "And I already know who did it."

He explained. Gilberto Rodríguez Orejuela of the Cali cartel had called on a special phone number about a half hour after the explosion. "Pablo," he said, "I just heard somebody put a bomb in your building." This was the first news about the bombing that Pablo had received, but he didn't give that away. I know, he said. Rodríguez said, "I already sent somebody to see if you're okay and your family's okay. Are you at the building?"

On the streets people were already saying this bomb was the work of the DAS, but Pablo knew the truth. Cali had planted this bomb.

This bombing attack on his family was something that shook him. But all he said was that he was going to confirm what he believed.

It didn't make sense to me. At times we would be doing business with Cali. We had even kept money in a bank they owned. Some people had worked without problems for the organizations in both Medellín and Cali. But Pablo felt certain about this.

Later he was able to confirm this claim. Knowing the country as well as he did, Pablo felt very definitely that it was impossible for the bomb to have been built in Colombia without him knowing about it. It had to have come from elsewhere. He remembered that a good friend of his that I will call Reuben had been in jail in Spain at the same time as Gilberto Rodríguez Orejuela, one of the Cali leaders. So Pablo made contact with Reuben, who told him that a member of the Basque guerrillas, the ETA, this person I will call the Maker, was also in jail at the same time. "I remember Orejuela talking to him all the time," Reuben said. "The Maker was well known for being part of the ETA and he was a specialist in bombs and weapons."

Reuben said that "after I got out of jail I was in Cali to pray at the town of Buga. I was in Cali and I saw this guy in the dining room of the hotel and he didn't even say hello."

For Pablo, Reuben agreed to try to get in contact with him. It was discovered that the Maker was in Colombia trying to make contacts to buy cocaine to bring to Spain. Anybody who wanted to be in the cocaine business knew about Pablo Escobar. So when the Maker got invited to Napoles he was happy to come. Pablo started talking to him. Definitely the Maker was having a nice time in that wonderful place. Finally Pablo said to him, "I heard you were in jail with a friend of mine. I need you to do me a favor. I need you to train some of my crew." In return, Pablo offered to give him good prices on cocaine, telling him, "I will put more merchandise in Spain very cheap, cheaper than anybody else, but please help me out training my people with the bombs."

And then Pablo asked easily, "Do you have any experience working in Colombia? You ever work for anyone here?"

The Maker replied, "Yes, as a matter of fact I met somebody in jail a couple of years ago and he brought me to Colombia to train some guys. I told them all the materials that were needed, how to put it in cars, how to activate them." Pablo asked the name of the man he had worked for. "I trained the Indian, some guy called the Indian, ordered from a guy in Cali. They said they were going to do it against somebody in the government."

"All right, I'm going to tell you what," Pablo answered. "I'm going to help you with the drugs. You're going to train my people. Here is $200,000 in cash to pay your expenses in Colombia. I'll give you more money, but that bomb was against me." The Maker was shocked. His face went white seeing he was surrounded by so many armed men, and he thought it was his last day on earth. "Yeah, it was against me, but don't worry. I'm not going to do anything to you because you didn't know. What I need you to do is work for me."

The Maker agreed to do this, because he saw that Pablo was a serious person, and he started training the bomb makers that Pablo was to use in this war. Later he went back to Spain with a different identity and did many deals with Pablo to put merchandise in Spain.

The Orejuela brothers, Gilberto and Miguel, found out that Pablo knew it was the Cali cartel that had moved against him. Gilberto called Pablo saying something like, "Please, patrón, I didn't do anything."

"Don't lie to me," Pablo told him. "Come on, it's too obvious. You called me right away when you put down the bomb. Do you remember your friend"—he said the name—"when you were in jail? We spoke with each other in an honest way. You did it. You started the fight so now be ready to get hit!"

Cali continued the fight. A couple of months after Monaco they did another bombing, this one coming against our mother's home.

At 4 A.M. they detonated a car bomb. My mother was in bed on the third floor and from the impact a huge picture of the Baby Jesus came down from the wall behind her, protecting her face and stomach, but her feet were uncovered. Some glass came down and cut her. She was brought to the emergency room by her friend Guillermina, who was always with her.

My sister Marina lived on the fourth floor with her husband and kids. She was six months pregnant and was rushed to the hospital where she gave birth to a premature baby. The baby had to live in an incubator for many weeks, but survived. One of the people who worked for her was killed.

On the fifth floor my older sister, Gloria, was wounded with shrapnel and was taken to the hospital. It was fortunate that no one in our family was killed. They destroyed the building and everything our mother owned. All the windows from the surrounding buildings were blown out. Pablo denounced the attack to the media, but the government looked away. The government prohibited the newspapers from printing stories about anything done to Pablo or his family so the people of Colombia did not know what was really happening.

When the war with Cali was starting Gilberto Orejuela hired a gang of very ruthless people of Medellín called Los Briscos. These guys were more into killing for the drug traffickers than dealing with the drugs. The head of this group got in touch with Pablo and said to him, "We are from Medellín so we have nothing against you. But Mr. Orejuela told me he wants to pay me $5 million for your head."

Pablo said okay, "But you're going to work for me from now on." He said he had to get together an army and wanted them to be part of it. Then he said, "Here is your $5 million. I'm going to prove to you how weak Orejuela is. Tell him you need $1 million for the guns to kill me and show him pictures of me getting in my car from a long distance. That way you can tell Orejuela you have tracked me and easily can kill me." The man was nervous but Pablo told him to go ahead, don't worry. So he met with Orejuela in Cali and showed him the pictures, and the Cali cartel offered him only $5,000. "See," Pablo said, "if he promised you $5 million if you were to kill me he would pay you only $2 million or something." That was when Los Briscos started working for Medellín. Los Briscos realized that Pablo didn't care about saving money like Cali did. And that made them want to work for Pablo.

But for Pablo that was also the last evidence he needed that the Cali cartel wanted to kill him. The question that never was answered completely was why Cali started this war. There are many who believe it was simple business: Pablo was making so much money and Cali wanted more for themselves. The American DEA said Medellín controlled 80 percent of the cocaine going into America. But other people believe it was the opposite; Cali controlled New York and Chicago and Medellín had Miami and Los Angeles. Then Pablo decided to do business in New York. So he sent Champion, the Lion, and Jimmy Boy to open up New York for Medellín. Maybe that started it.

Or maybe the war was started because Jorge Ochoa was arrested going to Cali and in return Rafael Cardona from Cali was killed.

Or maybe it was because Gilberto Rodríguez Orejuela had made strong relationships with powerful government officials. The government never went after the Cali people; instead they were considered *los caballeros*, the gentlemen of the drugs, while we of Medellín were *los hampones*, the thugs, because we used weapons to protect our property. It was said that Pablo liked to fight but Gilberto liked to pay bribes. Even the head of the DEA in New York said to the newspapers, "Cali gangs will kill you if they have to, but they prefer to use a lawyer."

For whatever the reasons the war started with the bombs. We stayed running, but by 1987 we were fighting against the government and the army of the Cali cartel. And we were winning because Pablo fought back tougher than anyone could have believed.

Seven

ONE OF THE TIMES I CAME CLOSEST TO BEING KILLED—until I was bombed six years later—was on a Sunday morning in 1987. My son José Roberto and I were in a modest car that would not attract any attention. We drove out of my farm at the head of a line of five cars, each of the others having a driver and a woman lookout. But each car had complete surveillance equipment and my car was equipped with gadgets that I had copied from James Bond. For example, I could press a button and release a cloud of fog so no one could follow me, or spray oil on the road, throw nails on the road or even release six tear gas bombs.

We were traveling on the road to Medellín when two big Nissan Patrols with eight officers in each one signaled for me to get over. When I stopped, these cars pulled in front of me and behind me. At the time this happened I had no problems with the justice system so I had not believed it necessary to use my gadgets. The police could not know that one of my bodyguards in the car behind me was recording the event. They asked me for identification and I handed them an ID that identified me as Hernán García Toro with the number 8.282.751. I wondered if they already had knowledge that I was Pablo Escobar's brother. The impossible thing to know about the police was whether they were working honestly or in the kidnap business. Or worse, if they were people just pretending to be police. There was no way of knowing.

The police were confused. They told me politely that they were looking for someone else and handed me back the ID. But then another policeman suggested that they take me somewhere so I could be "identified by our friend."

I was not showing any nervous signs. I have always been a tranquil person. When I got the García Toro ID back I handed it to my son to hide in his pants. Then I signaled him to go into one of the bodyguard's cars. It was a crime to use false documents and that was enough to send me to prison. We were in the middle of the road, causing a large traffic jam. These police were distracted. Finally one of them came back to me and asked, "Sir, can you give me back the ID please?"

I said, "I don't have it. I gave it to you and you didn't give it back. May I have it back, please?"

"What do you mean?" he said. "I gave it back to you."

I shook my head seriously. "No, you didn't. You took it away. I haven't moved. Please, I'm going to see my mother and I would like my ID back."

It seemed likely that they knew who I was, but they weren't certain. Finally they put me inside one of the Patrols and ordered everyone else to leave. I nodded, and they got in their cars and drove off.

The police could not know that my bodyguards had recorded all of the police so we could identify them. A bodyguard called Lorena got into the car I had been driving. Under the seat there was a walkie-talkie tuned in to Pablo's frequency. Lorena called Pablo and informed him of what was happening. She gave him the police officers' license plate numbers. "Don't worry," Pablo told her. "Try to follow him, but stay away."

They drove me around for a few hours. When we stopped, two men with their faces covered like bank robbers came over to the car. One of them looked at me and said, "He is Roberto." I was pulled out of the car and told to walk with them. I thought, This is the end.

They led me to a trail. It was about eleven o'clock at night. I remember looking into the sky and thinking, There is no moon tonight. I was resigned to my fate. It was freezing and they weren't talking. Finally I asked, "What are you going to do with me?"

"We're going to kill you," one of them said.

"That would be the end for you too," I said. I lied, "My brother already has your pictures and recordings. When we stopped, remember that red BMW? It took your pictures. By now my brother has all of your information."

They couldn't know if I was telling them the truth. They began speaking with others on their own walkie-talkies, trying to figure out what to do. They decided, "We aren't going to kill you. We just want $3 million."

We negotiated. In the forest, on a cold moonless night, we negotiated the value of my life. I told them I could only give them $1 million, but later we settled for $2 million. "I need to make my call to my accountant," I said. We returned to the police car and they drove me to a pay phone. I dialed a number that reached only Pablo wherever he was. "This is Roberto," I said to him.

"Can you talk?" Pablo asked.

"Yes."

"Are you kidnapped?" I told him the situation. He said he already had a lot of information from Lorena and they were learning more from the video. Phone calls were being made to the police working for us and within a short time we would know the identity of the kidnappers. He told me not to try anything, the money was nothing for my life. Then he told me to put the kidnappers on the phone.

The kidnappers thought they were going to speak to my accountant. I watched as the color drained completely from the face of the one on the phone. I knew that Pablo had told him, "This is Pablo Escobar. I have all your information. You are responsible for my brother."

We drove on country roads while we waited for the ransom to be delivered. As the night passed some of the police left us supposedly to go to places where the money might be delivered. I wondered if some of them had decided that kidnapping Pablo Escobar's brother wasn't such a great idea. I finally spoke with Pablo and he told me Carlos Aguilar, El Mugre, would organize the delivery. Two more policemen waited at that place.

We drove off another time. I was in the back seat with three policemen. I had established trust with these police, because we had stopped to eat and they had allowed me to use the bathroom. I kept looking for a way to escape, but I couldn't find one. I was still fearful that once the police had the money in their pockets they would kill me.

At four in the morning we were parked, waiting for the money to arrive. I knew exactly where we were, as it was a place I had suggested for the money delivery. It was a road I had traveled often from my farm to the city. After a half hour the cop sitting right next to me behind the driver had fallen asleep. I waited until the driver looked to be yawning, then jumped on the sleeping cop and grabbed his machine gun. I pointed the gun at the cops and told them to get out of the car. Now I was in control. I made them all crawl under the car, then I shot two bursts into the air and took off running toward a nearby river I knew very well. I threw the cartridge into the river and tossed the gun away, then crossed the river and escaped into the safety of the jungle.

I had saved my own life. By noon I had arrived at the farm of a friend and called Pablo. "Where do we need to send the money?" he asked. I told him the story. He scolded me for risking my life for a few million, but he was grateful that I was alive.

I never learned the fate of those policemen.

Most of the time, though, I personally wasn't involved in the violence. Although to be safe for a few years after that I traveled with as many as thirty bodyguards.

My brother had become a general leading his private army against the government of Colombia and the Cali cartel. He did what needed to be done for victory and sometimes it was very brutal. Too many innocent people were killed in this war. Drivers, bodyguards, cooks and maids, people walking on the street, lawyers, women shopping—thousands died in the bombings. But it's important to remember this: Pablo didn't start the bombing. Cali and the police continued placing bombs against us. Pablo, for example, owned the most beautiful farm I have ever seen; it was called Manuela and it was located in the Peñol. It had every luxury imaginable, soccer fields, tennis courts, horse stables and cow barns, even a wave pool with water slides. The police arrived there and looted everything, from beds to family pictures, putting it all in trucks. The caretakers were tied down and then they blew everything up. Pablo denounced the police to the government, but nothing was done.

Our mother had bought a small farm known as Cristalina with her own pension money from being a teacher, and they came there and tied up the caretaker with his wife and small children and blew up the house in a thousand pieces in front of them. Pablo had a mansion in El Poblado near a country club. Our enemies killed the two caretakers and they blew it up, including huge sums of cash hidden there. As always Pablo protested to the government but he was ignored. In addition to some cars kept at Napoles, Pablo had a famous collection of classic cars and motorcycles that he kept in a warehouse in Medellín; he had about sixty cars there, Fords and Chevrolets from the 1920s and the car that supposedly had belonged to Al Capone. Our enemies killed the guard and set fire to the building, destroying this irreplaceable collection.

Pablo began his war to defend himself from our enemies by transforming his sicarios plus dozens of other men into a trained force. The pilot Jimmy Ellard testified in court that he told Pablo that the security was not good: "And the best thing you can do is employ American Green Berets." He had contacts in America to accomplish that, he said. Pablo said thank you very much, but informed him that he had hired his own military people to do the training. Later it was learned that these were Israeli and British mercenary soldiers hired to train people in the methods of warfare that would be necessary.

The first targets were a chain of drugstores called La Rebaja that were owned by the Cali cartel. There were thousands of these drugstores around the country and in the months after we were attacked eighty-five drugstores were bombed. Because of Cali's bombing attack the war had spread onto the streets. People could not travel safely from Medellín to Cali as every visitor became suspect. Sometimes people found in the wrong place would just disappear.

The police and army focused their war on drug traffickers only against the Medellín organization. Secret police squads terrorized the city. They were responsible for many deaths, including innocents. These were the people who would drive through the barrios machine-gunning the young men standing there. Some of the survivors would be taken into custody to the Police School Carlos Holgüín, where they would be tortured to find out if they knew where Pablo Escobar was hiding. Most of these young men didn't even know Pablo, and a few days later their bodies would be found thrown in the streets. Their crime was being poor. Outside Colombia I'm certain people wondered why there was such support for the drug lords who were killing the police. This was a reason why.

Just being in the streets was often the reason people died. The brother of the girl with the pretty legs borrowed the car of a friend of his, for example. He didn't know that person was wanted by the police, so when they saw this car they shot it up and killed this innocent person. It was at this time that the bombings of the CAIs and the shootings really got going.

I also believe that the state also took advantage of the public fight between Medellín and Cali by blaming Pablo for crimes he didn't commit. There were many bombs during that period that the police said Pablo had placed that he had absolutely nothing to do with. We know Medellín was blamed for deaths that we had nothing to do with. So Pablo used to say, "If the government is putting the blame on me and I know we didn't do anything, it could work both ways." Meaning they could be blaming Cali for crimes they did not commit.

It was in the interest of the government to encourage conflict between the two organizations. The more we attacked each other the better for them. In 1989 at the airport in Bogotá, for example, presidential candidate Ernesto Samper was attacked and was shot seven times—although he survived and years later became president. Samper supposedly was friendly with the leaders from Cali. Because of that he was the kind of politician who might have been attacked by Pablo—but the real fact is that Pablo was not involved in this assassination attempt. Regardless of who did the shooting, the government blamed Pablo for it.

The first big attack on the government to cause major change in their policy took place in August 1989, during the political campaign for president. Six men were running for that office, but the most popular was Luis Carlos Galán, one of the founders of the New Liberals. It was believed he would win. This was the same man who had denounced Pablo as a drug trafficker years before when he served in Congress.

At a campaign rally in the town of Soacha, about twenty miles from Bogotá, Galán was starting his speech to about ten thousand people when several shooters hiding machine guns behind posters began firing at him. He was hit in the chest and died right there.

Many other people were hurt. In Colombia this killing was compared to the terrible assassinations of the Kennedys.

Many people had reasons for wanting Galán dead. He campaigned hard against all the drug traffickers and promised that if he became president he would follow serious extradition policies. In Congress he had blocked a bill that would have banned extradition. So everyone in the drug business could not afford for him to win the election. The DAS said the mastermind of the assassination had been Gacha, who was killed four months later. Pablo was not named.

Galán also promised to fight the left-wing paramilitaries if he became president, so those organizations had reason to want him dead. The wealthy families who controlled the life of the country by supporting friendly politicians were not happy that Galán had promised to open the government to the working people. He also had promised to reform the politics of the country so the politicians and police could not take money from the drug traffickers and emerald companies to look away while they did their business. So all of those people would have suffered if Galán had been elected president.

It took eighteen years after this assassination until Alberto Santofimio Botero, who was also running for president, was convicted of ordering the killing of Galán. The jury in Bogotá found him guilty after listening to the testimony of one of Pablo's main sicarios, who said that Santofimio thought that by eliminating Galán he would become president. The election of Santofimio would have been good for the drug traffickers because there would have been no extradition. The reason for the assassination was that Santofimio "was removing a political enemy from his path."

This was not the kind of question I would have asked my brother, and if there was not a reason for me knowing the answer he would not have offered it. But I know that it served the purpose of many other people and agencies for Pablo to be blamed for crime. To the world he was already becoming a vicious killer, so putting one more killing on him would make no difference.

But Pablo knew that the killing of Galán would cause a stern reaction, so on the night of the killing he called me and told me the police would be searching for us so my family should meet him at a hotel in Cartegena. By the time we got there Pablo and Gustavo were waiting. He wanted to send our families out of the country.

As he knew would happen, the government of President Virgilio Barco immediately declared a state of siege and smothered the country with police and military, raiding houses and buildings and making thousands of arrests. The government took almost one thousand buildings and ranches, seven hundred cars and trucks, more than 350 airplanes and seventy-three boats—and almost five tons of cocaine. Four farms owned by Gacha, the Mexican, were claimed by the government, in addition to some of Pablo's buildings and businesses in Medellín. This reaction was a big chance for the police and the army to settle old feuds because no one would dare object when they arrested a person and said he was a suspect in Galán's assassination. Many people were taken into custody, but none of them were the leaders of the drug operations.

President Barco also put back into effect the extradition treaty with the United States, which the Supreme Court had suspended a few months before. The cartel answered that it would kill ten judges for every person extradited. Right away more than one hundred judges resigned their office. Medellín began fighting even harder than ever before. In the first few days seventeen bombs were exploded against banks, stores, and political party offices. Some of these terrorist attacks were placed there by our enemies to create more confusion, but it was all blamed on Pablo.

The United States offered to send soldiers to Colombia if they were invited to help in the fight against the drug traffickers. The U.S. president, George H. W. Bush, said he would send $150 million in equipment to Colombia, as well as soldiers to help our government solve their drug problems. So now America was in the fight against

Pablo too. Pablo had never attacked the U.S.—he only defended himself from the Colombian government.

After ten days of this government crackdown, the leaders of Medellín offered a truce. Gacha called a newspaperman and said he would surrender all his farms and airplanes in return for amnesty. The father of the Ochoas, Fabio Ochoa Restrepo, wrote to President Barco, "No more drug trafficking, no more war, no more assassinations, no more bombs, no more arson . . . Let there be peace, let there be amnesty."

The mayor of Medellín also wanted the government to negotiate, saying, "This is the position of many people who believe that you have to talk to obtain peace."

President Barco answered by saying, "We cannot rest until we destroy the organizations dedicated to narcotics trafficking."

Pablo remembered the same appeals had been made after the death of Lara. He wrote to the newspaper *La Prensa*, "How much blood could have been avoided after the Panama talks. We want peace. We have demanded it shouting, but we cannot beg for it.

"No more the path of legal action," he finished. "Now it is with blood."

In September a homemade rocket was fired at the embassy of the United States from ten blocks away. It hit the building but didn't explode, and did little damage except that it made American diplomats in Colombia send their families home. President Bush answered by changing a presidential order that had prohibited the assassination of citizens of other countries who were terrorists—and drug traffickers were considered terrorists. This rocket was not fired by Pablo. It was all a setup to involve Pablo and have the U.S. retaliate against him.

In your mind part of you is always the person you used to be. For me, that was the bicycle champion. If I had paused to think about the journey I'd taken it would have been impossible; from representing the country I loved in the sport I loved to running through the jungle as police helicopters fired tracer bullets down on me. So I didn't think about it. I know that it seems difficult to understand, but it is true. Maybe that was my means of dealing with my reality.

Also I did not have conversations with Pablo about what was going on. I didn't try to talk to him about the violence that the police were committing against our family, friends, and employees. I know that wouldn't have done any good. The decisions Pablo had made in the past had allowed him to become one of the richest men in the world, so there was no reason for him to begin doubting his decisions. I know he felt the government had given him no choice but to fight. He believed that many in the government had made the choice to associate with Cali to try to destroy Medellín so they could take over the business. The proof of that came later, in 1996, when the 8000 Process scandal made it public that Cali was paying bribes to many politicians, even men running for the presidency. And what Cali wanted the government to do was use the legal system to rid the business of their competition. Even our prosecutor general once admitted, "The corruption of the Cali cartel is worse than the terrorism of the Medellín cartel."

So Pablo felt he was fighting everybody—but this was just the beginning. Soon there would be more enemies.

At 7:15 in the morning of November 27, 1989, Avianca Airlines flight HK 1803 from Bogotá to Cali exploded over the mountains outside the capital city, instantly killing 107 people. It was a terrible blow to the country. Even I was a little surprised when Pablo was accused of this crime. Why? The investigation discovered that a small bomb had been put aboard the airplane under a seat in the middle. When it went off it caused the fuel to detonate and destroy the airplane.

Like so many crimes committed in this period there were many possible motives. The first was that the man who had replaced Galán in the election for the presidency, his campaign manager, Cesár

Gavíria, was scheduled to be on that plane. That was true, but Gavíria saved his life by changing his flight and taking a private flight instead. So he was supposed to be the first target. But it also was said that the plane was destroyed because there were one or two informants from the Cali cartel who were going to testify against Medellín aboard. Also in September and October more than thirty thousand kilos of Medellín cocaine had been seized in the U.S. and the word was that Cali had given them the information where to find it, so some people believed the plane was destroyed because Marta Lucía Echavarria, the girlfriend of Cali leader Miguel Rodríguez Orejuela, was on board in seat 10B and this was to punish him.

I will say this: If I had any knowledge of this plan before it was carried out I would have done everything in my power to stop it.

Many people have told their stories about this disaster and the DAS and American FBI and the police have made their investigations and published their reports. The United States used the excuse that two Americans were killed in the crash to become involved, and two years after it happened Pablo and La Kika were indicted by the United States for this crime. La Kika became the very first person ever to be tried, convicted, and sentenced under the 1986 law against killing Americans anywhere in the world.

All those reports put together say that this is the way the bombing happened: No one will ever know for sure the reasons that this was done, but supposedly it was talked about at a meeting of Pablo, Gacha, Kiko Moncada, Fernando Galeano, and Albeiro Areiza. They had a copy of Gavíria's schedule so they knew he was going to be on that flight. The bomb was carried to the airport in parts in three different cars. The plan was to put five kilos of dynamite on the plane and have it detonated by a "suizo," meaning a person who is tricked into doing a job in which they will die. The ticket for the suizo was bought for the fictitious name Mario Santodomingo, who sat in seat 15F and put the package under seat 14F. It seems the suizo was told his job was to record the conversations of Cali people sitting in front of him.

As the plane rose into the air as instructed the suizo turned the knob on the "recorder." The bomb exploded a hole in the floor and side of the plane, and then blew up the fumes in the empty fuel hold. Everyone on the plane died and three people on the ground also were killed.

Right after the airplane was blown up a man claiming to be of Los Extraditables called a Bogotá radio station and reported that they had planted the bomb. Four years later the man who claimed that he made the bomb told the DAS that Medellín leader Kiko Moncada gave him a million pesos to recover the cost of the operation. So certainly others were involved, but the only name the world heard was Pablo Escobar.

The U.S. sent to Colombia its most secret intelligence unit, Centra Spike. Centra Spike flew small airplanes above the cities and applied the most advanced technology to listen to communications of interest. Their method was to spy on the ten people who Pablo spoke with most often and then the ten people that each of those ten people usually contacted. That's the way they built a map of the Medellín organization. They flew in total secrecy. When our contacts told us about this I had warned Pablo that the U.S. was eavesdropping. As an electrical engineer who specialized in communication I knew what was possible. But Pablo wasn't too concerned about that. He thought that if he had been listened to they couldn't have located him anyway; he used to say that he could have been anywhere in the world.

To use the information provided by Centra Spike, in 1990 Colombia organized an elite military unit named the Search Bloc. This consisted of seven hundred of the most trusted policemen, trained by the United States Army Delta Force, who had only one objective: catching Pablo and the other leaders of Medellín. To fight back, a bombing campaign was begun against the Search Bloc. The whole situation was completely out of control. The government thought about stopping the Search Bloc, but instead they added more soldiers.

There were more than a hundred bombings. This was all-out war. Judges were bombed. Newspapers who wrote in favor of extradition were bombed. Every policeman had become a target. The police of Medellín had stopped living in their own homes to protect their families and stayed together in secure places. Everyone in the city, probably in the country, were touched somehow by the bombing campaign. For example our cousin, "the girl with the pretty hair," was a student at college. She was registered there under a new name and only her best friend knew of her family. During the war against the police a bomb was placed in a police car near a stadium and when it exploded hundreds of people were killed and wounded. It was horrible. Even now I can't really understand or accept how it came to this. But there was nothing anyone could do to stop it. In that bombing the grandparents of another student were killed. When it was reported a few days later that Pablo's men had planted the bomb this student approached our cousin in the cafeteria filled with people. "Your cousin killed my grandparents," she screamed and started hitting her. She grabbed her by the hair and pulled her down.

The girl with the pretty hair started crying too, not for herself, but for the grandparents, for everything that was happening in our country. She grabbed the girl by the arm and put her into a corner. "Stop screaming," she said. "I want you to understand this has nothing to with me. I have the same last name, but I had nothing to do with this incident. I'm not like that. I can't go to Pablo and tell him 'Stop doing this.' I can't."

But later she did go to Pablo and ask him why he did such terrible things. And he told her, "You don't even know how many people that I care about are gone because of this war. This is what I have to do."

She said to him that he had two personalities. Sometimes he

could be so nice and kind, but on the other hand, "You can be so ruthless."

"They made me like this," he said. "I have to be strong. I have to fight back because people turned their backs on me. I know I'm not going to die like a regular drug dealer."

If there was one personal enemy Pablo had it was General Miguel Maza Márquez, the head of the DAS, a man who had made a vow to defeat the cartels. In an American trial a drug pilot testified that Maza had been involved in the cocaine business, that he had been told by a major connection that Maza was shipping between twenty and twenty-five kilos a flight. I have no personal knowledge of this; it could be another situation of someone trying to make a good deal for himself at the sake of an innocent man. But is it possible? In Colombia in those days anything was possible. Until the government focused on Medellín the money was so easy to make and the big people were not touched at all. The only people taking the risks were those on the lower levels who were actually doing the moving. It was well known that many famous people in politics in Colombia had been involved in small ways in the business. If Pablo or his high associates agreed to include your drugs in their shipments you were almost guaranteed to make a profit.

There was also the possibility that some agents were on the payroll of the drug organizations. A lot of poor people feared the DAS in that period just like the police for all the atrocities done in the city much more than they respected it. To them DAS wasn't the Colombian FBI, it was the police who came in the night.

Maza has said that Pablo offered him money through a lawyer to work with the cartel and that he turned him down. That I had not heard. But it makes good sense. So many politicians and policemen were happy to take money from the traffickers that there would be no reason not to make such an offer.

Pablo despised Maza, due to the crimes committed by him and

his agency. Numerous times Pablo had denounced these illegal acts to the Colombian government but everything was overlooked. Maza has claimed that Pablo made seven attempts to kill him. Maybe. There were many bombings at this time. In one car bombing Maza lived but seven of his bodyguards were killed. Maza proved to be a very lucky man. In December of 1989 the plan was to blow up the entire DAS building to kill him. This would be just like bombing the FBI Building in Washington, D.C.

At least a thousand and perhaps as much as eight thousand pounds of explosives were loaded onto a bus. One man was waiting in the lobby of the building. After Maza and his bodyguards arrived this inside man was supposed to contact the outside men with the bus and give them the okay. Then they were to direct the bus into the lobby of the building and explode it. But the plan went wrong in many respects. The man inside was waiting and waiting but he didn't see Maza arrive because he came into the building a different way than usual. Finally the inside guy decided to step outside—and when the bombers saw him walk out of the building they detonated the bomb—almost killing him too.

It was probably the biggest bomb of the whole war. The bus crashed into a car outside the building, and the whole front of the building came off as if it had been pulled away. The bomb was so strong that the engine of the bus landed on the roof of a knocked-down building blocks away. There was serious damage to buildings as far as twenty blocks away. At least fifty people in the DAS head-quarters and nearby were killed and as many as a thousand were wounded. It was written in newspapers that the walls of the building were covered in blood and, unfortunately, parts of bodies were found many blocks from the explosion. If the bus had managed to reach the building there would have been even bigger destruction.

But Maza survived. His office had been protected with steel and that saved his life. He said that he was almost the only person on his floor to survive the attack.

I always loved my brother, but my soul was not blind. I could see that there were parts of him that I couldn't recognize. Now more than ever we lived day to day. Each movement had to be planned in secret. There was no going back to Napoles or the places we knew. Even seeing our families was difficult as we guessed they were being watched. Gustavo, for example, would show up in disguise—like all of us he would wear a mustache, glasses, a hat, and even a wig—at the home of a friend without any announcement. He would wait in their small living room and during the next few hours his wife and some of his children would arrive. The family would show up at different times in different cars. They would share cups of hot chocolate, knowing the time was precious. When they left, Gustavo would hug them and even sometimes cry. When we saw the people we loved no one knew if it was going to be the last time ever.

No one can ever know with confidence how many people died on all sides in the drug war. There were so many deaths that the figure is lost. Certainly many judges and policemen and politicians died, and three of the five candidates for the presidency in 1990 were killed, as well as members of the drug organizations and our families and friends. When I turned myself in for a second time and was sent to the maximum security prison in Itagüi, we built a board as a shrine to honor the perished friends and family. There were so many good names on that board. So many innocent people died for no reason. All of it could have been avoided. That's the real tragedy; it all could have been avoided.

While the bombings continued Los Extraditables began kidnapping the elite of Colombia. The very wealthy and their families in most ways had been protected from the street violence, and because they controlled the power it seemed obvious that nothing would change until they were affected. The news said that the kidnappings were just a way to raise money by ransom, but money was never short. More than the money it was the pressure that these people could apply on the government to end the extradition treaty that was the real goal, and of course to let everybody know what kinds of corrupted officials were running the show with their gruesome murders. Rich people were taken off the streets, and most of the time their chauffeurs were killed to send the message.

The kidnappings of the wealthy had more effect than all the violence. The government used three former presidents to negotiate with the Extraditables. I think it's true that Pablo wanted the fighting to end. He knew that this was not a way to live—or to die. But the one thing that Pablo always insisted on absolutely was an end to extradition. Everything else could be negotiated. The business would end, he would give up some of his fortune, he would surrender and agree to serve time in prison, there could be some compromise on all points—but there could be no compromise about extradition. There were times we spoke about this and I saw his frustration.

The country was in chaos and confusion. Before in Colombia, the shadow world had been allowed to exist along with the public world and there was calm and stability in the country. The government had accepted and even worked with the emerald trade, the marijuana smugglers, and all the illegal businesses. It was safe for everyone to walk in the streets. Everyone was making money. The people outside the business almost never got hurt. But that was not true anymore. By attacking the Medellín cartel and especially Pablo, who had become a political figure when he announced his presidential aspirations, the government had forced them to fight back. This was the terrible result.

A few of the leaders that lived in the poor neighborhoods of Medellín were murdered for supporting Pablo's political career. I believe the real reason this war against my brother began was because of his politics, instead of the drug business. When Pablo used to get up on stage to give his speech to thousands of followers throughout the country his ideals were compared to that of presidential candidate

Jorge Eliécer Gaitán, who had been assassinated in 1948. Gaitan had been Pablo's idol. Pablo's ideals in his speeches were to work to eradicate poverty in our country, provide a chance for an education, health care, and decent employment for everybody in the country. He was proud that he had always shared his winnings with the country's poorest people.

The government attacks did have many successes. A lot of our people were killed by the national police, Cali, or by the elite troops of the Search Bloc. Hernando, who was the manager of Napoles, was with his family on a farm for a weekend. Our enemies showed up at the place and Hernando told his son to run and hide. These people took a tool and broke every bone in Hernando's hands and fingers and burned him all over his body with cigars until he was dead. Many of our employees were killed, including Ricardo Prisco and his brother Armando, who was shot by the national police as he sat in his wheelchair. Two of María Victoria's brothers, Pablo's brothers-in-law, were killed. Our cousin Luis Alfanso was killed and his parents, Lucy and Arnand, were beaten black and blue and burned and killed. Another cousin Rodrigo Gavíria, had his skull blown off by a machine gun, and another cousin, John Jairo Urquijo Gavíria, was shot as he tried to flee, as was their eighty-seven-year-old father, Luis Enrique Urquijo, an innocent man who had gone to church every day. My cousin José Gavíria was tied up in front of his wife and children and stabbed in the neck and allowed to die there. Our cousin Lucila Restrepo Gavíria was gunned down with her husband in front of her children. Now they all rest in the family cemetery with Pablo.

On August 7, 1990, Cesár Gavíria, Galan's campaign manager, became the president of our country. Gavíria immediately announced his new policy: The government would continue to fight against drug terrorism, the bombings and kidnappings and assassinations, but Colombia could not stop drug business without the cooperation of the rest of the world. He said, "Drug trafficking is an international phenomenon that can only be resolved through the joint action of all affected countries. . . . And no success will be possible in this area if there is not a substantial reduction of demand in consumer countries." There were many people who did not understand the important difference. This was interpreted to mean that there could be some agreement if the violence was stopped. But the new president's message was clear; he wanted to change the situation.

But any thought that real change might come quickly ended four days later when the Search Bloc found Gustavo in a guarded house in Medellín and killed him in a gunfight: Gustavo, who had been with Pable since the first day. The shame of that for Pablo was that Gustavo almost lived to see the war against the government won.

Three weeks after Gustavo died the daughter of a former president, Diana Turbay, was kidnapped. It's not possible to really know how that affected the government, maybe it didn't at all, but Pablo had proved to them again that their own families could not be protected. A week later the new president agreed that those drug traffickers who surrendered would receive reduced sentences. They would have to serve some time in prison for drug trafficking, but they would eventually walk out free to live the rest of their lives.

During the next few months the three Ochoa brothers surrendered and eventually got reasonable prison sentences, but Pablo refused until the government agreed to change the constitution and put in new justice laws. He never for one second forgot the sentence the Americans put on Carlos Lehder, life plus 135 years in a maximum security penitentiary. Better a grave in Colombia than a jail cell in the United States.

Today the situation in Colombia is the opposite. Drug dealers work differently. The sentences in Colombia are more rigid than in the U.S. because there by giving up the names of other people and some money it is possible to have a long sentence reduced. Many present-day drug dealers earn fortunes and after serving some time recover it. These sorts of benefits are reserved for the wealthy drug lords, not for the petty drug dealers.

The negotiations with the government went on for almost a year. Most of the meetings took place in the middle of the night at farms owned by Pablo outside Medellín. In 1990 the M-19 guerrillas that Pablo had long ago fought for the kidnapping of Martha Nieves, Pablo's friend's sister, had made a deal with the government that allowed them to end the violence, surrender their weapons, and become a political party, and in return they would receive pardons for their crimes. Pablo believed he should be granted the same offer. Why not? M-19 had been guilty of violence; it was their guns behind the raid on the Justice Ministry. And yet the government had allowed them an entrance back into society. So why not Pablo and his associates? Even before the negotiations began Pablo had decided exactly what he wanted and what he would give in return.

The attorneys and government representatives who came to these meetings were picked up at night by vans without windows and had to wear black glasses so they couldn't see anything. They were driven around for a time so they wouldn't know how far from the city they had traveled. Even our own representatives did not know where we were hiding or how to get directly in touch with Pablo.

Meanwhile, unknown to us, American airplanes were still flying over Medellín, listening to telephone conversations, trying desperately to find Pablo. Cali was also trying hard to find Pablo. There was no question they knew we were talking to the government and they wanted to find Pablo before an agreement could be made. At this time there were no criminal charges against me. There was no reason for them to arrest me. But people on the payroll had told us that Cali had put out an order to kill me. So, unbelievable as it seems, the safest place for me was in prison with Pablo.

The church played an important role in these negotiations. Even with his sins, Pablo remained a religious man. Like our mother, who was saved from death when a picture of the Baby Jesus of Atocha fell on her and protected her, he almost always slept beneath a drawing or painting of Jesus. During his telephone conversations with our mother they often prayed together. Father Rafael García Herreros appeared on television every night just before seven o'clock on the show *Minute of God*. The audience heard him say, "I would like to speak to Pablo Escobar, on the edge of the sea, right here, on this beach," but what they did not know was that Father García provided information for us about the progress of the negotiations, like when the government wanted to meet with our representatives, with his secret signals. For example, on his TV show he would say that they got a donation of 1,370,000 pesos, but what he was telling Pablo was that they were going to have a meeting on the 13th at seven o'clock.

When Pablo and I spoke on the telephone we also used a code. In the most dangerous time Pablo would call himself Theresita, the name of the nanny we had as little children, to avoid danger in case the phones were tapped. Theresita was a woman who did not wear shoes. She used to change our diapers, feed us with the baby bottle, and was with us until she died of cancer. When Theresita died I was saddened and thought why the scientists hadn't discovered a cure for this disease. This began the great search of my later life. I started to buy every book I could find about cancer. In 1987, when one of my favorite horses got sick with equine anemia, I started to research this disease, which is similar in many ways to the human AIDS virus. When all of our troubles began I had to put aside my desire to contribute to finding a cure for this terrible disease.

One of the most important people involved in these negotiations was Archbishop Dario Castrillón of Pereira, who had a special relationship with the president, having been the official at his marriage. Pablo also had a strong friendship with this priest; he had worked with the churches of Colombia for many years, giving money to provide food, clothing, and shelter for the parishes of Medellín and Antioquia. The archbishop was important throughout all the negotiations until the end, and at this moment he is serving in the Vatican. It was normal for Pablo to use a helicopter to visit small villages in Chocó or Urabá. Even during the worst times Pablo continued to help the underprivileged citizens in these government-forsaken towns. Pablo and I met with the archbishop in a house at the highest point in El Poblado to ask him to go directly to the new president with his offer. Pablo told him, "I've decided to surrender myself but I have to get some guarantees before that. I would like you personally to take this message to the president so there will be no mistake."

Pablo then listed the conditions that needed to apply if the war was to end. First, no extradition. Then he would agree to receive a sentence of thirty years, which would be reduced one third for his surrender and admitting to crimes. This sentence was similar to the punishment given to others who had taken a similar path. He thought the thirty-year sentence would actually require serving about seven years in prison with the benefits granted by the government.

As I sat there listening to him, for the first time I began to believe that maybe there was a way to end this horror and eventually return to our regular lives.

The search for Pablo went on during the negotiations. There were more killings, more kidnappings. During one of the police raids on a house, hostage Diana Turbay was killed, probably by police bullets, which Pablo had denounced during a communication to the government. A few days later President Gavíria made the policy that Pablo would be eligible for a smaller sentence if he confessed to his crimes. Pablo understood that to mean that the president was open to making a reasonable deal. There was a lot of negotiating, a lot of compromises, but eventually a deal for surrender was reached. The time was good for this. America had been paying Colombia millions of dollars and providing military assistance to go after the drug traffickers, but mainly to catch Pablo. U.S. president George Bush had been strong with Colombia about this issue. Including Carlos Lehder, our government had extradited forty-one men to the United States. But fortunately for all of us, right at this time Colombia was seated on the United Nations Security Council. The U.S president was attempting to gather support from the world to attack Iraq's Saddam Hussein to expel him from Kuwait. Colombia had voted against a U.S. military attack, and Bush wanted Gavíria to change that vote. Gavíria announced that no more Colombians would be sent to the United States for trial. Perhaps in return for our vote in the Security Council, the U.S. didn't make much of a protest. It has been said by our politicians that the Gulf War brought peace to our country.

Pablo and the government had made a deal. I remember the day we found out for certain that the government had agreed to the compromise. As always Pablo showed little emotion. He was happy, he was satisfied, but he was never a man to celebrate loudly. But I could see he was pleased. It seemed like there was finally a way out of this life. In return Gavíria got what he wanted most—the killings would stop. The kidnappings would stop. The bombings would stop.

The drug smuggling business? Ending that would be much more difficult.

With the agreement to end extradition the rest of the terms of surrender were finalized over several months. The terms that Pablo arranged allowed him and other members of the organization to plead guilty to at least one crime, and the other crimes would not be prosecuted. Pablo would be permitted to keep most of his property. The people who hated him most would be kept away from him, and in particular Maza would step down from his post as chief of the DAS. The government wanted to put Pablo into its highest security prison in Medellín, but of course that was not possible. He would pay for his own prison. As part of the agreement he insisted on approval of the guards. After searching for several weeks Pablo informed the government that a suitable prison could be made from a vacant building sitting on top of a mountain just outside Medellín. The building looked like a small school surrounded by tall electrical wire fences, but it had originally been built as a rehabilitation center. It was known as La Catedral, the Cathedral.

Pablo owned the building and all the land, although his name did not appear on the ownership papers. To hide that fact from the people it was registered in the name of a friend of the family, an old ironmonger, who exchanged it to the government of the city of Envigado in a completely legal arrangement and in return was given a smaller but desirable tract of land. It was not traceable to Pablo. The area measured about thirty thousand square meters.

Pablo had been very careful in selecting this place. The government had suggested two others, including Itagüi where the Ochoas were doing their sentence, but the Cathedral offered many advantages. The location was on the top of a hill overlooking Medellín, seven thousand feet above sea level, which gave us a view of anyone approaching from below. It would take considerable time for anyone to get up the mountain. It also gave Pablo a complete view of his beloved Medellín. As I said to him while we stood on the top of the mountain, "With a telescope, from here we could see the whole city." In addition, for security, Pablo purchased a small bodega at the base of the road going up the hill and gave it to an employee, Tato, on his wedding day. But inside was a phone wired directly to the prison, so people stationed there instantly could give us warning if anyone passed. I built an electronic system that was laid across the roads and gave us a warning signal. The buildings also were bordered by a forest, which provided good coverage from the air and also would allow us to hide among the trees if we had to escape. From the first, we knew that we might have to escape quickly, so Pablo planned for it. In the agreement Pablo signed with Gavíria the government was prohibited from cutting down any trees. Pablo also was concerned that Cali or another enemy might attempt to bomb us and a big advantage of the Cathedral was that early in the morning and late in the afternoon it was hidden in fog. The prison was surrounded by a ten-thousand-volt electric fence. As much as it was to keep the prisoners inside, the purpose of the security was to keep people out of the prison.

After the terms were negotiated the only problem remaining was the extradition treaty. So in June 1991, the constitution was changed to forbid extradition. From then on Colombians would always be tried for crimes committed in Colombia in Colombian courts. Or until the law was changed again long after Pablo's death.

In addition to the government, Pablo also made arrangements with the other drug traffickers. He believed he was serving his sentence for all the traffickers who would be helped by the new laws. It was agreed that during his time in prison he was to be compensated by them from the business. This was just as had always been done when one person gave up his freedom for others. "I am the price of peace," he told them. "I am making this sacrifice for you, so you should compensate me."

To get safely *into* the jail all of us had to plead guilty to a minimum of one crime, which would serve as an example for all of the crimes committed. Pablo confessed that he had participated in one deal that had smuggled twenty kilos of cocaine into the United States. Twelve of our men went into prison with my brother and me. Pablo helped them invent the crimes for which they pleaded guilty. Three of them agreed that they had collaborated to transport four hundred kilos of drugs. Pablo told each of them, "You confess that you borrowed a blue Chevrolet. You say you put the package together. And you say you drove the car. Remember, a blue Chevrolet."

During their confessions the three men described the color of the car differently. It didn't matter; these crimes were just for the record. By informing on each other as drug dealers each man was entitled to a reduction in his sentence for turning in a drug dealer.

I was the last person to surrender. At first, I didn't see a good reason for me to be with them in the prison. The police had listed no crimes against me, and I could be more helpful outside. I could watch our family and pursue whatever legal work had to be done. But Pablo called me and said that for me the safest place was with him inside the Cathedral. "They are looking to kill you," he said. I assume he meant Cali. But it could have been any of our enemies. "You'll be safe in here so give yourself up quickly."

When I presented myself to the government I was asked to which crime was I confessing. "I will confess to my crime," I told them. "It's Rh."

The people in the room were puzzled. The female district attorney said, thinking I was referring to some code used to identify a crime, "That's not a code. What are you trying to tell me?"

I smiled. "No, doctor," I said. "It's not a code. My crime of Rh is that I have the same blood as my brother Pablo."

Eight

OUR SURRENDER IN 1991 WAS THE BEGINNING of the final end of
the story of Pablo Escobar. We had spent the three months before
the surrender at a farm called Skinny Dog. Pablo had given it that
name on the day it was bought, when he saw the owner's skin-and-
bones dog. He insisted that this ordinary dog be part of the deal,
and the farm was named for him. It was high enough on a mountain
in Envigado to provide a long-distance view. We had a quiet time
there—long enough for the skinny dog to grow fat.

On the morning of Pablo's surrender he woke up much earlier
than usual, at 7 A.M. We ate breakfast with our mother, then Pablo
began making plans to meet the helicopter that would take him to
the Cathedral. The surrender would begin as soon as the Assembly
voted to outlaw extradition. That vote was taken right after noon.
The war was won. We all got ready for the move.

I think the whole country was waiting.

We drove in a convoy to a soccer field in Envigado. A big crowd of
our people was waiting there to offer protection. Pablo was dressed
as always in blue jeans, blue socks, sneakers, and a simple white shirt.
He was wearing a Cartier watch and carrying his Sig Sauer and a

Motorola radio with two bands of twenty-five frequencies. By the time we got to the field the helicopter was landing. He hugged me and climbed on board for the flight. Father García and the journalist Luis Alirio Calle were waiting inside to fly with him. There was still great danger; there were many groups that did not want Pablo free to talk to the government. So the defense minister closed all the airspace in the region, writing in his own diary, "Not even birds will fly over Medellín today."

When the helicopter reached the top of the mountain Pablo got off and walked directly to the entrance. He handed a soldier his pearl-handled gun as a symbol of the end of the fighting—but people who were there told me that as soon as he got inside he took another gun. It took a few more days before all of us had surrendered and were safely inside. Officially there were fourteen of us.

The first few days there were very busy. Among our first visitors was our mother, who arrived with a rosary and a pot of cooked meat, Father García, who took our confession—we asked God to allow us to get out of this situation and protect our family—and friends like Colombia's famous soccer star René Higuita. Pablo had helped discover him as a young player and brought him to the notice of the professional teams. They had stayed loyal friends. The media tried to make a scandal from Higuita's friendship with us, but no one paid attention; he didn't even lose his TV endorsements of products.

There were many other things that had to be done quickly. While Pablo's people living outside would continue the business and pay whatever bribes had to be paid, we needed to have our own access to money. As much as $10 million in cash was packed tightly into ten milk canisters, which were covered with salt, sugar, rice, and beans, even fresh fish. We told the guards that these canisters contained our weekly food ration, so they let them inside. Eventually they were buried near our soccer field. Other money was stored in tunnels hidden under our bedrooms that could be reached only by trapdoors under the beds. Weapons that we might need to protect ourselves were also brought in that way.

To communicate with our associates outside we also installed eleven telephone lines, a cell telephone system—which was now available—a radio-telephone system, and nine beepers. It was written that we had carrier pigeons to carry messages, but that wasn't true. We had the lighting system prepared for our needs, so that if planes flew overhead we could quickly turn out all the internal lights with a remote control that I built—or when we needed to slip outside we could do the same thing.

Security was always the primary concern. In addition to our bodega watching post, there were four guard stations along the twisting mountain road to the Cathedral. These were manned by the army, who were never permitted inside the gates, but in truth we were allowed to hire half of the jail guards, and the good mayor of Envigado hired the other half, so these guards mostly were friends of ours. The government paid them very little, so they were often persuaded to work with our needs in exchange for additional cash payments, good food, and colored pieces of paper. An arrangement had been made so that these pieces of paper could be exchanged in Envigado for home appliances, electronics, clothes, and even Colombian cash, and the owners would be paid by our people.

When our protection was done, we prepared the Cathedral for our pleasure. When we arrived it was a simple place. It wasn't like a regular prison with bars and cells, but it wasn't especially comfortable either. With the help of my son Nico, we changed that situation. Nico had acquired a soda truck and received permission to bring cases of soda to the prison. But the crates of soda formed walls and inside those walls was whatever we wanted. He brought in Jacuzzis and hot tubs, television sets, the materials needed to build comfortable bedrooms, whatever we wanted—including the first of the many women to stay there. It was a hectic period and much was done to transform the prison into a much more tolerable place.

I also brought two bicycles inside with me, a stationary bike and one of my own Ositto riding bikes, so I could keep in shape. Among the things that Pablo brought with him was a large record collection, including classical music, Elvis's records he'd bought when we had visited Graceland, and his signed Frank Sinatra records that we'd received when visiting Las Vegas. For reading he brought in a collection of books, from five Bibles to the work of Nobel Prize winners. The books I brought included a text on having a super-memory, and books on horses, cancer, AIDS, and bicycles. We also had a large collection of videotapes, naturally including the complete set of *The Godfather* movies and Steve McQueen movies, including *Bullitt*.

Eventually we turned the prison into a comfortable home. We had all the necessary electronic devices, including computers, big-screen televisions with video systems, beautiful music systems, even a comfortable bar with the best champagne and whiskey. Outside we had a good soccer field with lights to play at night, paths to walk where we could be hidden from the air by thick trees, and good places to exercise. Within a couple of months we had made it a reasonable place.

Immediately there were stories written that we were living in luxury, that the faucets in the bathroom were gold. That it was just like Napoles. That wasn't true at all. It was safer for us than moving between hiding places, and we made it comfortable—it wasn't an ordinary prison, but still it was a prison. We no longer had the freedom to make our plans to go where we wanted or see whoever we wanted when we wanted to see them. Everything required planning. But soon we had settled in. We fixed the kitchen and brought in two chefs to prepare international foods for us—we knew them as the Stomach Brothers. We had sufficient entertainment, sports and exercise facilities, security, arms, and a lot of money.

But it was not luxury. Some of our mattresses were on cement. The furniture was simple; the walls were decorated mostly with paper posters, although Pablo did have a couple of nice paintings. And our clothes were basic. In Pablo's closet, for example, were his jeans and shirts, and many pairs of sneakers—some of them ready with spikes on in case we had to move quickly.

The difference between this prison and the world we'd lived in for the past few years was that now our enemies knew exactly where we were, but they couldn't get to us. Instead of tracking us and trying to kill us, the government was responsible for protecting us. It was a difficult political situation.

President Gavíria had his own needs. To restore Colombia as a safe place for foreign companies to do business the Gavíria government had to have peace in the streets. People had to feel safe to come here. Ending the war was the beginning of that.

I spent the first months there without being charged with a true crime. After several months a government prosecutor came to the prison to accuse me. "The charge against Roberto is that he has accounts outside Colombia with millions and millions of dollars in them."

At that moment there was no law in Colombia against keeping money in foreign banks. I told the judge, "That isn't illegal, and if you read the law you see that I have the right to negotiate an agreement with you. I'll give you half the money and then you make the other half legal for me."

The judge refused this offer. Instead the Colombian government made an agreement with other countries to freeze the bank accounts. Some of these accounts are still frozen.

Meanwhile, outside the prison the drug business continued to prosper. The arrest of the legendary Pablo Escobar did nothing to change that. Members of our organization continued to do their deals, the Cali cartel stayed in serious business, the other cartels kept working. When someone fell, other people stepped forward to take his place. What was different was that the violence had abated.

While we were there we did try hard to change our situation. Pablo had as many as thirty lawyers working most of their time in our effort inside the judicial system. The soccer star Higuita volunteered to try to make peace between us and Cali. Eventually with the help of Father García he spoke with the Rodríguez Orejuela brothers, but to no good. They were too stubborn. Pablo told me, "I don't believe in the word of those two." As we discovered later there was good reason for that. A DAS agent who was helping run the prison security discovered that Cali had bought four 250-pound bombs from people in El Salvador and was trying to buy a plane to drop them on us. They were not able to, but on occasion our guards suddenly would begin firing their weapons at airplanes hovering too long in the area or coming too close to the Cathedral.

Time passed very slowly. I exercised, rode my bicycle, continued to read everything possible about AIDS and making my research, and I worked with my brother. Pablo would spend his days on the telephone, reading, and visiting with his attorneys. He even began studying Mandarin. In the evenings we would sit in rocking chairs watching the lights come on in the buildings of Envigado. At those moments, when we watched the normal life of others, it was hard not to think about people being with their families in an ordinary but comforting way.

As before, Pablo continued to try to help the people who most needed it. He received hundreds of letters every day. The world knew he had surrendered and wrote to him with their requests. Letters came from around the world, from Europe, Asia, and basically everywhere else, and most of them asked for money or advice on how to make money. Four or five of our employees did nothing but organize these letters. They were put in piles for family, for friends, for people who needed help with their health especially with cancer, for students needing money for education, and for business letters. Pablo would read most of these letters and often send a crew to investigate the cases and verify the information. If it was real they would hand money to the people.

I remember a few of the letters. One odd letter came from a man in Africa who owned the elephant that was the mother of the elephant we'd had at Napoles. It was his idea to have the mother and daughter together living at Napoles. He included a picture of his elephant and his request for money.

A person wrote from America that he had seven different bank accounts and would be very happy to hide Pablo's money in his accounts.

There was a letter addressed to myself and Pablo; it included a photograph of a gorgeous seventeen-year-old blonde wearing a wedding dress. She wrote something like, "I'm a good girl. I have just finished high school and my dream is to be an attorney but I don't have the money. I am a decent girl, but it would be an honor if one of you can take me. I am a virgin and that is all I can offer. I am not a whore, but I need the money for my college career."

Pablo sent a representative to her house. Although we never became involved with her in any way, we did pay for her college. But that was typical. The pleading letters were hard to read: I am dying and my children have nothing . . . I need an operation so I can walk and support my family . . . They are coming to take away our house . . . The government helped none of these people, so their only hope was Pablo.

Countless other people would gather at the first gate at the bottom of the mountain and send handwritten notes, *boletas*, with the guards to ask for assistance. Sometimes they wanted money but other times they just wanted Pablo's advice about the problems of their life. To them, Pablo was a man of the streets like they were who had risen to the very top of the mountain.

Most important for our daily lives was the fact that we were able to receive visitors regularly. This was not supposed to happen, the only official visiting days were Wednesday and Sunday when our families came, but it seemed like there were always people there. We had bought two trucks, a Chevrolet and a Mazda van. In the back of them we built a fake wall, leaving a space we called the tunnel that was big enough to hide as many as twenty people. The people who used this method to come see us were those who did not want their visit known publicly, others who had committed crimes and were not legally allowed to be there, or people we did not want our enemies to know were there. Usually they would be picked up in the night and driven to our bodega. From there those people who could show ID to guards were placed in the seats and those who could not were put in the hidden tunnel. At the checkpoint the guards would ask, "What are you taking there?"

The password was "Materials."

Each time a truck left the bodega we were called and told who was coming up.

In addition to our family and friends, politicians visited us, businessmen, priests, the greatest soccer players, and some of the most beautiful women in the world. There were many parties and in attendance were the beauty queens of Colombia and other countries, including famous actresses, models, and the prettiest girls at the universities. We would see a beautiful woman on television or in the newspapers and she would be invited. There was never any danger to them and for their visit they would receive a very nice gift. Often by their own choice they would stay the night, and leave after breakfast the next morning in the tunnel. In fact, between many of our bedrooms we had built small hideouts, so the girls could stay there without anyone being suspicious.

No one was ever pushed to come if she felt uncomfortable. One of the girls at the university remembers being approached by a friend who asked her if she wanted to go to a lovely party, for which she would be well paid. "What do I have to do?" she asked.

"Nothing. Just be beautiful."

There is a magazine in Colombia called *Cromos* that publishes pictures of beautiful women. We would pick out women from the pages and invite them to the parties. One of the very first women to stay at the Cathedral was a twenty-year-old beauty who had just been fourth in the Miss Universe pageant who I had invited—she arrived there and stayed for five days. From these visits several people fell in love and there were some marriages at the Cathedral. And one of these women I fell in love with, she was a beauty queen and we had three beautiful children together before our marriage had a bad end. As I learned eventually, she had not fallen in love with me, but instead with my bank account.

It should not be surprising that there was a lot of sex at the Cathedral. We were young men, many of us rich, and confined inside the walls of a prison. Who could protect a woman better than the men of Pablo Escobar? Even our parties were moderate, with nice music and dancing.

Later, photographs found at the Cathedral after we'd escaped, of blow-up sex dolls and some of our men dressed as women, were printed in magazines to try to embarrass us. The impressions of those photographs were not true at all; these toys were jokes, the dress-up part of a costume day we had as our entertainment.

The beautiful women were never invited there during the weekly family visits. During the years we'd been running we had only been able to spend brief periods with our families. Being in prison allowed us to finally spend time safely with our wives, children, and families. In fact, Pablo had three beds put into his bedroom so his whole family could sleep in that room with him when they visited. He even had a small playhouse built for his daughter and a go-kart for his son.

There were always many people there when our families visited. Pablo would stay in his bedroom, which was right off the main living room, and invite those people he wanted to see into his room. Often through one of the trusted people there with us, he would hand out cash to the family. One of those people who came to visit was his seventeen-year-old cousin, who he called Pelolindo, the girl with the pretty hair. She came there dressed in her high school uniform with her mother and sisters. Like other members of the family, they had not seen Pablo in all the years we'd been on the run. And during that time she had become very beautiful. "When we were invited into his room," she remembers, "he looked at everybody but he focused on me." He said he didn't really remember too much about meeting these girls when they were children. "The way he looked at me that day, I felt shy."

She returned a few days later, this time dressed as a young woman. At first she was invited into his room with her two sisters. Each of them spoke of their wishes, although Pelolindo asked for nothing, and then returned to the living room. As they were about to leave Pablo asked her to return to his room. Her two sisters moved with her but he stopped them, "I didn't call you." When they were in his room he wondered why she hadn't asked for something. Everybody always asked him for something, he said.

"I don't see you like that," she said. "I'm not here to ask you for anything. I don't like to do that." In response he planned and sponsored her high school graduation trip to a Colombian island in the Caribbean, San Andrés. All that he asked in return was that she would call him when she returned.

When she returned from the island he invited her to come back. This time she went with her cousin. To go up the mountain they were hidden in a false area of a jeep. "I went up there because I felt something special with him. I know he felt something too. But he was always respectful to me. And it did not feel like we were in a prison; instead I felt like we were in a very private place. I was nervous and anxious. But then I began to visit him often, sometimes four or five times a week. One day with him felt like a week." And this continued for several months.

The truth is that their relationship never was sexual. Many stories have been written about Pablo and young women, but he was very quiet about that. In public he was always a gentleman. And with Pelolindo it remained sweet and innocent. When she came to the Cathedral they would take walks and talk. As she remembers, "Sometimes at night we would go to the soccer field and he would turn on the lights, and the two of us would play soccer. He'd pretend to be the goalkeeper and he would challenge me to score a goal. Score a goal! After showing me he could stop me, he would let me score.

"Sometimes after that we would cuddle and hug and watch TV," she tells. But there was never sex between them. "If he had not been killed that probably would have happened in time, but it did not." This girl suggested to Pablo that he put together albums of all the political cartoons about his life, an idea he embraced, and together they began putting together these books by hand. A few hundred were done, but only ten were done by hand and those had Pablo's signature and thumbprint in gold on the cover. One night as they were working together she said to him, "The way I know you, sweet and romantic and caring, I can't believe the other side of you is true."

He smiled, she said, then responded, "Do you know who I am? Do you know who you're talking to?"

"I know. But right now I see you as Pablo Escobar." Often he asked to give her things. Once two of his men showed up at her school with a new car for her. And Pablo gave his word that he would use his contacts to help her have a successful career as a singer. Pablo's wife knew about these visits and was not happy about them. But there was nothing she could do—and it remained a flirtation. A happy innocence.

He never told Perolindo he loved her or he'd missed her when she wasn't there. But each night when she left he wanted to know exactly when she was coming back.

Pablo eventually came to trust her so much that he allowed her to have the combination to the safe in which he kept many thousands of dollars and pesos. Several times he let her open the trapdoor below his bed and go down alone into the hidden room where cash was kept. There was always a lot of money going out of the room, she remembers, but it stayed full of piles of cash.

Within a few months she began cutting his hair and taking care of his nails. In fact, there was a night Pablo decided he should be a blond, so she returned the next time with blond dye—but also black in case he didn't like it. She dyed his hair blond to hide his white hairs. He looked in the mirror and hated it. He would be even more of a target as a blonde than black-haired. "Put it back black," he said instantly, deciding the blond made him look too much like a woman.

As they became close, they talked about the hardest topics. One night he asked her, "What are you going to do if they kill me?"

She was surprised at that question. Pablo thought about life, not death. One time he had showed her the photograph of himself and Juan Pablo taken in front of the White House and told her that in the future he was going to go there and do business with the American president. He said, "After I get back on track, I'm going to be president of Colombia." So she hadn't expected a question about death. She tried to laugh it away. "Oh Pablo, I don't think you're going to get killed. If they take you to another prison I know with the power you have you're going to escape from there."

"I'll try," she remembers him saying. "But if something happens to me what are you going to remember most?"

"I will remember the way you look at me. The intenseness of your eyes, because I know you don't look at me as your cousin." To that, Pablo did not respond.

Their relationship changed because of a second cousin. This cousin was killed by Pablo's enemies when they got of ahold of him and he would not snitch on Pablo. For that he was killed. That event scared Pelolindo and she suddenly stopped going up there. Instead she had excuses. When Pablo called her home her mother would tell him, "She has gone to a party." After a week of such excuses he said he needed to talk to her immediately. She came up to the Cathedral but Pablo could see there was a distance. "You're afraid," he said.

She admitted that she was. Pablo explained that there was no reason to worry, and promised to keep her safe and help her build her singing career. And he gave her a gold comb with "Pelolindo" inscribed on it. She admits, "That was the first time I spent through the night. It wasn't a night of passion, but the feelings were very deep. I felt loved that night. I told him that love isn't only sex, that I would make love to him in my own way. I kissed his face and his hands and that night I saw tears in his eyes. I asked him why. 'After all this that I've been through this is what I wanted, this is love. I know my wife loves me, but I don't think in the same way.' He asked me, 'Are you ready for something?'

"'What for?' I said. I thought he wanted to have sex, but it wasn't that.

"'Are you ready to approach the family?'

"'No,' I told him. 'No, I'm not going to do that. Are you crazy?' Eventually though, in a different time and a different place, I know we would have had physical love together."

After leaving the Cathedral in the morning, she went to collect a $2,000 payment for a singing job she had done. She was with a male friend of hers, and on the road called Las Olmos they were kidnapped by four police in uniform, driving in two taxis. These men took everything from them as well as all the equipment in their car. That evening, when Pablo's man went to her house to pick her up, her mother explained that she had not come home since the morning. Pablo put out the word.

The kidnappers received a phone call telling them, "This is Pablo Escobar's cousin that you're fucking with." They returned the money and gave them back the car. Then they left quickly. The second she got to her home the phone was ringing and Pablo told her, "You have to come here now!" When she arrived she told him the whole story, and learned about his own phone calls to find her.

"I told him, 'You are my Superman.' He didn't say anything, but it was one of the few times I saw him smile. And that was the last night I ever saw him, because at that moment we didn't know that the government was planning to take him away from there." This was June 20, 1992.

We spent 396 days inside the Cathedral. We celebrated many events there, including holidays, marriages, and birthdays. Pablo turned forty-two there and we enjoyed a feast including caviar and pink salmon. Musicians played for the guests and our mother gave him a special Russian hat she had bought during a recent trip there. But when I think of it all maybe most memorable were the days Pablo's beloved soccer teams visited us there.

René Higuita's Nacional team arrived first, on the celebration of Las Mercedes, the patron saint of prisoners. Pablo wanted us to play a real game against them, except as he warned them, "Games here last about three or four hours, without rest and only two changes are allowed. A tie is settled with penalties." They wore their official uniforms; we wore the colors of the German team. Pablo was a good player but he was guarded hard by Leonel Alvarez, and when Pablo complained, Alvarez told him, "This is how we play soccer, brother." Nacional went ahead 3–0, but eventually the game was finished 5–5. In penalty kicks I believe René helped us, missing his own attempt, then allowing my brother's left-foot kick to get into the goal for our victory. There was no consideration of the fact that maybe they had played easy with us. We won, that's what mattered.

Within a few days the professional teams from Medellín and Envigado also came to the Cathedral to play against us—and they also could not beat us! From those days until our stay there ended, the flag of one of those teams always flew outside the perimeter. And if that flag was not that of Pablo's favorite Medellín team, after everyone went to bed he would quietly make certain that it was.

Pablo believed he was serving his time for all the people in the organization. He had given himself up to end extradition. With Pablo Escobar in prison the government could say the war against drug trafficking was being won. This really wasn't true.

Because we were in the Cathedral did not mean our business stopped totally. Pablo continued to know what was going on in Medellín and throughout Colombia. People would call him and tell him what was happening. Not one single load left that he did not know about. But it was expensive being there; there were still people on Pablo's payroll who expected to be paid. Sometimes helicopters from the outskirts of Medellín would land in our prison and fly away carrying money to keep the business operating. But all of that stayed possible because the people doing business paid Pablo his fees in cash.

Two of the biggest organizations paying their percentage belonged to Pablo's friends Fernando Galeano and Kiko Moncada. They were making a lot of money using the route through Mexico, called Fany, opened by Pablo, and thanks to him without fear of extradition. But then Pablo found out that they had done five loads without paying him a cent. They had cheated him out of millions of dollars. As business that made no sense. They were earning millions of dollars, the money they needed to pay Pablo was nothing for them. So Pablo knew that this was much more than the dollars and the lack of respect, this was an attempt to take control of the whole business. But Galeano and Moncada were friends, men he had trusted. In Pablo's mind, men he had gone to jail for.

Pablo found out from a friend where Galeano had hidden the money and he sent people to collect it. It was more than $20 million in the coleta. Galeano and Moncada wanted it back, denying what Pablo knew to be true. He told them to come to the Cathedral to discuss the business.

They died as expected. Probably they thought they were safe coming to the prison. They were killed after they left the Cathedral. The sicario Popeye confessed that he killed Moncada and claimed that Otto killed Galeano. It doesn't matter who killed them, they were still dead. Their families pleaded to have their bodies and they were told where to dig them up. Pablo then called all the accountants for those people and told them from now on they were responsible to him. All the properties of those families, the boats, the planes, the cash, were put in the names of Pablo's loyal people.

Then Pablo specially called the principal people from both of those operations to come to the prison. Most of them were brought up the mountain secretly in the tunnel. "I am declaring an emergency," Pablo told them, reminding them all that even in prison he was still the leader, the patrón, of the Medellín cartel. While the cartel of the old days was gone, Pablo meant all of the drug traffickers of Medellín. He told them that if they stayed calm nothing would happen to them—as long as they continued to pay their monthly quota, their tax.

Pablo believed he had to take these steps to protect his own interests, which were being stolen from him. This was business, the people he was dealing with were equally guilty to him, so I don't believe he thought the government would be protective of them. But it turned out they made a good excuse for the government to take the actions suggested by the United States.

Pablo did not want to escape from the Cathedral. Inside we were all safe, outside there were many enemies waiting for all of us. It is clear to us why President Gavíria decided suddenly to take actions against us, and that was because the Cali cartel was pressuring the government through their political ties. We know letters were written from the Cali cartel to the minister of defense telling about the way all of us were living inside the prison: guests of all sorts coming at all times, good sports facilities, the fact that we had money and weapons and that Pablo had continued in the business. But it's hard to believe the government did not already know about the way we lived inside the Cathedral. When stories about the deaths of Moncada and Galeano became known to the public there were complaints that the government was too weak to act, so perhaps Gavíria was embarrassed and felt he needed to show how tough he was. There were also comments made later that the government was forced to act when it learned Pablo was planning an escape. Pablo was not planning any escape. And then there was the pressure from the United States. The drug trafficking from our country to America had not decreased even slightly when Pablo surrendered, and when the news that he was living easy was made public the American government objected and offered even more assistance. Whatever the reasons, in July 1992, President Gavíria decided that Pablo had to be moved to a more difficult prison.

Pablo had always been nervous about this possibility. He believed that the American DEA wanted to kidnap him and bring him to the United States. He even thought some of the planes that flew over the prison had been sent by the DEA to take pictures. I remember he read a book by the Charles Manson prosecutor that said the U.S. should send commandos to Colombia to kill the drug traffickers.

I felt that this was coming two days before when the small priest came to warn me. For the first time I told Pablo the whole story, when the priest had visited me before and what had happened. Pablo believed me. I asked him, "Is it true that they are going to come for us?" I know he went to his informants in the government and army and they told him that indeed it was true. Someone at a very high level of the army told him he needed to move. Others told him that there was an order from the U.S. that either the Colombian government had to bring him to America or they would come to our country.

The next few days there was a lot of preparation in case we had to leave quickly. There was a lot of nervousness those days, as if we were waiting for a tornado.

It came as a breeze. We had set up a communication system that made it possible to find Pablo or myself wherever we were; we even had speakers above our beds. One morning at 10:15 we received a warning that four truckloads of military were coming up. Soon after we were officially informed that representatives of the government were coming to speak with us.

Pablo and I started to get ready to leave in case we had to go. We knew it would be difficult in the daylight but there was nothing else we could do. One thing for sure, Pablo was not going to let them take him anywhere without a fight. At noon the assistant minister of justice, Eduardo Mendoza, and the director of prisons, Colonel Hernando Navas, got to the gate and explained that President Gavíria had ordered the army to search our bedrooms.

Pablo remained polite, inviting these two men to come inside to discuss this situation. "I'm sorry," he said to them. "But I have made a deal with the government of Gavíria. The police and the army are not permitted inside this prison. If you want, you can bring the regular prison officials to do this search, but I will not allow the army and even less the police. Please remember, gentlemen, I fought a war with the police and this policy is the result."

The assistant minister looked very upset. To make the situation more comfortable, Pablo offered to allow soldiers inside, but only without weapons. The two officials accepted this, but when contacted, the president refused. Breaking his pact with Pablo, he insisted the army enter with their weapons, that there could be no compromise. I think he was concerned he would look weak if he accepted Pablo's offer.

But Pablo was just as strong. "They can't come inside with weapons," he insisted. "No one's coming in here armed to kill us." The government men tried to calm the situation, but Pablo insisted: "We don't know what their intentions are. I do not trust my life with them." There was no solution to this standoff and we all waited to see what would happen. What happened was that the government sent many more soldiers, as well as helicopters and airplanes. We learned from sources that two loaded Hercules airplanes had left from Bogotá to Medellín, and already truckloads of soldiers from Bogotá were coming up the mountain to replace the troops from Medellín that were patrolling the prison's perimeter.

After dark the government officials decided to leave. "Let's go to sleep tonight," Mendoza said. "We'll come back tomorrow to figure out how to solve this." But just at that moment Pablo got a phone call from an army general we trusted. He informed Pablo that the government planned to capture or kill him, or even extradite him. Pablo took me aside and explained the situation knowing that we were the only two who knew what was going on. Our options were narrow. The first thing he decided was to keep the government officials as hostages. He explained to them: "I'm sorry, but you can't leave here right now. We need you to ensure our own security while we figure out what to do."

The situation could be solved only by the president, but Gavíria refused to get on the telephone. Pablo's lawyers tried many times to contact the president, but it was clear that the president had his own plan. Pablo did not want to leave the Cathedral, but he had no choice. We all believed the army wanted to come in and kill us. It was time to leave. All of us except me got armed with the weapons that had been hidden a long time, including a machine gun and rifles. Pablo had an Uzi on his right shoulder and his Sig Sauer stuck in his waistband. Without saying anything I left the prison building and slipped into the cool night. I was going to prepare our escape route. The fog was drifting in, which gave me some cover. Pablo and I had walked the perimeter of the prison many times, searching for the ideal place to get through the wire fence. We were convinced this was the only place in the entire perimeter we could leave unseen. Months earlier I had buried wire cutters near the place we had selected. The nearest soldiers were about eighty meters away. Pablo and I had carefully selected this place to go through the fence because it led directly to a gulley, a trench cut in the ground by a stream that served as a natural tunnel. The wire fence was thicker than I thought it would be, and much more difficult to cut. I had to be very quiet because sounds flow easily in the night. One of the most difficult challenges we faced was getting through the high-voltage fence. Everybody was worried they would be electrocuted, and truthfully they would have preferred to be shot dead instead of fried. My engineering knowledge allowed me to bypass this system. Eventually I cut a hole just barely large enough for our men to slip through one by one, and then I went back to the prison building.

Inside the prison our hostages were terrified. They had been captured by Pablo Escobar so probably they abandoned hope. They were scared quiet and lost all skin color. Colonel Navas took a glass of whiskey and said, "This could be the last whiskey I will drink in my life." Then he went to a Bible and read Psalm 91. Finally he asked for a telephone and called his family to tell them goodbye. He told us he didn't even know what his mission was when he was ordered to fly to Medellín.

Later in the night Pablo ordered the prisoners taken to his bedroom. He had tried many times to contact the president, even through Father García, but Gavíria would not accept the phone calls. There was no longer a question of leaving for us. Pablo said clearly, "Either we flee or we all die." Pablo and I went to the hidden room and packed ourselves with cash. We heard airplanes circling above and I flipped a switch that operated the lighting system I had installed, and the Cathedral went into darkness. The dark prison was lost in the fog. But inside the lights going off scared everyone, especially the hostages. It was explained to them this was necessary for security but I don't know how much they accepted that.

Outside it was very quiet. We could hear the birds and insects and occasionally a soldier yelling. Inside radio stations were broadcasting the story. They all got it wrong: One said the army had taken control of the Cathedral and there had been casualties. Another said Pablo had been captured and was already on an airplane to Florida. But all of them spoke of this military assault. They gave us some good information. Pablo used the mobile phone to speak with his family. The reports terrified them. "Don't worry," he told them. "Don't listen to the news. The situation is being resolved directly with the president." I called my children to tell them the same thing. And then Pablo and I both called our mother.

We had thought about this night many times. Pablo always walked around with the laces of his sneakers open and we all used to say, the day Pablo ties his sneakers is the day we're in real difficulty. There were already as many as two thousand soldiers surrounding the Cathedral. An air controller we paid informed us helicopters from Bogotá had landed in Medellín. Things were now happening fast. Pablo gathered all of us and told us who would be leaving and who would be staying. He picked the most fit knowing we would have to move fast. Then he bent over and tied the laces of his sneakers.

He said to me, "Roberto, let's put our radios on the same frequency." We visited the hostages, told them to remain calm, that this situation would be solved without bloodshed. Then he told them he was going to sleep for a while and would see them again in the morning. There have been stories written that the guards were bribed and we just walked out the door, that Pablo and others were dressed as women, that we paid more than $1 million to leave. With all the soldiers around, many of them from Bogotá, bribing all of them would have been impossible. Instead, Pablo decided we would slip out of the prison one by one at five-minute intervals. It had started raining, so the dark of night, the thick fog, and the rain gave us good cover. Pablo went first and took a good position to see everything that was going on around him. I waited with the hostages a few minutes and told them that I was going to lie down. Then I went back to my room to make my final preparations.

I put on boots, put new batteries in the radiophone, and took my transistor radio so I could hear the news. I finally put on my raincoat and my old bicycling hat with the message *Bicicletas El Ositto*, Bear Bicycles. It was time to leave. There were only a few things we left behind that mattered, for Pablo it was his collection of records by Elvis and Sinatra. I left the bicycles I loved and my mini-lab for cancer and AIDS research. I walked slowly through the dark, empty building. It was a strange feeling. I looked for the lights of the city below the mountain, but Medellín was hidden in the fog.

I walked toward the fence where I thought Pablo and the others were waiting, but something happened. In the dark I got confused, I got lost. And for the first time that night, I felt panic. I felt completely alone. There wasn't much I could do, I couldn't make a sound because the soldiers were too close. Like in a race, I took deep breaths to find a place of calm inside me. I knew Pablo would never leave without me. He had often told me that he would not leave. I walked slowly—and finally saw movement. It was one of our people.

They were all outside. I slipped through the fence and joined them. It was almost 2 A.M. As we left I heard some panicky shouts and thought it was the priest warning me that we had to get moving. Slowly, but gradually, we went down the mountain, careful to keep our footing on the wet ground. One slip could mean death.

It was a difficult descent. There was a large straight rock face we had to climb down. The biggest and strongest went first, and allowed other men to stand on their shoulders to make a human ladder. That part completed, we found a steep slope covered with thick, thorny brush. We pushed on as silently as possible through the bushes, holding hands to make a chain. We kept moving forward toward the morning, not knowing where we were going. Finally, after more than two hours we came into a clearing near a stable. The fog had thinned. We paused and looked around, and were stunned and dismayed to discover that we were only a few hundred meters from the prison. We had almost been going around in a circle. If anyone had been looking in this direction from the prison they easily could have seen us. If they were shooting, we were an easy target.

The one advantage we had was that seven of us were wearing army camouflage uniforms and if people in the distance saw them they probably would have mistaken them for the army. Pablo figured we had less than two hours to find safe cover, so we began moving faster. Looking back over our shoulders, the Cathedral looked so big, so strong, like from some movie. We managed to snake down the hill into the neighborhood of El Salado by daylight. The city was coming alive, people were leaving their homes to go to work, and children were on their way to school. For them it was a normal day, for us it was the end of our old lives as we walked into the unknown. Once again we were fugitives of justice.

We were filthy, covered with mud and sweating, our clothes torn. The people who saw us thought we were ordinary street people. No photographs of Pablo had been seen by the public in more than a year and he had gotten heavier, so no one recognized him. The rest of us were not known. Pablo decided to go to the farm of Memo Pérez, an old friend who had worked for him in many different important positions.

Memo's groundskeeper answered the door. After a second of shock he recognized us and quickly had us come in. It was the first time we could relax since the government came to the Cathedral. We were wet and exhausted. But within the hour there was a heavy banging on the door. We grabbed our weapons and got ready for the fight as the butler, Raúl, opened the door. It was some neighbors who had seen us move in, coming with hot food for our breakfast. It was an amazing gesture. Several of these people formed a neighborhood watch for us, standing on the nearby streets to warn us if the army arrived. Someone else took our filthy clothes and washed them as we cleaned ourselves and shaved. By the time we put on our fresh clothes we felt refreshed and ready for whatever happened next.

We learned from the radio what had happened on the top of the mountain. At about 7 A.M. Gavíria had ordered General Gustavo Pardo Ariza, commander of the Fourth Brigade, to attack. The radio said that as they burst through the main door they screamed that everyone should get on the ground, but when the commander of the prison guards tried to fight back he was shot and killed. Months later we would learn the truth that he had turned to open the door and was shot. The army then stormed through the prison, shooting and setting off explosives looking for us. They discovered the hostages safe in Pablo's bedroom, but still they continued shooting and tearing up the place. They captured the five of us who had stayed behind, and arrested twenty-seven guards on suspicion of cooperating with us. The radio reported that the purpose of the raid was to move Pablo out of the Cathedral to a more secure prison.

While this was going on we were enjoying fresh coffee. We could hear the helicopters circling above the city. We knew we couldn't move again until dark. We felt no joy or excitement about our escape. We believed we were forced to flee, that the government had broken its agreement and there was no way of knowing what would be done to us. There was nothing else we could do if we wanted to live.

I called my son Nicholas from the radiophone. I gave him number hints so he would know which frequency to switch to so we could talk safely. When we had contact I told him to call the national network Radio Caracol and tell them Pablo and I were hiding in a secret tunnel beneath the prison and that we were well armed and had enough food to hold out for a month. Nicholas also told the reporter Dario Arizmendi that Pablo was willing to surrender if we were guaranteed that we would be returned safely to the Cathedral and the original terms of surrender respected.

Inside the prison the government forces heard this interview and began searching for this secret tunnel. They started digging with heavy construction equipment and using explosives in the fields to find it. Pablo stood at windows of the farm looking at the mountain. "The only thing they're going to find is the money in the barrels," he said, meaning the $10 million we'd buried. Pablo wasn't concerned about that, his thoughts were about what our next steps should be. He wanted to surrender again, but only with the same guarantees as before.

We waited throughout the day, listening as the reports on the radio became more frantic. Someone told the radio station that Pablo had ordered the killing of the attorney general, defense minister, and other officials if the government continued to pursue us. Other people phoned in bomb threats supposedly from us. It was ridiculous. In the afternoon I called the station and told them that Pablo had made no threats to anyone, that all we wanted was to return to the former situation—with protection. It didn't matter; the whole city was in a panic. Schools in Bogotá held bomb evacuation drills, people went to the stores to buy groceries afraid that stores would be forced to close. At night the president went on TV and told people to be calm, promising if we surrendered he would protect our lives and defending his policy of giving leniency to drug traffickers who gave up. But he did not promise to restore the situation.

In the United States newspapers wrote that we had shot our way out of prison and that we had escaped in a rain of gunfire. Some senators threatened to send troops to Colombia to kidnap Pablo and bring him to the United States for trial.

During the day we made plans to move again. I called an employee we trusted and told him in coded language to find the friend I would jog with before our surrender and tell him to get three cars and at midnight meet us at the iron door at the entrance to the farm. He knew the place, the gate of a farm where my friend and I would end our daily runs. After dark we left and walked through the woods, staying off the roads. We stopped briefly at another farm owned by one of our friends, and from there called our families to confirm that the cars were going to meet us, and then told them not to worry and not to believe the radio reports. After eating, we kept going. As we walked we could hear the explosives going off at the Cathedral as the search for the tunnels continued. Each step had danger.

When we passed one farm five German shepherds came bursting out after us. El Mugre was bitten on the leg and started bleeding. We fought them off but we couldn't shoot at them because the noise would bring attention. Fortunately Pablo had candy in his pocket and tossed it to the dogs, who went for it and calmed down. Pablo stayed with the dogs until the rest of us had moved away, and then joined us. We got to the meeting point about 1:30 and the cars were waiting for us.

At 3:30 in the morning we arrived at a farm owned by a friend. First thing, Pablo cut the phone lines. Instead we used a clean cell phone to call our families—although now we didn't call our mother because clearly the government would be listening for that. Instead Pablo and I agreed that I should go see her.

My face was still not easily recognized by the government. One of our drivers took me there before dawn. "It's me, Mom," I said to her. "I came to tell you that we are all right." She came out of her room and we embraced. I held her tightly and for that one moment I could almost forget our situation. The important thing was to tell her that the tunnel story was not true, that we had just made it up to oc-cupy the army while we escaped. I could only stay a short time. She insisted that I wait while she prepared food for us, just like the way she would make lunch for her boys Roberto and Pablo when we rode our bicycles to school. It was my mother, I had to wait. I kept nervously watching through the window, afraid the police would show up at any second. In the life of the city another day was starting. She packed a meal of chicken and rice in pots and gave them to me. She also gave me a note for Pablo and urged me to continue praying. Then she kissed me twice, "One for you and one for Pablo."

By the time I got back to the farm some of the others had left us. Pablo had decided we should move separately to be harder to find. We rested there a few days, believing we were safe. We kept track of the TV and radio coverage and listened to the many untrue rumors. Supposedly we were being seen everywhere. After a few days Pablo made a tape for the radio, again offering to surrender if our safety was guaranteed and we were allowed to return to the Cathedral, giving his word he would not start a new campaign of violence. Then he closed with: "From the jungles of Colombia." Of course we were not there, but the government believed that and sent troops and helicopters.

The search for us was intense. The army rushed troops into the region. The president was on the TV almost every day trying to explain what had happened. Everyone seemed afraid that the violent days were going to start again. But while all this was happening we were watching it on TV. Mostly those first few days we stayed quiet, just waiting for the situation to calm down so we could move again. Our lawyers continued to try to make a new arrangement. But this time the government did not want Pablo to be in prison. This time government officials wanted to kill him.

Nine

I HAVE OWNED HORSES FOR MANY YEARS. For a time the man who took care of my horses was called Doll. He was called that because he had a very attractive face and long hair. Doll was a very nice person, but like so many others he wanted to make more money, he wanted to be in our business. I told him, "Don't get involved. You know what you're doing with the horses. Do that."

No, he insisted, I need to make more money. No. We had that discussion many times and he would get angry when I refused him. Finally one afternoon I had to go into the jungle with Pablo. But before I left I bought Doll a motorcycle.

After twenty days Doll showed up at the farm where we were hiding, riding his motorcycle. Once again he asked to make more money. He wanted to be my bodyguard and do everything for me. Finally I said okay. "If you want to stay, stay here." The next day about five thousand soldiers surrounded our farm. Helicopters were flying overhead, it was chaos. We had to run to get away. We spent twelve days in the jungle sleeping on hammocks while every day the army flew by dropping bombs everywhere. When we were safe in the jungle I asked him again, "You still want to be in the business?"

"No," he said.

Doll returned to the horses, and I took care of him like my own son. We had learned how hard it was to be on the run. It's not life. Pablo knew that and wanted it to end; he wanted to negotiate a second surrender. The U.S. had offered several million dollars as a reward for the capture of Pablo and myself. As time passed he accepted that we could not return to the Cathedral and told the government he was prepared for "the most humble and modest jail" in Antioquia, as long as he was given firm guarantees he would not be extradited or moved again. He telephoned a reporter and told him he would even accept going to a military base, anywhere but a police station. This was a discussion he and I never had, but I think he knew it was his only chance to enjoy a real life with his family again. For us, the safest place was in jail. But Gavíria did not want Pablo in chains again.

This time the world was chasing us. Probably never had so many different organizations been trying to kill one criminal. Some people call it the biggest manhunt in history. And while they were after that one man, many others died. We found out later that Gavíria had told the U.S. government that there no longer were any restrictions; he invited them to be an army in Colombia. The U.S. Army sent people from the elite group Delta Force to work with our army and police, the American covert operations group Centra Spike and the Search Bloc, while agents from the FBI and the Drug Enforcement Agency inspected the Cathedral to find clues. On the other side of the law was Cali; some of the Galeano and Moncada people went to them to offer some help. They knew all the places that Pablo favored and all the people who worked with him. And they were pleased to give that information to Cali. Also there was a new group supported by Cali, the people that became our worst enemy, Los Pepes.

Los Pepes, meaning the people persecuted by Pablo Escobar, was headed by the Castaño brothers, Carlos, Fidel, and Vicente, in addition to Diego Murillo Bejarano, known as Don Berna, a trafficker himself. Many of these people were former associates of Pablo's, people that he had defended from extradition. What happened was that when their father got kidnapped by the guerrillas they got so tired of all the kidnappings for ransom that they formed an army to fight back, just as Pablo had done so many years earlier. They made their own force, five thousand people, ten thousand people, all over Colombia. Carlos Castaño believed that Pablo had a plan to kill him because he thought this army was trying to take over the jungle laboratories. Carlos responded by joining the armies searching for Pablo.

Most of these organized groups started sharing their information. Also coming to Colombia to hunt Pablo were individual bounty hunters from all parts of the world, from the United States and Israel and England and supposedly Russia, hoping to become rich by collecting the reward money, which was many millions of dollars.

All of these people against Pablo, with all this technology and information, with all the money they could need—but they couldn't catch him. Or me.

While they thought we went into the jungle, Pablo decided we should go to the place safest for us, the center of Medellín. Our city. I was staying in an apartment on the fourteenth floor I had bought quietly a few years before. The apartment was comfortable with a good location. With me was one bodyguard and living in the apartment was a woman and her five-year-old son. I traveled under the name Alberto Ramírez. After four days there I needed to go outside. I put on my disguise, a wig and beard and glasses, and dressed in a black suit, so mostly I looked like a rabbi. On my feet I had special shoes I had made, a black coating over sneakers, so they matched my suit but if I needed to run I could. My bodyguard was also in full disguise. I was with the woman of the apartment and her boy, who provided even more cover for us.

The elevator doors opened on the fourteenth floor and looking back at me was a man I had known well—he also was a person the government wanted badly. In my disguise he seemed not to know me. We greeted each other politely as strangers. I got off, he got on. The doors closed.

That afternoon I walked through the city feeling total joy. The people, the noise, the free life, it had been more than a year since I'd felt any of it. Even in disguise, even as a fugitive, for a time I could feel free. I knew that no one would suspect that one of the men most wanted in the world was walking easily through the city, eating an ice cream cone.

We couldn't go back to the apartment. I was much more wanted than the fugitive I had seen. I was concerned that he had recognized me and would give me up to make a good deal with the government. We couldn't go to any family homes because they would be watched. So instead the bodyguard and I went to a flophouse, an any name check-in hotel to hide with the woman and her son. This boy was really rambunctious and one day he was playing around and he hurt his head and his mother had to bring him to the hospital. In the next few days my friends bought and rented five apartments in different parts of the city so we might move easily if necessary. I found out later Pablo had done the same thing. He was always with Otto and Popeye.

My decision was to write an anonymous letter to this fugitive warning him that the police knew where he was living and were ready to pounce. I wanted to worry him into leaving right away. Then we went with the lady of the apartment and her son into the beautiful mountains and camped next to a stream. Unless you have lived in prison it's not possible to know the feelings of those few days. There are few places lovelier than the mountains of Colombia. It was a place to rest.

The fugitive had left the building fast when he got the letter, so it was safe to return. But truthfully, I felt more comfortable moving around every few days. We had good people living in all the apartments so they were always prepared for us to stay there. Eventually I met with Pablo. He had allowed his beard to grow, shaved off the mustache he'd had in prison, and wore glasses and a wig. Together all of us went to a private home where the owners were expecting us. While all around the country men waited for Pablo's orders, only the five of us knew what was really going on. Our plan was to stay away until a new compromise could be found, and then surrender again.

Pablo gave us the rules we would live by. Each trip outside from the house had to have an exact time. If that person did not return in that time, in difficult situations we would wait an additional ten minutes, then we would leave. Pablo worried that one of us would be captured and tortured to give up our hideout. At the end of each trip it was necessary to circle the house three times before coming inside, while the people inside watched for the police.

Pablo knew that it was no longer safe to contact our families by phone. Instead he would write long letters to his family, demanding that they burn these letters after they had read them. He created a special system of delivery. He would hire three or four young boys on bicycles to make a chain, but insisting they always ride against traffic. That way no car could follow them. The letter would be delivered to his employee, either Alvaro or Limón. He also made many recordings for his children, giving them advice, telling stories, singing and reminding them of his deep love for them. One story I remember he told for Manuela was about a special horse he rode to escape from one of the farms.

It was dangerous for us to go outside, but sometimes it was too tempting to resist. One night as we walked by the governor's office Pablo wanted to show us a demonstration. Borrowing a cigarette from Otto he approached the uniformed guard and requested a light. The guard politely lit the cigarette. Pablo thanked him and asked him for the time. Again the guard responded nicely as we walked on.

"See what I'm telling you," Pablo said to us. "They will only find us if we are betrayed or careless." He told us stories of smart guys who had died only because someone had given them up. If we walk with confidence, he continued with confidence, no one will ever suspect our true identities. No one.

When we were outside we moved about the city in a fleet of taxis owned by Pablo. Each of these taxis was equipped with a big antenna that made it possible to make mobile phone calls. Most of the calls Pablo made were from these moving cars, which would make it impossible for anyone to find the place from where the call was made.

After spending three weeks together Pablo believed it had become too dangerous, so we went our separate ways. We would get together late at night about every three days, spending the time playing cards, talking, and barbecuing in the backyard. It was during this period that Pablo had the closest escape of his many close encounters. He told me that his bodyguard Godoy would take a plain car every few days to meet the boys carrying the mail. This meeting was always at seven o'clock when the streets were most crowded. That day Godoy returned to the house in the car as usual. When Pablo heard the horn signal he ran downstairs and swung open the twin doors of the garage. Godoy drove in quick—and two men on a motorcycle came racing in behind him before Pablo could close the doors. One of these young men—almost kids—pulled a gun and pointed it directly at Godoy's head and screamed, "Get out of the car, motherfucker."

Pablo was frozen. He couldn't know if these men recognized him or if this was just an ordinary Medellín crime. "Give them the car," he told Godoy. "Don't worry about the package. Just get out."

The young man turned the gun on him. "Don't move, motherfucker," he said. "I got a bullet for you too." These two street robbers had done what the police and soldiers of Colombia and the United States could not do, what the Cali cartel and the paramilitaries and the bounty hunters and Los Pepes could not do—they had put a gun two feet away from Pablo Escobar.

But they didn't know it.

They stole the car and the letters and drove away. Pablo left that house right away and never returned or paid attention to it. He went into the forest with his family for a few days of complete safety. He knew he could last forever in those woods, but for him that wasn't living.

More dangerous than any of the enemies we had fought before was Los Pepes. Their members had been part of us, so they knew much more information than anyone else. It has never been proved, but it has been strongly suggested that Los Pepes was really working with the government. According to the Colombian *Caracol News*, published December 22, 2007, ex-paramilitary Salvatore Mancuso, before he was extradited to the U.S., had officially accused former Colombian president Cesár Gavíria of joining forces with them to assassinate Pablo Escobar, and kill all our organization's members.

One reason to believe that is true is that the government never tried to stop anything they did. Even more, because the vigilante killers of Los Pepes moved in secret it is pretty much known that after the sun went down members of the other government organizations put on their masks and became part of Los Pepes. In fact, information between all the forces, the government as well as the death squads, flowed easily. When only the government knew the secret place where members of our family were staying, for example, that place was attacked by Los Pepes. A clear example was that only the former attorney general, Dr. Gustavo de Greiff, had known where Pablo's wife and two children were secretly secluded, and protected. Nonetheless somehow the killers from Los Pepes found out that location and his family was attacked with a grenade launcher fired from the ground to the fourth floor. Fortunately nobody was injured. Pablo was devastated by that news, which ended any possibility that he might safely turn himself in.

Pablo fought back. The fear of the people had been realized. The violence that rocked the country had started again. And also the kidnappings of important people. It had all gotten completely out of control again. The country had become one battlefield. Colombia was under siege. People were afraid to go out of their homes even to the shops or the movies. All in search of one man. There was nothing that the government would do to stop it.

Los Pepes couldn't catch Pablo, nor could they find me, so instead they began killing anyone who was part of our organization. They didn't go just after the sicarios; instead they went after people working for Pablo who couldn't defend themselves. They killed many of my accountants. Pablo's main lawyer who was negotiating with the government, Guido Parra, who had also worked with the government, and his fifteen-year-old son were assassinated by Los Pepes and a note was left around their necks for Pablo: "What do you think of this exchange for your bombs now, Pablo?" Los Pepes killed lawyers who had worked for Pablo, preventing them from trying to work a compromise with the government. They killed the sicarios. They killed people who did business, people who had worked at Napoles, anyone who had an association with Pablo or with me. My closest friends were Guayabita, El Negro, Chocolo, my trainer from my bicycle life Ricardo, and my friend since I was fifteen years old, Halaix Buitrago. None of these had connections to the drug business. They were friends who would visit me at the Cathedral to play cards, kick a ball, and help me fill the days. Los Pepes kept track of them. After our escape Halaix went to live safely in Europe. This was not the same El Negro who worked for Pablo, and he and his wife, Marbel, moved to Argentina with members of their family and my own for safety. But Ricardo and Guayabita were kidnapped and tortured to try to get information about finding Pablo and their bodies were found dropped on the street next to the Medellín River. Chocolo was a psychologist and he was on vacation with his wife and six-year-old daughter in Cartagena; he stopped at a traffic light, and in the usual way two motorcycles came alongside and started shooting with machine guns. Chocolo died right there, but miraculously his family was saved.

Los Pepes would come out of the night, unexpected. Five sicarios very close to Otto were staying in a house, along with a sixth person who worked for them at his house. Supposedly nobody knew they were there. These were tough men who had been involved in a lot of violence. One night they were having a party with five lovely girls. The house man was upstairs, and he just happened to look out the window when as many as ten cars suddenly appeared. The doors flew open and maybe forty men, all of them carrying guns, all of them with their faces covered, came running out. The house man climbed out the window and went onto the roof to hide. There was a lot of shooting. Probably two of the sicarios were killed right there. The others were alive, maybe shot, and dragged into the cars. The house man lay still on the roof for at least five hours. When he came inside he found the women tied up.

No question the sicarios were tortured to provide information about where Pablo was. Their bodies were thrown into the street the next morning.

But this was just typical, almost every day about six bodies would be in the streets, usually with notes on them telling everyone that this was the work of Los Pepes and taunting Pablo. Los Pepes attacked everyone and everything touched by Pablo Escobar. Pablo would denounce these acts on repeated occasions without any response from the government.

This was a war, I understand that, but so much was not necessary. I owned a championship horse, Terremoto, meaning earthquake, that was the joy of Colombia. Our country takes pride in its beautiful horses and this was a pure Colombian horse. I was the only person who would ride Terremoto, and he was softer than a Rolls-

Royce. He was easily worth $3 million, but his value as a horse to breed other Colombia champions was even greater. I knew the police were looking for this horse to take it like the rest of my property, so it was hidden on a farm in Manizales. One evening the trainer of the horse was at a restaurant when gunmen showed up. They took him outside and put a gun to his head. They demanded, "Where is the horse? Where is the horse?" He didn't want to tell them, but they threatened to kill his whole family right there. So finally he told them where the horse was kept. Then they killed him.

They kidnapped the horse. A few days later the horse was returned, tied to a post on Las Vegas Street. But the horse had been castrated, its value to the nation as the father of champions destroyed. Its worth in dollars was gone. And then they had starved the horse so he was just bones.

They destroyed beauty without caring. Terremoto, fortunately, survived. But his promise to the Colombia horse business was never fulfilled.

But Los Pepes' biggest target was our families. If they couldn't catch Pablo, they would try to kill those people he loved the most. Two of the houses owned by our mother were bombed, our sister's house was set on fire—so badly that a priceless Picasso was destroyed. The fear was so strong and our mother so scared she would sleep in the bathtub because it was the safest place in the house against bombs.

The most loyal of our sicarios fought back hard, but the circle of people around Pablo was getting smaller. It became safer for us to move around with very few people. Once I had thirty bodyguards, now I lived with only one. The main protection we had came from the people of Medellín, who believed in Pablo. At times we stayed with different people in the poorest sections of the city and these people shared with us whatever they had. The inner city was the safest place for us now. Once Pablo was staying in an apartment when there was a lot of noise outside. The soldiers had entered the area and were searching house by house. Pablo didn't panic. Instead he sat with the resident of the apartment on the balcony, both of them leaning over a chessboard. The soldiers came closer and closer. Pablo was wearing a hat to keep the sun off him and had changed his appearance with his usual disguise of wig, beard, and glasses. Also, as I've mentioned, because he was not getting exercise he had gained a lot of weight eating fried rice and plantains and his whole body looked much heavier than in pictures. As a soldier passed directly below the balcony Pablo asked him, "What's going on?"

The soldier responded, "Somebody called in that Pablo Escobar was staying around here."

Pablo laughed at that. "Pablo Escobar! I hope we're all safe from him."

"Don't worry," the soldier told him. "If he's here we'll find him."

We found out later that more than seven hundred men spent all their time searching for Pablo. They looked at thousands of houses and apartments. The Centra Spike, Search Bloc, and Delta Force listened to conversations all around the city, but particularly to our family, and still they couldn't find Pablo. Meanwhile, the drug trafficking to the United States didn't even slow down, the product was just coming from different people. Pablo Escobar had become a symbol of drugs to the United States, but stopping him was not a solution to the problem.

Was I afraid? For myself, no. I was resigned to the situation. I had lived under the possibility of immediate death for so many years now that it just didn't make me worry. But for our family, yes I was afraid. Los Pepes was making targets of completely innocent people without any interference from the government. We took every possible step to protect them. In November of 1992 plans were made for the family to go to Bahía Solano on the Colombian Pacific Ocean, where they would be safe. Pablo made arrangements for a helicopter to take them there. When it arrived they loaded everything they needed and climbed on board. Finally they were going to be safe. When the helicopter took off I think they all breathed deeply.

And that was when this helicopter tangled in the telephone wires, and everything suddenly went crazy and it started dropping fast. There was a lot of screaming. It hit the ground hard. Everybody was hurt; there was blood all over the place. When it hit the ground the helicopter burst into flames and the people on board were afraid the fuel was going to catch fire and explode. But they got out as fast as they could. Nobody knew why this helicopter had gone down and their fear was that the police or Los Pepes had shot at it and were waiting for them to come to the ground. A dump truck was coming down the road and my son Nico stopped it and pushed the family in the back, so if shooting started they would be protected by the truck's metal sides. The driver was so frightened he peed in his pants. But he drove them away from the site and later Nico gave him $3,000. With that he was so happy he told Nico, "If you come around again and I can help you, please call me."

Later I was able to send my wife and some of my family to Argentina, some others to Chile, and some of the others went to Germany. In those countries they were safe.

Pablo knew the situation had to be changed. The president had continued to say that if we surrendered and stopped all the violence he would guarantee our safety. Finally Pablo and I realized that the best thing would be for me to surrender again and in custody I could negotiate for him the terms by which he would give himself up. We were having discussions with high people in the government and they told me, "Fine, fine, Roberto, we will protect you. We'll provide what you need and take it from there." The only promise they gave me was that I would be treated with respect.

The plan was that I would surrender first and then two days later

Pablo would follow me. The night before my surrender Pablo and I met with our mother and other family at a farm outside Medellín named La Piñata. They were brought there in a van disguised as a bakery truck. We wanted to tell them about this decision, rather than letting them hear it on the news. "This is the safest for all of us," I explained. "And you can visit me without having to make all these secret arrangements." When they had left, Pablo and I reviewed all of the houses and caletas I had in place so that he might use them if necessary.

We spent our last few hours together the next morning. I was to surrender with Otto. Pablo and I walked to the garage door. At that time we believed this was only a temporary parting; we would be together again soon in confinement. I gave Pablo two mobile phones that we would use. We hugged each other as brothers and I drove away at about 4 A.M. I left very sad, Pablo and I were inseparable. I did not want to leave him alone, just like he too had the same feelings, but that was the road that was inevitable. That was the last time I would see him.

It was always a possibility to me that the government would kill me rather than accept my surrender. In the arrangements I told them that Otto and I would surrender at a place more than a hundred kilometers outside the city, but that was never the plan. Instead the day before I had called a news reporter, Marcela Durán, and informed her that she should be waiting at a furniture store called Deco: "The people from the attorney general's office will pick you up and bring you to where we are. We want you to be a witness."

The government men went to the supposed meeting place way out of the city while we went to the furniture store. Marcela Durán was in shock when she saw us, and pleasantly complimented me, saying I looked snappy. I always have been a good dresser. I cared about my appearance and wore brand names, but nothing too fancy.

Together on October 7, 1992, she went with us to the jail, which was only about one mile away, and watched as we surrendered safely.

I wanted to help make the arrangements for Pablo's surrender, but no one would speak to me about that. Without a deal he would not come in, knowing what was waiting for him.

I was put into a small prison cell by myself for the first ten days. Most of the time I was treated like a dog. I slept on the floor, but at least the food was decent. The agreements we made were forgotten. If it would not have been for the mobile phone I had smuggled inside the jail in a radio I would not have been able to communicate with Pablo. I called him and told him how everything had gone out. The Colombian justice system did not allow me to have a lawyer, and I had to sue them to acquire one. It took the government a long time to determine what charges I should face, although everyone knew my real crime was being Pablo's brother. I was never charged with any drug crimes or crimes of violence. Instead they claimed that I was involved in stealing a horse to use in terrorist actions, which did not make sense as I had more than a hundred horses, and carrying guns without legal permission. Also they had passed a law that made it necessary for the first time in our history to provide proof where your money had been earned and they charged me with that, and finally they charged me with escaping illegally from the Cathedral. They were making up all of these cases—except the escape, which I did, but only because we believed they were coming to kill us that day. The proof of that was that we immediately tried to make arrangements to surrender again. Originally they wanted me to be in prison for twenty-five years, and then they decided I should be in prison for forty years, and then it was fifty-eight years. So from the first day in prison I had to start fighting for my life.

After a month I was moved to a maximum security prison and my life changed forever. I was treated more like a normal prisoner. My attorney, Enrique Manceda, was allowed to bring a TV for me—although no one knew that inside that TV was a mobile phone. Unfortunately before my case could go forward Enrique was murdered. After having the mobile phone I spoke often with Pablo. I was one of the very few people he still could trust. Mostly he was traveling by himself, no driver, no security, and no friends. The people who got close to him now too often got killed. He moved around the city like a breath; he was never seen, but the government knew he was there. He had to stay away from all the places we knew because they were being watched; he had to stay away most of the time from all members of his family, as they were also being watched. They wrote letters to each other every day. Just getting his letters to them and from them required secret plans and secret codes. A good friend of Gustavo's known as Carieton came to work for Pablo after Gustavo was killed, mostly just to carry this mail to Pablo. Carieton was the only one who knew where the family was hiding. When Carieton wanted to meet with the person who would get the mail for Pablo he would say to them, "All right, let's meet at your mom's house." Since this person's mother had died that meant they would meet at the cemetery. Another favored meeting place was the entrance to the biggest rum maker in Colombia. When they were to meet there Carieton would say, "Let's have a shot of rum at three o'clock." In this way Pablo was able to communicate with his family.

He was like a phantom; people would meet him and not know it it at all. One day he was wearing a costume and was going to a soccer game at the stadium. In the taxi he talked to the old driver. The driver told him he was struggling. "It's tough. I'm worried because I'm behind on my payments and they're trying to take away my taxi. It's all I have and my family is huge."

Pablo told him, "If you don't mind, give me your phone number and address. Don't be scared but I know somebody who might be able to help you." The next day he sent some money for his debts to this old man's home.

From the days of beautiful living at Napoles and taking helicopter rides with Frank Sinatra in Las Vegas, Pablo was now staying secretly with regular people in their homes, and never for more than one or two days. For example, Pablo told an assistant whose name I would not use in order to respect him and the good deeds he did, "Don't be scared if I show up at your house one night because I'm staying in different places in the city."

"That's not a problem," this man said. Then he informed his wife that Pablo Escobar might stay over for one night only and she shouldn't be scared. Perhaps a week later he came home to find Pablo sitting in his living room watching the television alongside the man's seven-year-old daughter. Later they were having dinner with the TV still on when a public announcement showed a picture of Pablo and offered a $5 million reward to anyone "If you tell us where Pablo Escobar is."

The seven-year-old child looked at Pablo and laughed. "Oh, sir, you look just like him."

They all laughed. The man explained to his daughter that Pablo was his uncle who had come to visit him. But she shouldn't tell anybody.

There were some very close escapes. One time Pablo was staying outside Medellín and the American planes intercepted a phone conversation and sent men to the house to grab him. Pablo and a bodyguard escaped into the forest and hid. While they watched from above the house as the soldiers searched for them, Pablo listened on a small transistor radio to the big game between Medellín and Nacional. Suddenly he whispered urgently to the bodyguard, "Listen, listen." The bodyguard got very nervous. Then Pablo explained, "Medellín just scored!"

In another situation Pablo was staying for a few days at a farm outside the city. I had warned him many times to never spend more than a few minutes on the mobile phone, but sometimes he couldn't stop himself. He spoke with his son, Juan Pablo, or myself, almost every day trying to find terms of surrender that would be acceptable. But he had learned not to make calls from the exact place he was staying. This time he had walked up into the woods to make his call and could watch from there as the army raided the main house. As always he was listening to a soccer game between Medellín and Nacional on his small transistor radio. Just as his bodyguard approached Pablo and whispered that the police were close and they had to go, Medellín was awarded a penalty kick. Pablo said, "Let's just wait for the penalty kick." When Medellín scored Pablo looked up and said calmly, "Now where did you say the police were?"

Several times Pablo had to run away from his life of only a few minutes earlier, leaving everything he possessed behind him. The newspapers would run stories about how close the Search Bloc had been to catching him, finding hot food or making him leave without shoes. That's what they claimed, but they couldn't catch him. More than a year went by since my surrender and still the world was looking for Pablo Escobar.

In prison there was little I could do to help him. I know I was watched carefully, hoping that something I did or said would give away his hiding places. But I had my own difficulties. I was trying to fight my legal case while also caring for the safety of my family.

The hardest part of it all was the feeling that in jail I could have no control over my own life. In the Cathedral we had to stay in that one place, but within the fence we could do what we wanted. In this prison my life was controlled completely.

Those feelings I had about not being able to help Pablo were magnified many times when my son, my beautiful son Nicholas, was kidnapped. Nico was never involved in the business, until later when he risked his life to make peace with Cali and Los Pepes. But on this day in May 1993, he was driving with his wife and son, as well as an employee and a bodyguard, from his farm to Medellín. They stopped at a restaurant on the road called Kachotis. Almost instantly after they sat down police cars surrounded the place, and the police yelled for everybody to get down on the floor. Then they came in with guns and took Nico out. Nobody else. So it was clear this was their plan from the beginning.

While this was happening I knew nothing about it. There was little I could have done anyway, and it made me crazy when I found out.

These police put Nico in the back of a car and drove away. As Nico remembers; "Within a few minutes we reached a police checkpoint. They were stopping cars asking drivers for ID. When our car stopped I started screaming, 'I'm kidnapped! I'm being kidnapped!' Nobody paid any attention to me, so obviously they were part of the corrupt police group.

"We kept driving. I didn't think about what was going to happen to me. They drove me to a farm in Caldas, a town near Medellín, and there they tortured me trying to get information to find out where my uncle Pablo was. They tied me to a chair and started kicking me. That was the beginning. I didn't have a clue where he was so I couldn't tell them anything. Honestly I was never afraid. Maybe that's part of my blood, but I was not afraid of death. They returned me to the same neighborhood where they had caught me. I don't know why they didn't kill me. But soon after I got back Pablo called me. He had me picked up and we spent two hours together as he asked me questions."

Pablo was getting desperate to save the family. This was when we made arrangements for my family to leave the country. Nicholas went with his pregnant wife and children, his mother and his seventy-eight-year-old aunt, all huddled together. They went to Chile, where, as Nicholas remembers, "It was tough because when the police found out who we were from the Colombian government informants there, they didn't want to let us into the country. Finally I had to pay some money to the police in Santiago to allow us to go through the gate.

When we left the airport three cars were following us. I started driving all over the city and they followed me. I went faster they went faster. Just like in the movies. We were scared. We didn't know if they were going to take us and hand us back to Colombia or kill us. It didn't matter that we were innocent, that we had nothing to do with the wars between Pablo and the cartels and the government. They wanted to use us to catch Pablo. I turned into a huge parking lot and shut the car and we all hid below the windows. We waited, the cars drove around looking for us for hours and hours. Finally they went away.

"I waited some more, then started the car. Two blocks later they were waiting for us. I raced. On the road I saw a police station and I stopped. It was better to be taken out of the country than killed."

Eventually from Chile my family went to Brazil. They were not permitted to land in Brazil; instead they were sent to Spain. Again, they were not permitted to leave the plane, because the Colombian government had warned all these different countries and the persecution against my family continued. So from Madrid they went to Frankfurt, Germany. There, Nicholas remembers, "I spoke to an immigration agent since I had studied there and knew German and he told us it was true that everybody in Europe had information from the Colombian government that the Escobar family was trying to hide in Europe so don't let them in. 'The president of Colombia gave the order to my superiors,' he told me.

"Finally we pleaded, 'Please let us get in, they are going to kill us, we are innocent. It would be better for everybody. We're not going to do anything bad. Please call your superiors.' It took some time, but he got permission for us to be there. That agent was so human he saved us."

Pablo was not so fortunate. María Victoria, Juan Pablo, and Manuela were not permitted to leave the country. There is a story I have heard that Manuela would walk the halls of the security hotel the government had put them in singing little songs that Los Pepes were going to come and kill her.

Through the months I would speak to Pablo almost every day on the mobile phone. He always spoke from a moving taxi. But he was very much alone and lonely. Much of his money was beyond his reach, too many people of the organization were dead or had surrendered, and it was dangerous for him to be in contact with his family. A contact inside the Search Bloc would tell us that their new listening tools allowed them to track every phone call of interest. The government would not negotiate. In the city he only went out in complete disguise and now he stayed away from the most popular areas, instead going outside the city. When possible he liked small places where he could sit and drink black coffee with pastry. For Pablo it seemed that the safest answer was to go into the jungle and work with his new movement that he was forming called Antioquia Rebelde. So in November of 1993 that is what he began planning to do.

He had just moved into an apartment in Medellín in an area near the soccer stadium Atanasio Giradot. With him was our cousin Luzmila, who prepared his meals and did the errands for him, and one of my best men, Limón. Nobody in the family knew Pablo was staying there. Luzmila told her sons that she had a job taking care of an older man and she was going to earn good money. But with the torturers waiting, it was important that nobody knew where Pablo was staying. I personally had sent Limón to work for Pablo and before he went to meet him I had him pick up a different mobile phone. That phone was a terrible danger. On Sunday November 29, a woman who was working for me had smuggled in some secret letters hidden in the soles of her shoes, shoes that had been made for that purpose. One of those letters came from a source who warned that if Pablo continued talking on those phones he would be caught. I wrote immediately to Pablo this letter: "Brother, lovely greetings.

I hope that when you get this note you are all right. Next Thursday you will be one year older, and that is a gift of God He can give us. Brother, I'm really worried; I just received some information, which tells me your mobile is being intercepted, they are triangulating the signal, you could get caught if you keep it up. DO NOT SPEAK OVER THE PHONE . . . DO NOT SPEAK OVER THE PHONE . . . DO NOT SPEAK OVER THE PHONE."

When my mother arrived for her visit I gave this letter to her and gave her instructions where to take it. I told her it must be done very quickly. She knew it was for Pablo, and so she was worried. I did not lie to her, but I did not tell her the complete truth. "Mother," I said, "they have Pablo's phone intercepted, and it's not convenient for them to know who Pablo is talking to, because we are negotiating again with Gavíria's government."

His big worry always was his family. Pablo was trying hard to get them out of the country, away from Los Pepes. In April he had tried to send them to the United States but the American DEA stopped them from leaving in Bogotá, keeping them under the death sentence from Los Pepes. In November Pablo called my son Nico, who was living in Spain with his family, and requested that he go to Frankfurt to meet María Victoria, Juan Pablo, and the rest of his family. "Uncle," Nico told him, "I don't know if this is safe. We had so much trouble getting into Europe."

Pablo replied, "I have no other choice right now. I want my family to be away and I want you to please help me out and take care of my family while I fix this situation here in Colombia."

Of course Nico would do that. He returned to Germany, to the same airport he had arrived at months earlier. María Victoria, sixteen-year old Juan Pablo, and five-year-old Manuela flew to Germany, but they were not permitted to get off the plane. There was no legal reason for this, not one person on the plane had done anything illegal. None of them had sold or transported drugs. As I have said, their crime was their Escobar blood. So they were told they had to return to Colombia. They were told that being allowed into any country in Europe was only possible "upon the immediate surrender" of Pablo.

For Pablo surrender was sure death. According to his sources he was going to be murdered once in custody.

When Pablo's family was deported from Germany the government ordered that they be put into a famous hotel in Bogotá owned by the national police. This was incredible; the government was holding the entire family hostage. The government of El Salvador had offered to protect them, but the Colombian government wouldn't talk to them. Worse, they were being protected by the police, which was known to be working with Los Pepes. Then the government threatened that it was going to take away the protection from the family.

Pablo made phone calls telling people what would happen if his family was harmed, but besides that there wasn't much he could do. He would still go out of the apartment; in the last days of November he took the risk of attending a soccer game. But now the Search Bloc, Centra Spike, Delta Force, the police, Los Pepes, and Cali were getting closer to him. They had set up the family and they knew that Pablo would do anything, even give his own life, for them. So the planes continued to fly overhead listening for his conversations, the experts with phone-tapping equipment drove through the city, soldiers roamed through the streets, all of them searching day and night for Pablo.

Limón, the person staying with Pablo, was superstitious. He believed in witches and fairies, the luck of the four-leaf clover, even the power of spells. Pablo didn't take any of it seriously, but he enjoyed Limón's predictions. On the last day of November he was reading the newspaper when a big, ugly fly started bothering him. He rolled up the paper and tried to kill it, but failed. When he sat down again to read the fly landed on his right ear. Limón said nervously, "Patrón, this is not good. This means bad luck. Something is going to happen." Pablo tried to kill it again, but again the fly escaped.

Pablo told Limón to kill it, which he tried to do, but again it landed on Pablo's leg, and Limón just let it out the window. I'm sure Pablo laughed.

At night Pablo sent our cousin Luzmila to the store to buy a present for me, a copy of the new *Guinness Book of Sports Records*. Pablo was an expert on our sports, particularly soccer; he knew the details of every World Cup final ever played and would always quiz me to make sure my knowledge kept even with him—and I would not lose any sports bet. When Luzmila returned he wrote a note to me in this book and asked our cousin to send it to me in prison.

The next day, December 1, was his forty-fourth birthday. Writing this, it is difficult not to think of the great celebrations we had enjoyed in years earlier, from when he was a boy to the parties at Napoles with hundreds of people. Now he was almost alone. Luzmila made his favorite breakfast and he read the notes that had arrived the night before from his family. Manuela had written, perhaps with some collaboration with María Victoria, "Even though you are not here, we have you hidden in a corner of our heart. Happy Birthday, I love you Dad."

María signed her letter of good wishes and long life with the mark of her lips.

My card to him expressed my love for him and my hopes for his long life. After reading them all he put them in a paper bag and for security asked Luzmila to burn them. She does not remember if she burned them or not.

For dinner that evening the three of them enjoyed seafood from one of the best sea food restaurants in Medellín, Frutos del Mar, with a bottle of Viuda de Clicoff champagne. Limón failed to open the champagne so Pablo tapped it gently against the wall. The cork shot out, hitting Limón on the chest. They laughed and Limón said, "Thank God it wasn't a bullet, patrón."

The three people raised their glasses in a toast, but Pablo insisted a fourth glass be present, "Which symbolizes the presence of my family that cannot be with me today." His toast was, "For my family, for the good health of all."

"God bless you forever," toasted Luzmila.

Limón offered thanks to God for the chance to work with Pablo, saying, "God crossed our paths."

They raised the glasses to toast once again, but as Luzmila remembered later the glass slipped from Limón's hand and fell to the ground—and landed standing up without breaking. To Limón everything that happened in life was a sign from the other life. This one, he said, was "a sign of bad luck. Something bad is going to happen."

I know that Pablo respected the fears of Limón, but never took superstitions very seriously. He probably wanted to comfort him when he said softly, "You don't die the night before." After dark he put on his disguise and went outside. Early in the morning he managed to get inside to see our mother. She was still living in the secure apartment he had established for her. Getting there was difficult and dangerous, but this time Pablo risked it because he needed to tell her goodbye.

Pablo had finally accepted that the government would not make an arrangement with him for his surrender. There was nothing he could do in Medellín for his family. He needed to get back his power if he was going to make them release María Victoria and his children. So he was going to leave the city and go into the jungle to form up with his new group. "This is the last time we're going to be seeing each other in Medellín," he explained to our mother. He was going into his new life to set up Antioquia Rebelde, he said, which will fight for freedom. "We will establish an independent country called Antioquia Federal. I'll be the new president." And as president he would be free from the legal system of Colombia.

Our mother did not cry. Instead she told her son that she loved him and walked him to the door. He slipped out into the early morning.

My mother was a very strong woman with good feelings; she was a beautiful woman with blue eyes. She was a devoted Catholic with a charitable heart for Medellín's needy. During her youth she was a teacher with perfect penmanship, which I dearly remember. After ending her teaching career my mother had created a group for retired teachers for which she would provide the money needed to enjoy different sorts of activities like arts and crafts, music, singing, and anything fun.

Pablo knew he had to limit his time to under two or three minutes, but he was getting too careless. On his birthday he had called the radio station to inform the Colombian people that their government was holding his family hostage, and he had called his son. With their sophisticated equipment the Americans had located the general area where he was staying, but not the precise spot. They were getting too close.

That night in my dreams the priest came to visit once again. But this time it was a happy dream. I don't remember the details, but when I woke on December 2, I felt excited, like everything was going to be fine. For no reason I was filled with joy. I was feeling love for my family, I was feeling happy to be alive.

Pablo got up about noon that day, the usual Pablo, and organized his day. The day was gray, with hints of rain in the air. The early news was sad; the son of Gustavo, Gustavito, had been killed in a raid by the national police. Pablo asked Luzmila to go to the store and buy some things he would need in the jungle, like pens, notepads for writing letters, toothpaste because he used so much of it, some shaving supplies, and medicine. He warned her to return back to the apartment by three o'clock. If she had not returned by 3:30 he reminded her, he would be forced to leave for safety.

It was just another day for her. After she was gone Pablo got into the taxi with Limón and drove around the city while making his telephone calls. The Search Bloc was listening to him, armed and prepared to attack wherever he was staying, but he was moving and they couldn't track him. He called María Victoria and spoke with her briefly, then spoke with Juan Pablo. A German magazine had requested to do an interview and given his son a list of forty questions. I suspect Pablo thought that maybe he could appeal through this magazine to the German people to accept his family, and inform them of the inhumane treatment that they received from the Colombian government. As they drove, Limón helped him write down the questions. Questions like, Why did they depart Colombia for Germany? Why did they pick Germany? What happened when the family landed there? Why were they refused entry?

I guess Pablo must have felt secure because he went back to Luzmila's apartment and continued speaking on the telephone from there. He was never this careless. But this time the Search Bloc was able to find the right street. They went to the wrong place first, but Pablo knew nothing about it. Then they found the right place. Only the people who were there on December 2, 1993, know what happened. I know the official story they told. I also know what I believe.

At the moment this was taking place I was in my cell opening up the gift-wrapped book that my brother had sent to me. With it came a short note that read: "My dear brother, my soul brother, my best friend. This is so you learn a little more of the sport, and perhaps someday you could beat me in sports trivia . . . I send you a hug." He signed it with two letters, "V.P.," and to this day I have never understood this signature. Pablo always singed his letters to me "Dr. Echaverria," and the most secret letters were signed "Teresita." But "V.P."—I didn't know what it meant. I can only think about two assumptions: "Victoria Pablo," and the other would be *Viaje Profundo,* which means "profound trip." I have asked many people, including my English teacher Jay Arango, what he thought the initials could mean. There has been no satisfactory answer. But while I sat there in my cell, wondering for the first time, the events that would become history were taking place.

In the official reports the government said that probably Pablo and Limón heard a noise downstairs when the police came inside. The reports all claim that the government shot only after Pablo and Limón began firing at them. That I do not believe. There is no way they wanted to capture Pablo and risk that one day he would be free. He was going to die there.

These reports say that Limón was shot first on the roof and fell to the ground. Then Pablo tried to run across the roof to the back of the house, carrying two guns with him, but he was shot there and collapsed. Limón had been shot many times. Pablo had been shot three times, in his back, in his leg, and just above his right ear. There have been many stories about the source of the third bullet. The claims are that it was the Search Bloc shooting. Some people claim Pablo was killed by an American sniper from another roof. But after he was shot and fell on the roof, the Delta Force Americans posed for pictures with him like at an animal hunt.

That's the story, but this is what I believe happened: The police barged in through the doors and Pablo told Limón to see what that noise downstairs was. When Limón went to see he was shot numerous times, and died right there near the entrance. While Limón was heading to the door Pablo decided he would escape to the roof. There on the roof Pablo looked around and saw he was surrounded. He would never allow himself to be captured or killed by the government. Pablo had always said that he would never be caught and taken to America. In my mind there can be no doubt about what happened. Pablo understood that there was no escape, and did not want to be a trophy for those who were out to kill him. He did as he always had said he would: He put his own gun to his head and deprived the government of their greatest victory. Truly, he preferred a grave in Colombia over a jail cell in the United States. At the end, in his last hour, he stood fighting like a warrior. And when there was no hope, he committed suicide on that roof.

In front of the building the police fired their weapons into the air and started screaming, "We won. We won!"

Luzmila had been late returning to the building. As always, she took a cab to a point a few blocks away from the building and walked the rest of the way. But this time people were running to the block. She stopped a young policeman who was carrying his gun and asked what had happened. "It's Pablo Escobar," he said to her. "We just caught him! We just shot him." Luzmila dropped the packages she was carrying for him. She sat down on the curb and cried.

Soon our mother and sister Gloria approached the building. The police let them through. A friendly cop helped them. The body they saw on the ground was Limón, not Pablo, and for a few seconds they could believe that the wrong man had been identified, that Pablo lived. Then one of the police told them, "His body is up there on the shingles." They led her up the steps to see the body of her son.

I was in my cell and I heard the news on the radio. Pablo Escobar was killed by the DEA and the Colombian police. Of course I couldn't believe it. It did not seem possible. The TV was turned on and it was on all the channels. Pablo Escobar is dead. It didn't seem possible to me. He had survived so much. We are all mortal, certainly, but the death of a few of us strikes harder than so many others. It was not that I ever believed Pablo could cheat death, but I thought it would come at a time much later. It was hard for me to accept. Finally I too began crying for my brother, for everything that had happened

Pablo had been prepared for his death. He had left a tape for Manuela. On this tape he is telling her that God wants him to live. So he was going to go to heaven and he decided to leave this tape for her. Be a good girl, he says. Be a good daughter to your mom, he says. Don't worry about death, you are going to live on earth for one thousand years—and I will be protecting you from heaven.

That night a radio station spoke with Juan Pablo, who was still terribly upset at the death of his father. Juan Pablo struck out with anger. His language was harsh to the police. He threatened revenge. I contacted Juan Pablo and told him of the problems this could create for himself and his family. I asked him to call back with an apology. He did this, explaining he had spoken too quickly because he was upset and wanted to apologize for his actions.

We have always to remain calm, I told Juan Pablo. I reminded him that even at the most dangerous moments his father would never show distress, never show anger or fear. Calm, I advised him.

Pablo's body needed to be identified in his coffin. Pelolindo, the girl with the pretty hair, went to the funeral home the next day. She would know him by his hand. In the times she had manicured him she had noticed that his index finger, his pointing finger, was short and square. If I see his hand, she had steeled herself, I will know it's him. At the funeral home the coffin was opened. Our family had not been allowed to change his clothes, so he was bloody in that coffin. When she approached the coffin she took his hand and held it. It was the hand of Pablo Escobar.

There were many thousands of people at the funeral. It is tradition in Colombia that at the funeral six songs are sung for the body. Pablo had told the girl with the pretty hair, "If they kill me I want you to sing for me. I don't want anybody else to sing to me at that place, I want you to sing."

It was his wish. She was in shock, but it was a promise she had vowed to fulfill. "You are the brother of my heart," the song begins. It continues, "Every journey of my life and every day you are there for me." Which of course is how I will feel forever.

While the funeral began as a solemn affair, soon the people of Pablo's city came inside to the funeral home and took the coffin outside on their shoulders. Approximately ten thousand people joined the procession carrying Pablo on his final journey through the streets of Medellín.

On December 3 the *New York Times* announced the death of Pablo Escobar on the front page. "Pablo Escobar, who rose from the slums of Colombia to become one of the world's most murderous and successful cocaine traffickers, was killed in a hail of gunfire. . . .

"The death is not expected to seriously affect cocaine traffic."

Ten

THE DAYS WERE LONG FOR ME. There were times it seemed like I was flying through time without any destination. I had been in jail for fourteen months but almost all of that time I had lived with hope that Pablo would be able to find a way for all of us to be free one day. So this was not just the death of Pablo, it was the death of my hope. Now each day seemed longer than all the days I'd been there.

Pablo had been the center of the universe for so many years it was difficult to find any solid land without him. At night I would lie in bed thinking about Pablo when we were kids, remembering our many escapes, feeling the special days of Napoles. I thought about our father and the things we used to do at his farm when we were only seven years old, and sometimes when I did I would remember his face and talk to Pablo as if he were in my cell with me, "Pablo, remember what we did." At night I would tell him that I missed him, and pray for him, "God be with you, you shall be with God." And then I would sleep and dream about him.

In my mind, he was there with me.

For the next weeks I was too sad to worry about my own legal situation. The days were so long for me. On December 18, I went to the prison's church to pray for my brother. Afterward I began speaking with the church's priest, and he told me, "Mr. Escobar, I'm going to tell you something true. I had a dream of Pablo and he told me to play the number 21 for a raffle for a motorcycle. I won that motorcycle." There had only been one hundred numbers in the drawing, but it was still shocking to me because that number had meaning: Pablo was born on the 1st of December and died on the 2nd of December.

I was thinking about the meaning of this when I returned to my cell. But as I went there a guard said to me, "Mr. Escobar, you got a letter from the prosecuting attorney."

"What is it?"

"It's in there," he told me, pointing at a small room. "You have to read it in there." I walked into this room. A prison guard of the government gave me an envelope with the initials INPEC, the prison system, written on it, and the other required seals from the control posts. Because of security I always had been careful not to open my own mail; instead I had paid someone to do it for me. But this, this I was sure was an answer to an appeal that I had made and I was anxious to know the outcome. I picked up the envelope, which was heavier than I had expected. I remember the weight in my hand. I tore it open and when I did the only thing I saw was a green wire. Maybe I knew it was a bomb before it exploded. That I don't remember.

The bomb exploded in my face. My eyes were gone. The explosion had lifted me off my feet to the ceiling, breaking the ceiling tiles with my head. The world was black. I smelled the blood. God, I thought, don't let me die here.

No one came to help me. I began to crawl to the door, but when I reached down to support myself with my right hand I knew my hand was badly damaged; my fingers had peeled like a banana, the fingernails had been blown off. I knew I had to live. I tried to drag myself the few feet to the door. I heard people shouting my name. Roberto! Roberto! But they seemed so far away. Later I learned that the bomb had blown all the electricity or perhaps somebody had switched off the electricity thus preventing my rescue. Nobody could help me right away; they were looking to find me. Finally they came.

I was left alone for several hours in a room in the prison. I think they were waiting for me to die. Earlier that day a doctor friend of mine had come to visit. I had told him that I was going to start my research on AIDS again, and he had been pleased to hear that. Then the doctor arrived in the room where they had left me and began working to save me. He wiped away my blood and gave me some medication for the intense pain I felt all over. Three excruciating hours it took them to take me to the clinic. I asked for a mirror but of course I couldn't see anything. The bomb had also damaged my hearing. At the clinic they did the work necessary to save me. My family came there quickly and I told them to leave right away for their own safety. They refused. "If you die, we die with you," my mother said.

The doctor offered little hope. After his examination he told my family that it was not possible I would get my vision back. My eyes were as dark as raisins. "We have no option," he said. "We have to take his eyes out. They are completely destroyed. If we don't remove them they'll get infected and he could die from that." My face and hands were burned, my nose was in pieces, and my ears had been sliced. I had shrapnel all over my body.

My mother refused to let him have my eyes. She promised she would go anywhere in the world to find the doctor to help me. Immediately she began this search. It was in Bogotá that she found Dr. Hugo Pérez Villarreal, a military doctor. In this clinic they did the surgeries on soldiers wounded badly in the war against the guerrillas, so my injuries were not unusual for them. Dr. Pérez agreed he would operate, but he did not offer me much hope for recuperation.

Two or three days later I was taken to Bogotá from Medellín for the first of my twenty-two operations. That was the beginning of the most terrible time of my life.

It was never discovered who had sent the bomb. But this jail was maximum security. In that prison there were five different control posts to get through; it was guarded by the army, the police, the DAS, the correctional officers, all equipped with cameras, metal detectors, and X-ray machines. When you passed all that there were still many steel bulletproof doors. Nonetheless, they were able to introduce the bomb without any suspects ever being apprehended. The government was so corrupt it could have been sent to me by anyone. Many of our enemies would have wanted my death.

I had no future. I was in prison where my enemies could reach me. My brother, who might have forced protection, was dead. I couldn't see to help myself. I recall that the former president César Gavíria had guaranteed my life but still that happened without any corresponding consequences. In 1994, the former president of the United States, George H. W. Bush, was coming to visit Colombia and to impress him with how strong our justice system was, my sentence was made fifty-eight years, although by Colombian law the maximum was thirty years. That difference didn't matter at all, for me it was longer than life. I kept fighting and after time they reduced my sentence to twenty-two years and finally after much negotiation, to fourteen years and eight months.

So many of these years are buried deeply in my memory, where I don't want to find them. Two months after my first failed operation the doctor tried a cornea transplant. At that time the doctor didn't give me just a new eye, he gave me hope. The transplant failed, mainly because I was immediately transferred back to the prison when I desperately needed thirty days of bed rest and care in the hospital. In the jail the prison officials failed to give me the required eyedrops for the new cornea. But the hope survived. I knew that I needed to live, not for me, but for my family. They had depended on Pablo and Pablo was dead. It was my responsibility.

There was unbearable pain. After the first operation on my cornea one of the nurses, I don't know if by mistake or on purpose, put alcohol in my eye. I don't have the words to describe my pain. There were days then I felt certain I would die, and it was not an unwelcome thought. On the way back from the second operation on my cornea one of the guards let the stretcher fall onto the floor. On the ground I couldn't move, afraid I would destroy the cornea. In addition to destroying my body, the government tried to destroy my hope. My sentence had been reduced to fourteen years, eight months, but that had been challenged. I remember one day before Bush had arrived in Colombia, I had gotten a letter from the government. A guard had to read it to me. It said that the government was never going to give me a reduced sentence, execute me in the electric chair, or release me. There was no hope for me, this letter said. No matter how long I lived, it would be in prison.

I had nothing left but hope so how could I give that up? I was moving back and forth too often between the prison in Medellín and the hospital in Bogotá. It was a perilous time for me. Although I was blinded and wounded badly, that was not enough for our enemies. I was being protected at that time by the Colombian army, not by the police. It didn't make a difference, no one would be sorry if Roberto Escobar was dead. My enemies made several efforts to make that happen. Once a cook in the hospital said he had been offered $100,000 to put poison in my food.

There are three things I fear the most: surgeries, prison, and glasses for vision (as I had been so proud of my athlete's good sight), and I was suffering from the three. I am grateful to two plastic surgeons, Dr. Juan Bernardo and Dr. Lulu, because they reconstructed my hands, fingers, nails, and face almost to perfection.

I was in a special part of the prison with members of the guerrillas. Not the leaders, but important people with power. They helped me survive, doing everything for me from helping me get dressed to even giving me the injections. And also I had my mother, a very remarkable human being.

She would die for me. After we knew about the plot to poison me I wanted to eat only food brought in specially for me from the outside stores. "Oh don't worry about that," my mother said. "I already ate the food a half hour ago and nothing happened to me."

I was angry. It wasn't only me she had; there was the rest of the family. I told her that was the wrong thing for her to do. And she said to me, "I'm an old woman. I've lived a long life. I don't want to see another of my sons die." And so to save the life of her son my mother would risk poison.

There were other attempts to kill me. I was outside on the patio with one of the guerrillas when I heard the noise of a bullet hitting a wall. It wasn't a big sound because the shooter had used a silencer. When we heard the spat against the wall the guerrilla threw me to the ground for protection. The guard who fired the shot was not captured and there was no investigation. I was told later that he had been hired by Pablo's enemies.

There were nights of terror. Two days after I had been through another surgery I was lying in my bed in a military hospital in Bogotá with many tubes stuck into my arms and legs. At seven o'clock all the visitors were supposed to leave, but with money that easily could be changed. So at about that time a member of my family went out to bring me some food. I lay there by myself, in my own darkness, listening to the radio.

I heard only the shot. A loud snap that echoed through my body. Then I heard a lot of screaming from the guards and I thought they were trying to kill me once again. Without pause I jumped out of my bed and the tubes got pulled out of my body. I pushed myself against the wall and started feeling for the door to the bathroom. I moved along it as quickly as possible, knowing any instant another shot might be made, until I found the door. I put myself inside and locked the door. Then I lay down on the floor. And I waited helpless for whatever was going to come.

In a couple of minutes I heard people coming into my room and crying out. "They killed Roberto too," someone said. "They killed Roberto."

I screamed for help and the door to the bathroom opened right away. Thank God, one of the guards said. I found out what had happened. Not too far from my room two young guards were playing gun games. One of them had taken his gun and put it under his chin, saying that "if I take a guerrilla I'm going to kill him like this." He was just joking with his friend, this kid. And boom, he accidentally killed himself.

There was a lot of running after that. When the tubes ripped out of my arms I started bleeding. There was blood all over the place and when the guards came into the room they guessed I had been shot too.

But these situations were happening too often. There were people who believed that without Pablo's power behind me there would be no danger to them to assassinate me. Because it had been the government's fault that a bomb had destroyed my eyes and my ears they eventually agreed to let me live in the hospital clinic. So from 1994 to 2001 I lived inside the clinic.

I also remember when I was being transferred to Bogotá from Medellín for my third cornea transplant. I was traveling in a private plane, and when I arrived to the airport at 7 P.M. there was supposed to be an army unit waiting for me with an ambulance to take me to the hospital. The plane arrived but there was not anybody there waiting for me in the darkness. There were six people, my mother, the pilot, the co-pilot, two guards, and myself. The pilot, co-pilot, and one of the guards got off the plane to get to a phone and find out why nobody had come to pick us up. I was totally blind and needed that transplant urgently, because my cornea was almost perforated;

my eye had collapsed and had been reinflated by gas extracted from some rooster's crest. I was in Dr. Hugo Pérez Villarreal's silk hands. When I was sitting in the plane with my mother, behind us a guard was playing with his gun, and it went off, the bullet hitting the plane's cables and barely missing the gas tank. My mother threw me to the ground trying to protect me, and so did the guard, who had frightened himself.

I believe that accidental shot saved my life. I think they left me alone in order to set me up and kill me by an armed force, but with that noise the airport security arrived to see what had happened. My mother and I were on the floor of the plane. On the radio the guards said that there had been an attempt on my life.

After the ambulance arrived I was taken to the military hospital and put in a room to prepare for my surgery. Five days after my transplant, when I was a little better, a nurse came in to bathe me. She closed the door and whispered to me that she was really grateful to my brother, who had given her mother a house. She was trembling when she told me that a man had approached her and told her to inject me with something to kill me.

That night the priest, who was always by my side, said to me, "Roberto, you are going to suffer plenty, but nothing is going to happen to you. I am always going to be by your side."

I made an agreement with the government in 1995. For my safety they allowed me a whole floor of a clinic in Medellín. They supplied me with twelve security officers, six from the police and six from the army. In addition, I always had six of my personal bodyguards. I had eighteen people next to me every day, seven days a week, for six years. In the clinic I had fourteen bedrooms and I had to pay the state $1,400 a day for every single day. But I was safe there, and I had my operations, one after another after another.

But before I could move there I knew that somehow I had to make peace with our enemies. The war was done, Pablo was dead,

Gustavo was dead, Gacha was dead, the Ochoa brothers were in prison, and the Medellín cartel had become fixed in history. But still the enemies threatened to kill our family. There was no reason for all of us to be living in fear. I thought, if they kill me okay, but what about my mother and my children and Pablo's children? I tried very hard to make contact with the leaders of Cali. I sent letters to the people through my lawyer, Enrique Manceda. I spoke with people who could reach them and asked to be heard. But I got no answer back. It was always silence.

Enrique Manceda was one of the few good lawyers who had survived the Cali attacks. At that time he was living protected from Los Pepes on one of the farms my family still owned. I didn't trust the telephones, so I sent him a fax asking, "Do you have the guts to go and face the Cali cartel?"

Enrique responded to me, "I have family too. I've been at this farm for more than six months. If they want to kill me they are going to have to kill me face-to-face." This brave man went to Cali only with a very well known sports journalist and there they met in a nice restaurant with an attorney for the Cali cartel. All of those years of fighting, the billions of dollars earned and spent, the way Medellín and Cali changed the world, and here it came to two lawyers sitting opposite each other in a fancy restaurant.

Their lawyer, Vladimir, listened and agreed to speak with the heads of Cali. He believed they would listen to him and said to come back a week later.

To make my point strong, I suggested that Enrique return to Cali, but this time with my son Nicholas. And when my mother learned that Nico was going to go there she insisted she go with him. Living with a death sentence every day was not a real life, she said. Let it end. There was nothing to be done to stop my mother when she was determined. These were two people the cartel wanted to kill, so we were saying that here is your opportunity to stop the killing.

They met with the leaders of Cali, the Rodríguez Orejuela brothers, José Santacruz, and Spatcho. It was a big big surprise to these men when my mother and son showed up. At first the meeting was very cool, except for Spatcho, who most accepted the possibility of peace between the warring groups. My mother was not afraid of them, which made them wary. "Whatever is done is done," she said to them. "Too many people have been killed. We don't want that anymore. Roberto is very ill. Somebody sent him a letter bomb and he is only just alive.

"We have only two options. Either you say okay and let's live in peace or you can kill me now because you want us dead and here I am. You can kill me and my grandson, Roberto's son, or we can make peace."

For Cali there were reasons to have peace. The members of the Cali cartel told my mother that the worst thing they had done was collaborate with the government by giving information that helped them kill Pablo, because now there was not anybody to take the blame for the drug trafficking.

She told them that they had made a big mistake because "Pablo wanted to end the extradition. That was for everybody. He wanted to be part of the government and end that."

Santacruz then said, "That was not a smart thing for us. Now that Pablo is dead every single thing that happens in this country will be blamed on us. Now the DAS will be after us."

That was true. With Medellín gone, the government had started looking for Cali. Rewards had been posted. They were on the run and there wasn't time to worry about revenge. Spatcho spoke for them. "Ma'am, I feel a lot of respect for you. I have a mother also and she worries about me. This is the end of the war. I give you my word." He told the others that it was time to make peace, that maybe it should have been done sooner.

Then they hugged and kissed, like in the movies. The meeting lasted less than a half hour. And that is how the peace was achieved with the Cali cartel.

Two weeks after this agreement I got a letter from one of the leaders asking me for $2 million to seal it. That had never been part of the discussion. I wrote back telling him, "You're breaking your word because you said you were going to be in peace and now you're asking for money. Two things about that: I won't send you a dime and if you continue with the war you're going to have to kill all of us because nobody is going to fight back." I sent a letter to some members of Medellín's cartel who were in jail, telling them that nobody was going to fight back.

Spatcho spoke to this man and fixed the situation. He called me in the clinic to tell me it was done.

But Spatcho was correct that with Pablo dead the government would move after Cali. Within two years, on July 4, 1995, José "Chepe" Santacruz Londoño, one of the three leaders of Cali, would be arrested. In January 1996 he escaped his prison in Bogotá and in March he was killed in Medellín.

At the beginning the police blamed the killing on Medellín, which was not true. But that talk was very dangerous for us, as the peace was very thin. One of the very first people to know about Chepe's death was my son, who was told by a friend and confirmed it with the newspaper. Nico called people in Cali to tell them and even broke the news to Santacruz's wife. The problem for Cali was that it was still too dangerous for anyone to come to Medellín to bring home the body. So Nico and I decided that this was a big opportunity for us to show our good faith. Nico was going to bring Chepe's body home to Cali. There was still a great hatred in the air because of the war, many Cali people had died too, so this was a very brave thing to do.

There was a woman in Medellín who was in charge of the funerals of each person in the cartel. She had made hundreds of thousands of dollars burying our people. Nico asked her to do the same honors for Santacruz. "We don't want to make a big deal," he told her. "We don't want the media to know."

She didn't want to do it. "Why are you bringing him here? This is the worst enemy you ever had." She was afraid the Cali people were going to show up and start shooting.

Nico told her it was safe. He had conferred with the wife and it was agreed that he was going to bring the body home. But the first problem was finding a coffin. Chepe was a huge man, tall and big. The woman had one coffin big enough but it was very expensive. Nico told her he would buy it, choosing it as if it was for himself.

I knew this war had to end and this was the best way. "It was a weird feeling," Nico told me. When Pablo had been killed he was out of Colombia, "but when I saw the body of Chepe, even after all the terrible things that had happened, I felt very sad. I saw this person who had been so powerful, so rich, who had always been sur-rounded by people, so all alone. I had tears."

The second problem at the funeral home became clothes for the body. Nico recounted, "The man from the funeral home told me, 'We cannot do the service with these clothes. Everything is de-stroyed.' There was blood all over. He was wearing blue jeans and a T-shirt all covered with blood. He didn't even have shoes on. It was three o'clock in the morning, and where could I buy clothes for a man that big at that moment?

"I'm also a big man and I was thinking maybe some of my clothes would fit him. At first I thought jeans and a shirt but then I had an idea. The only time I wore a tie was on my wedding day. As I looked through my closet I took out the tuxedo I had worn that day. I ironed it myself. I brought it to the funeral home and it fit perfectly. So he would go home in my tuxedo.

"At 4:30 in the morning a very gorgeous young woman arrived at the place. She was crying and screaming that she needed to see Chepe. She was devastated and couldn't believe that Chepe was dead.

He had given her everything, paying for her education and helping her family. When I allowed her inside she became even more hysterical. She started kissing his body and pleading with him to not leave her alone. She climbed into the coffin and was hugging and kissing and wouldn't let him go.

"There was always a question why he was hiding in Medellín. I think he made the decision to spend his last days with this beautiful girl."

It was difficult finding a way to move the body to Cali. Nobody in Medellín wanted to rent us their airplane, for fear of retribution from Cali. It finally cost a lot of money, but we had given our word that Nico would go to Cali and return the body of Santacruz to his wife.

It was almost dawn. The journalists had begun showing up at the funeral home but still nobody knew that Pablo Escobar's nephew was caring for the body of his once hated enemy. Nicholas was careful to stay away from the TV cameras and the journalists. To bring the body home without incident he rented four funeral cars and put coffins in each one. Two cars left the place and the journalists went after them. While they were driving around the city Nico lay down in the back next to the coffin and the car went directly to the airport. At the airport the police stopped the black car for inspection. And when they opened the back they were shocked to almost heart attacks to find Nicholas Escobar hiding there. The police told the journalists, who came quickly. It became a mess at the airport as the officials did not want to let Nico go, but he paid a lot of money and everything was approved.

Even the short flight to Cali was difficult. A large airplane came too close to their small plane and it started shaking. Nico almost laughed at the thought of dying right next to Chepe Santacruz's body. Finally they landed and a crowd of journalists was waiting. Nicholas was looking for the wife but she was nowhere. After a moment a cab driver approached him and said, "Nicholas, a lady sent me. Please get in my cab."

The body of Chepe had been returned, and the peace between Medellín and Cali was now solid.

It was also Nico and my mother who ended the fighting with Los Pepes. Even after Pablo was dead they continued to exist, becoming an army. Nico was living in a beautiful apartment in Medellín, an apartment that now belongs to the Colombian government, who seized it even though Nico was never involved in anything illegal. In that apartment Nico got a phone call from a friend who told him the son of his neighbor was scheduled to be kidnapped. Nico went to the neighbor and told him this information. This neighbor then told another person what Nico had told him, and that person went to Carlos Castaño and said by mistake, "Nico was going to kidnap this person." A few days later Nico received a telephone call from Carlos Castaño, who had worked for Medellín before founding Los Pepes. "I need to talk to you," he said.

Nico and Carlos had known each other for years. They agreed to meet to talk about this problem. When my mother heard this plan, again she insisted on going with him. Also going with them was the man Nico had warned.

They met at Carlos Castaño's farm in Montería. "I'm not kidnapping," Nico said. "I don't believe in that. My uncle is dead and we just want to live in peace." To prove that, Nico introduced Carlos to the neighbor, who was sitting right next to him.

Everything got cleared up and my mother told Carlos she wanted to talk to him. Carlos agreed, but only after a game of pool with Nico. He had heard that Nico was the pool master of Medellín and wanted to challenge him. They played; Nico won two games. Then the conversation began with Hermilda. She started talking to him like a son, never raising her voice. "You don't know how much I've suffered in this war," she said. She was crying but she kept her composure. "And I cannot imagine the pain your mother is feeling. Please, can't we go back to a normal life?"

Carlos agreed and they prayed together. Then she kissed him on the cheek, the man who had been a leader in killing her son. But she accepted that, she understood the reasons, and wanted it to end. All of it. And after this meeting, it did. She had forgiven Carlos.

The Medellín cartel was done. Pablo was dead. Our enemies had moved to other wars. And I was alone in prison, blind and wounded.

It was difficult in prison filling all the empty hours. In the clinic-prison my life was basically talking to lawyers and having operations. After one of the many efforts to fix my eyes I opened them and, for the first time, I could see light. It wasn't much, it wasn't total sight, but it was amazing. It felt like someone had opened a window on life. I could see shapes and movement. It was very dim, but it was there. It was beautiful. But strangely I didn't feel that excited. I had been through so many unbelievable experiences that I no longer could get excited or feel very sad. I had learned to be calm no matter what happened in my life. I was happy, but not like most people would imagine.

That same day the strange priest appeared again in my dreams. Why I have never known. He has been there for me for the good and the bad, but he stays with me.

I did different tasks in prison. I learned braille. I renewed my knowledge of electronics and fixed the radios and televisions and CD players for the police guards. Once I even built a traffic signal that worked by battery; just like a normal one with green, yellow, and red. (Truthfully I did need some help from my bodyguards to put the right connections together.) In the prison they had an exhibition and this traffic light won first prize.

I also made candles. In Colombia you can take years from your prison sentence if you study or do good works. I sent my bodyguards, Sander and Germán, who were like my guardian angels, who helped me do everything in the hospital, to buy all the materials I needed to make candles. Making candles is easy. Soon my bodyguards were so bored they were making them too. It was funny, all the people sitting there making candles. And then the nurses saw that and they started making them also. Most of the candles we would give to the church and they would give them to the poor people to sell for milk or bread. The poor people did not know that the brother of Pablo Escobar had made the candles, although the priests kept some of them as souvenirs.

In Colombia on December 8 we light candles on the streets to celebrate the beginning of our Christmas holiday. I remember one time we lit more than one hundred of the candles we had made around the clinic. I could see a little bit and it was beautiful. Then we prayed. When I was in the clinic I continued my research on AIDS with the help of a bacteriologist, and Dr. Juan Carlos Tirado from the clinic, a man who became a friend. In the clinic everybody was very nice to me.

I always had hope that one day I would be free. The years passed by and my lawyers argued with the state and my family grew up. In the prison I had three more children, two girls and a boy. Meanwhile the flood of cocaine into America did not slow down, just different people got rich from it.

Pablo was never forgotten. Around the world his name grew in legend. In death he was the greatest criminal of history. In Colombia on the anniversary of his death thousands of people still march in a parade, then go to his cemetery to pray for his soul—and to give him honor. And our mother, until her death, slept each night with one of his shirts beneath her pillow. She was never ashamed to be his mother. As a baby he had told her, "Wait till I grow up, Mommy, I'm going to give you everything."

But no one could have imagined the cost of making that promise come true.

I served my sentence. I thought about my brother often, but not too much about those days. It was not because of the pain those memories brought, but because it is always better to think about the future. When it was close to my time being served I was taken to the office of a judge who told me, "Mr. Escobar, you might be leaving soon. We need you to talk. We need you to start telling us which members of the government Pablo had paid to change the constitution to cancel extradition. We need to know which members of the army and the police were involved."

During my term I had spoken with many different people. From New York the prosecutor of La Kika, Cheryl Pollack, came and we spoke. The DEA man on that case, Sam Trotman, came and we spoke. When possible I was able to answer their questions. But never did I mention a single name of the people who had helped my brother. I told this judge, "I can't do that."

The government offered me a house outside Colombia and protection for my family if I cooperated with them. "We will maintain your family," they said.

When still I refused they promised me more consequences. I had spoken to the judge and DA and told him that I was not going to betray any of the many generals, colonels, judges, congressmen, or anybody from the government that had helped my brother or other members from the cartel of Medellín. The government was upset and one day before I was released a government official came to the hospital with two envelopes. The first one was opened and said I would be free the next day. After all those years I would be a free man once again. My mother was there and she kissed me.

The government man started crying. The second envelope was charges of kidnapping against me. Supposedly on August 18, 1991, I had detained a man who owed me money until it was paid. The penalty was between four and six more years.

My mother heard this charge and fell on the floor.

It was a lie. I had been in the Cathedral on that day. In addition, more than ten years had passed since the accused crime, longer than our statute of limitations. But still they brought the charges against me. I served four years more before my full trial on this charge. When these charges were read they were all about Pablo Escobar, Pablo Escobar, Pablo Escobar. Roberto Escobar is the brother of a criminal who committed terrorism, sold drugs, killed people, and committed other crimes.

I told the judge that they were supposed to judge me for who I am. I said, "I'm not here to pay for my brother's crimes. I beg you, the law of Colombia, to judge me, Roberto Escobar, for the things that I did, but don't judge me because I am the brother of Pablo Escobar."

The prosecutor made them focus on the detainment and I presented my evidence to prove I wasn't guilty. Finally in 2004 they had to allow me to leave the prison a free man. I had to pay large penalties of money and property to the state, but I was free. I was never accused of crimes of violence. In April of 2008 I received a notification from the prosecutor, which said they had made a mistake in holding me for all those years and I also received a $40,000 settlement for their error.

I am living on a farm now, like my father, with some cattle. I own some land. The days of the wars are long behind me. I don't visit with many people from those days when Pablo seemed to own the world. There are still many people in prisons in my country and the United States who will stay there for the rest of their lives, but others like me have finished their sentences and have moved on.

Not too much of Pablo's possessions remain. I was able to get back from the judge some of Pablo's possessions from the Cathedral, in addition to some of the racing bikes my company had made. I still ride, but close behind a car that I can just see in front of me. I also walk to stay in shape, and I don't drink or smoke. I dedicate my time to my family. I still continue to work on my AIDS project, which has become a reality. I believe I have helped alleviate the suffering of a lot of patients and there is research being done based on my discovery.

I have never returned to Napoles. It is a shell, falling apart and lived in by the homeless. The roof has holes and there are rusted bodies of Pablo's classic cars. People have come there and pulled apart everything for their use or for memories of Pablo. Only the rhinos have survived; the herd has grown much larger and they live near the river. Some of the rhinos have traveled more than three hundred kilometers upriver, and with those rhinos lives Pablo's memory. They are too big to move, too dangerous, and the government does not know what to do about them.

And finally there is the money. It is impossible to even imagine how much money remains put away somewhere, probably never to be discovered. People who managed millions of dollars got killed without telling anyone where the money was hidden. Or they took the money and disappeared when Pablo was killed. I feel sure there are undiscovered coletas in houses all throughout Colombia—but also in New York and Miami, Chicago and Los Angeles, and the other cities in which Medellín did business. I am also certain there are bank accounts in countries whose numbers have been lost and forgotten and never will be opened again.

And there is money hidden and buried in the ground.

For me, it's over. I still have the pains from the bomb and from my memories. I live quietly with the help I need. And also with the knowledge that whatever is thought about my brother, from the people who loved him to those filled with hate, he will live forever in history.

Acknowledgments

This book, with its language and logistical difficulties, required the assistance of many people. For obvious reasons some of them have asked not to be identified. To those people, we certainly respect your wishes, but we also want to express our appreciation to you for your invaluable contributions.

We especially would like to acknowledge the hard work done by Alex Orozco, who was instrumental in putting together this project and who fostered it through many days and nights, and whose phone bill must have been enormous. In addition, Michael Planit brought together many complicated components into one sensible and cohesive unit, creating the business structure that enabled everyone to contribute to the best of their ability.

Our literary agent, Ian Kleinert, originally with the extremely capable Frank Weimann of the Literary Group and later with the newly founded Objective Entertainment, worked diligently to find us the best possible publishing situation, and eventually put us together with the extraordinarily respected executive editor Rick Wolff of Grand Central Publishing in America and Jack Fogg at Hodder & Stoughton in the U.K., both of whom have been tremendously supportive throughout the process—and pushed at all the right times.

Among those people we can thank publicly we especially want to offer our thanks to Magistrate Judge Cheryl Pollack, a relentless prosecutor and a respected judge, who offered us her memories and her transcripts; and DEA agent Sam X. Trotman, who was in charge of America's investigation of Pablo Escobar, and whose exploits and courage should one day result in his own story being told. In addition we offer our gratitude to Florida attorneys Fred A. Schwartz and Alvin Entin, Guylaine Cote, Ron Cloos, Robert Zankl, and Pat Mitchell for their contributions and Richard Canton for his personal stories.

We would also like to express our thanks for their space to Jerry Stern and Penny Farber. And the amazing work of the Geek Squad of Cross County Mall, in New York, for saving the day.

It would have been impossible to complete this book without the unfailing assistance of Tito Dominguez, who was always there to answer questions, create contacts, and interpret their answers. Tito also has an amazing story to tell—and we can't wait to see the movie.

Working in two languages is especially difficult, and we would be remiss not to thank Suzanne Copitzky and her crew at the Karmen Executive Center in Seattle, Washington.

And David Fisher would like to express his personal appreciation to Roberto Escobar. What he did was very difficult, but this was a story he wanted told, and I am very proud to have worked with him.

And, and always, David wants to recognize his beautiful wife, Laura, who makes his days shine brightly; and his sons Beau Charles and Taylor Jesse.

Index